The Spider-Man of the ye██ ████████ ███ fell from the sky, landing on an offshore oil platform. Peter Parker has no idea.

W9-CJF-901

the AMAZING SPIDER-MAN 2099

WRITER **NICK SPENCER**

ISSUES #32-34

ARTIST	**PATRICK GLEASON**
COLOR ARTISTS	**MATTHEW WILSON** WITH **DEE CUNNIFFE** (#34) & **CHRIS O'HALLORAN** (#34)
COVER ART	**RYAN OTTLEY** & **NATHAN FAIRBAIRN** (#32) AND **PATRICK GLEASON** & **MATTHEW WILSON** (#33-34)

ISSUES #35-36

ARTIST	**BAZALDUA**
COLOR ARTIST	**STEVE FIRCHOW**
COVER ART	**TONY DANIEL** & **EDGAR DELGADO**

VC'S **JOE CARAMAGNA** LETTERER	**KATHLEEN WISNESKI** ASSISTANT EDITOR	**NICK LOWE** EDITOR

SPIDER-MAN CREATED BY STAN LEE & STEVE DITKO

COLLECTION EDITOR **JENNIFER GRÜNWALD**
ASSISTANT MANAGING EDITOR: **MAIA LOY** ❀ ASSISTANT MANAGING EDITOR: **LISA MONTALBANO**
EDITOR, SPECIAL PROJECTS **MARK D. BEAZLEY** ❀ VP PRODUCTION & SPECIAL PROJECTS **JEFF YOUNGQUIST**
BOOK DESIGNERS **STACIE ZUCKER** WITH **JAY BOWEN**

SVP PRINT, SALES & MARKETING **DAVID GABRIEL** ❀ EDITOR IN CHIEF **C.B. CEBULSKI**

ZING SPIDER-MAN: 2099. Contains material originally published in magazine form as AMAZING SPIDER-MAN (2018) #32-36. First printing 2020. ISBN 978-1-302-92022-7. Published by MARVEL WORLDWIDE, a subsidiary of MARVEL ENTERTAINMENT, LLC. OFFICE OF PUBLICATION: 1290 Avenue of the Americas, New York, NY 10104. © 2020 MARVEL No similarity between any of the names, characters, persons, and/or utions in this magazine with those of any living or dead person or institution is intended, and any such similarity which may exist is purely coincidental. **Printed in Canada.** KEVIN FEIGE, Chief Creative Officer; DAN BUCKLEY, dent, Marvel Entertainment; JOHN NEE, Publisher; JOE QUESADA, EVP & Creative Director; TOM BREVOORT, SVP of Publishing; DAVID BOGART, Associate Publisher & SVP of Talent Affairs; Publishing & Partnership; ❀D GABRIEL, VP of Print & Digital Publishing; JEFF YOUNGQUIST, VP of Production & Special Projects; DAN CARR, Executive Director of Publishing Technology; ALEX MORALES, Director of Publishing Operations; DAN ❀GTON, Managing Editor; SUSAN CRESPI, Production Manager; STAN LEE, Chairman Emeritus. For information regarding advertising in Marvel Comics or on Marvel.com, please contact Vit DeBellis, Custom Solutions & rated Advertising Manager, at vdebellis@marvel.com. For Marvel subscription inquiries, please call 888-511-5480. **Manufactured between** 2/28/2020 and 3/31/2020 **by** SOLISCO PRINTERS, SCOTT, QC, CANADA.

87654321

32

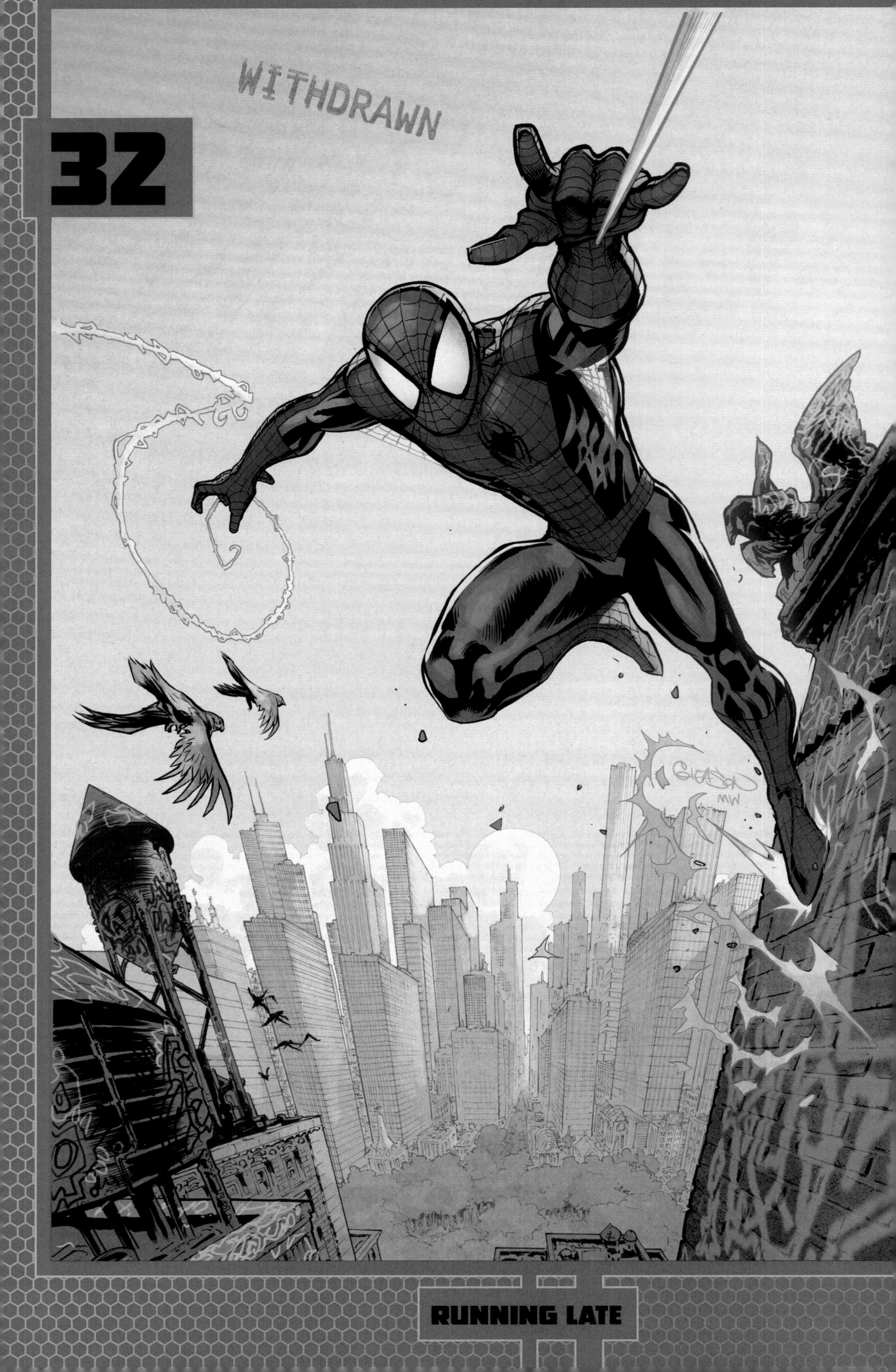

RUNNING LATE

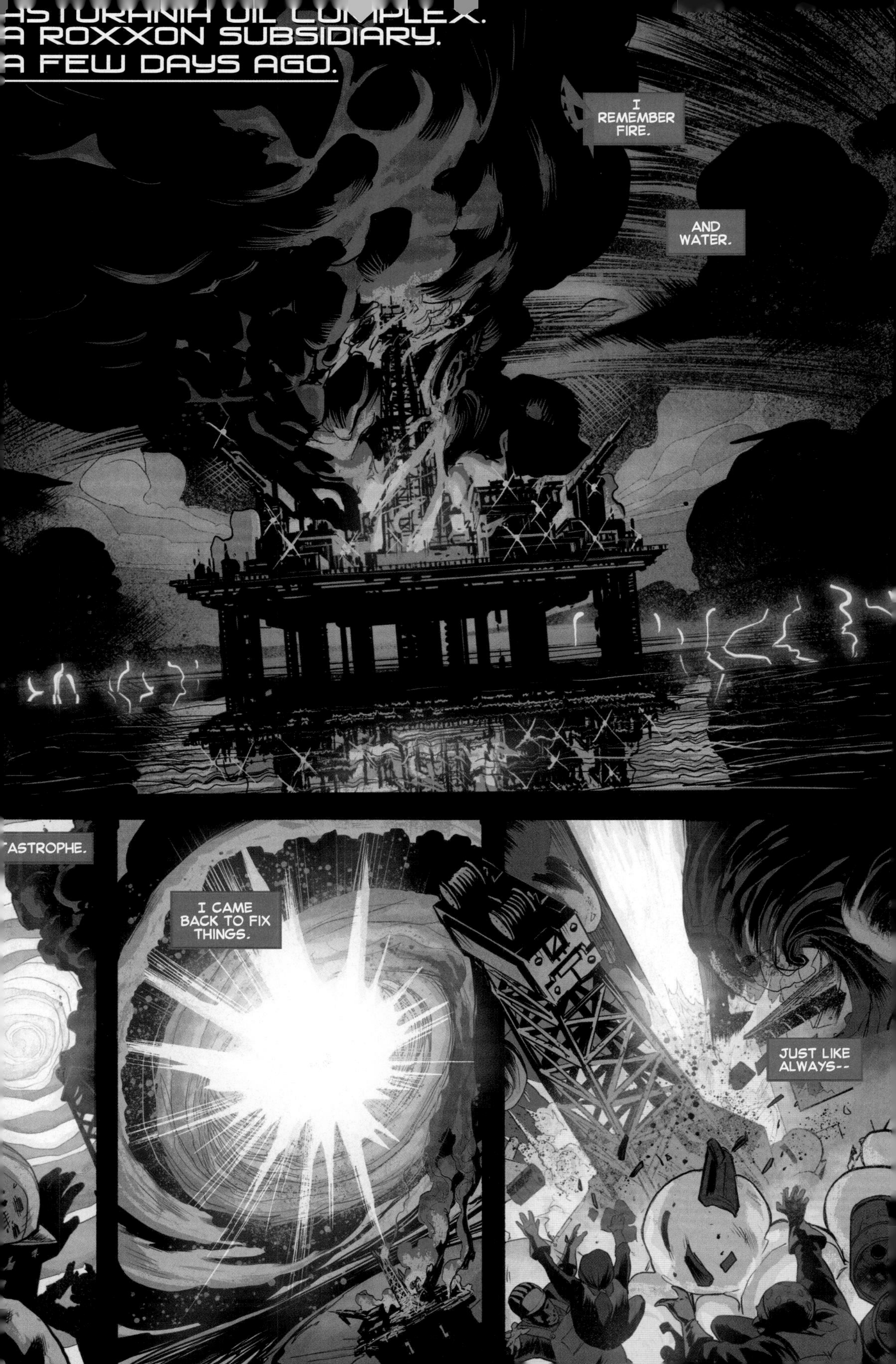
A ROXXON SUBSIDIARY.
A FEW DAYS AGO.
I REMEMBER FIRE.
AND WATER.
ASTROPHE.
I CAME BACK TO FIX THINGS.
JUST LIKE ALWAYS--

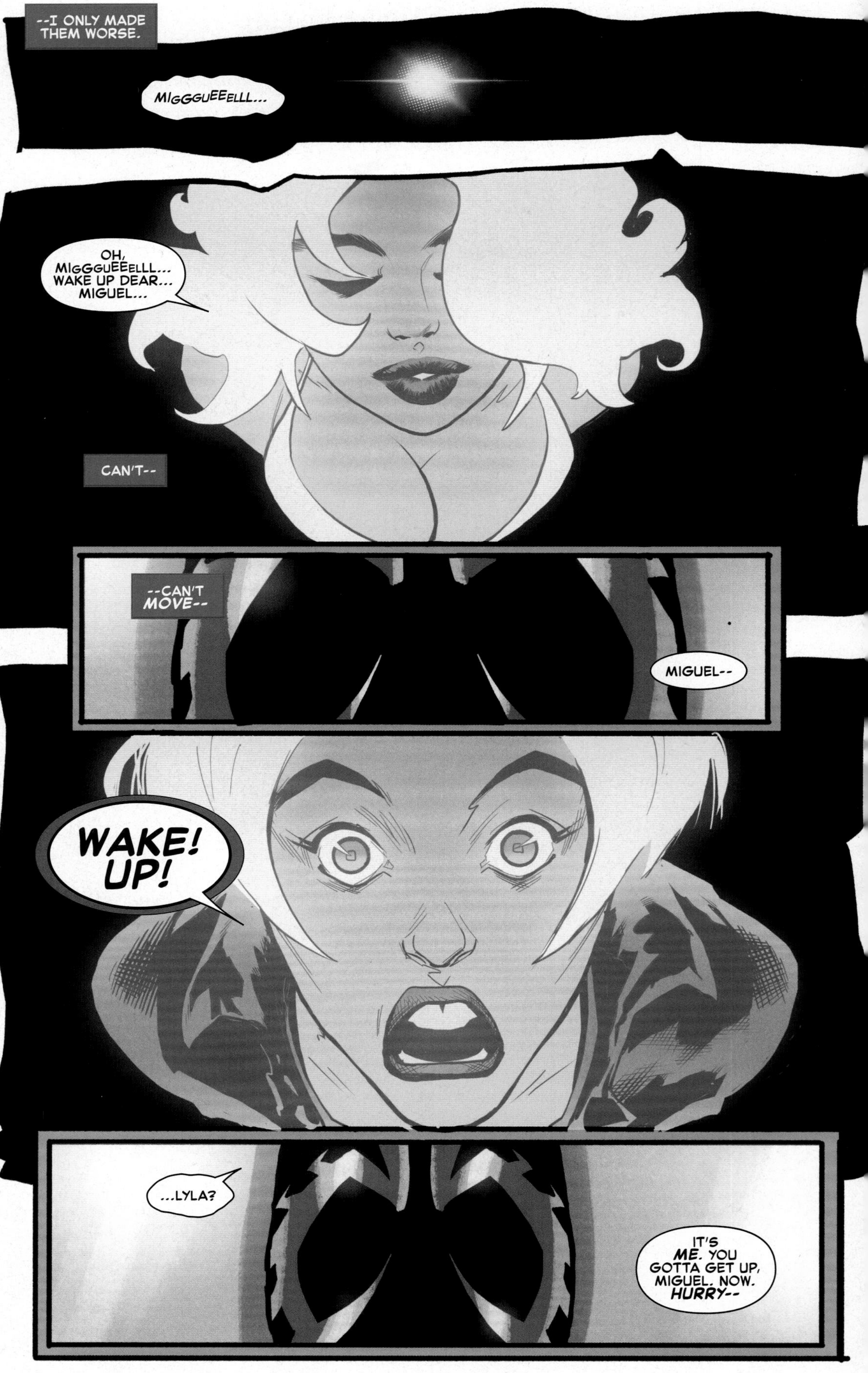
--I ONLY MADE THEM WORSE.
MIGGGUEEELLL...
OH, MIGGGUEEELLL... WAKE UP DEAR... MIGUEL...
CAN'T--
--CAN'T *MOVE*--
MIGUEL--
WAKE! UP!
...LYLA?
IT'S *ME.* YOU GOTTA GET UP, MIGUEL. NOW. *HURRY*--

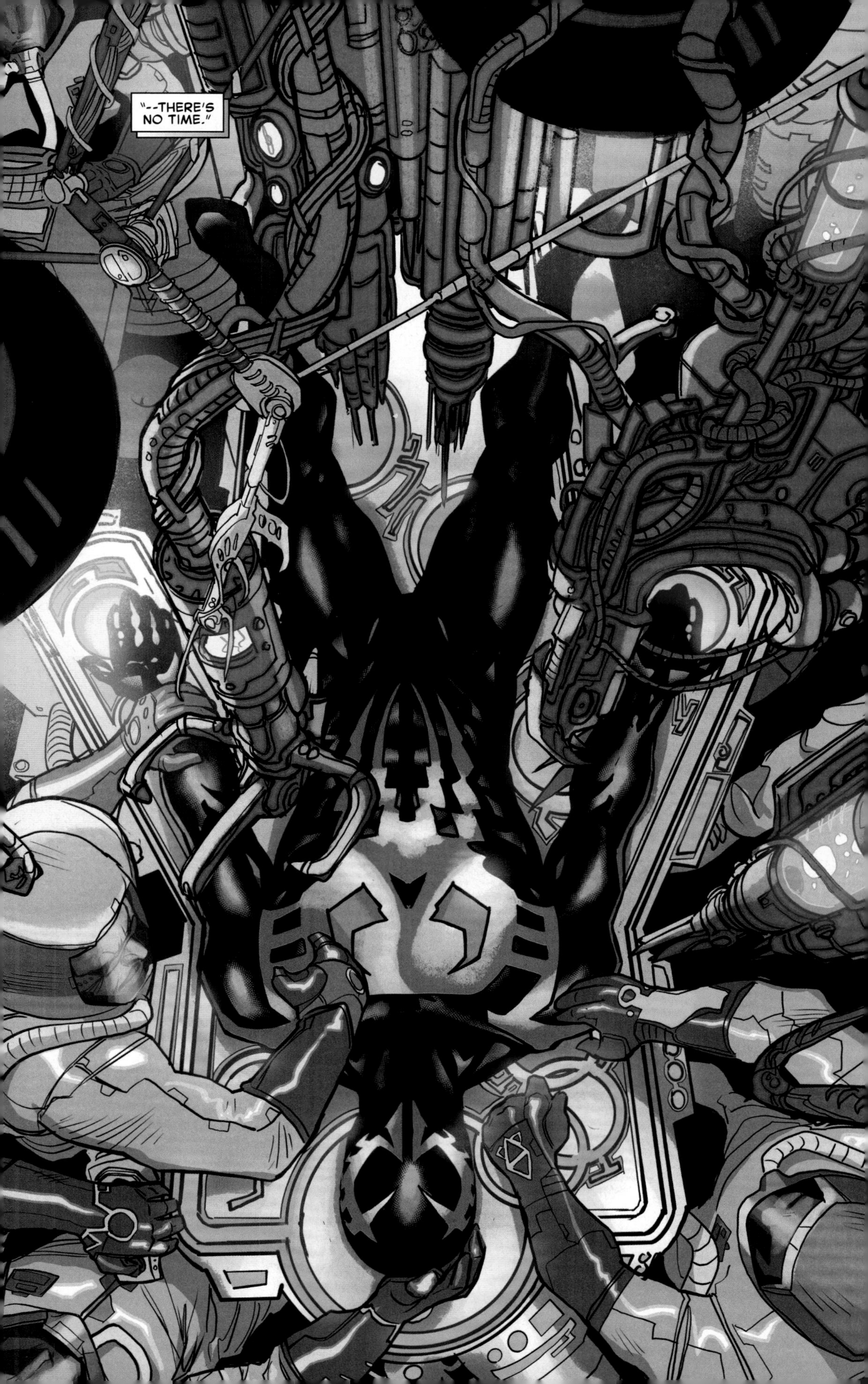
"--THERE'S NO TIME."

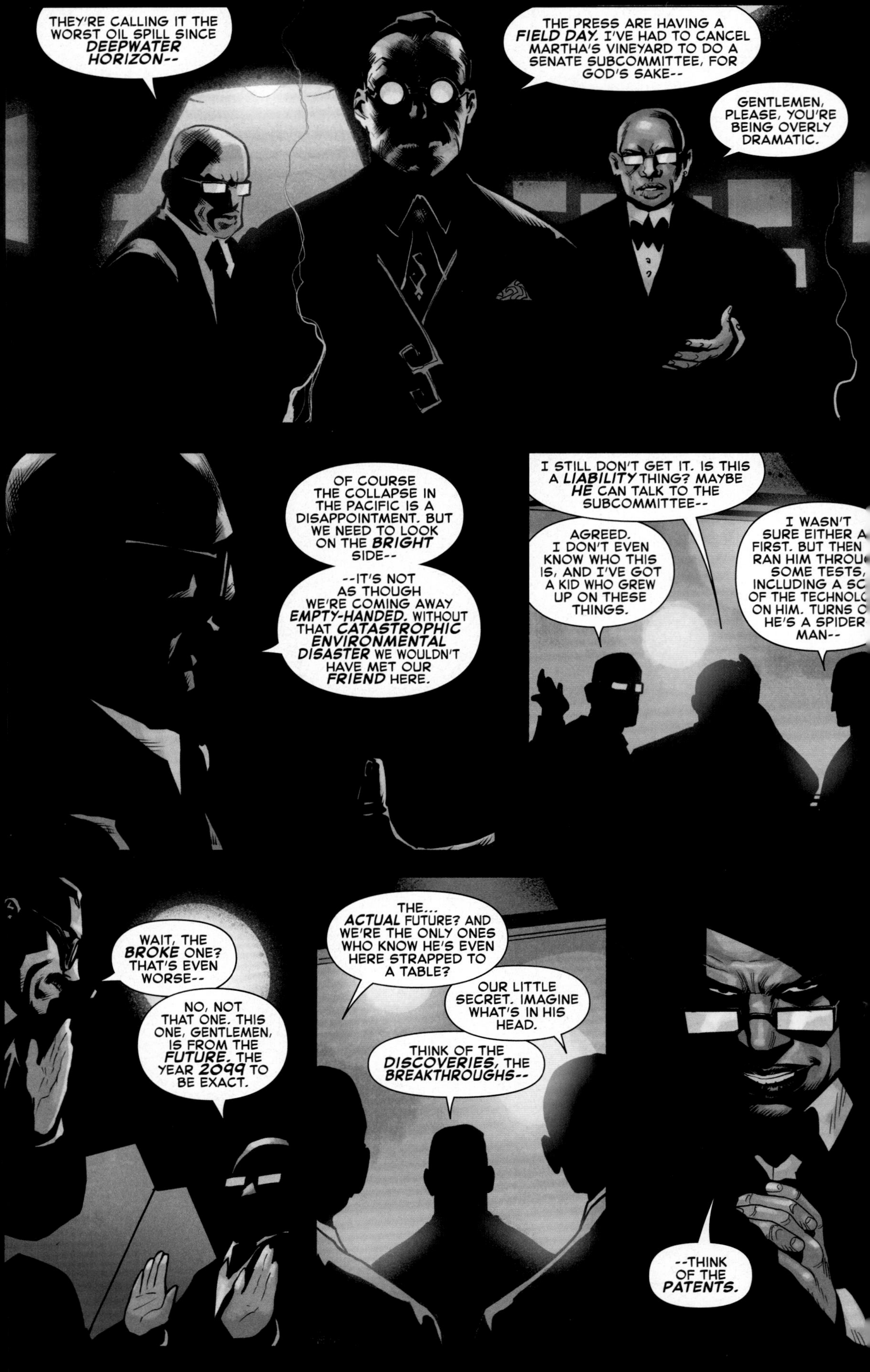
THEY'RE CALLING IT THE WORST OIL SPILL SINCE DEEPWATER HORIZON--
THE PRESS ARE HAVING A FIELD DAY. I'VE HAD TO CANCEL MARTHA'S VINEYARD TO DO A SENATE SUBCOMMITTEE, FOR GOD'S SAKE--
GENTLEMEN, PLEASE, YOU'RE BEING OVERLY DRAMATIC.
OF COURSE THE COLLAPSE IN THE PACIFIC IS A DISAPPOINTMENT. BUT WE NEED TO LOOK ON THE BRIGHT SIDE--
--IT'S NOT AS THOUGH WE'RE COMING AWAY EMPTY-HANDED. WITHOUT THAT CATASTROPHIC ENVIRONMENTAL DISASTER WE WOULDN'T HAVE MET OUR FRIEND HERE.
I STILL DON'T GET IT. IS THIS A LIABILITY THING? MAYBE HE CAN TALK TO THE SUBCOMMITTEE--
AGREED. I DON'T EVEN KNOW WHO THIS IS, AND I'VE GOT A KID WHO GREW UP ON THESE THINGS.
WAIT, THE BROKE ONE? THAT'S EVEN WORSE--
NO, NOT THAT ONE. THIS ONE, GENTLEMEN, IS FROM THE FUTURE. THE YEAR 2099 TO BE EXACT.
THE... ACTUAL FUTURE? AND WE'RE THE ONLY ONES WHO KNOW HE'S EVEN HERE STRAPPED TO A TABLE?
OUR LITTLE SECRET. IMAGINE WHAT'S IN HIS HEAD.
THINK OF THE DISCOVERIES, THE BREAKTHROUGHS--
--THINK OF THE PATENTS.

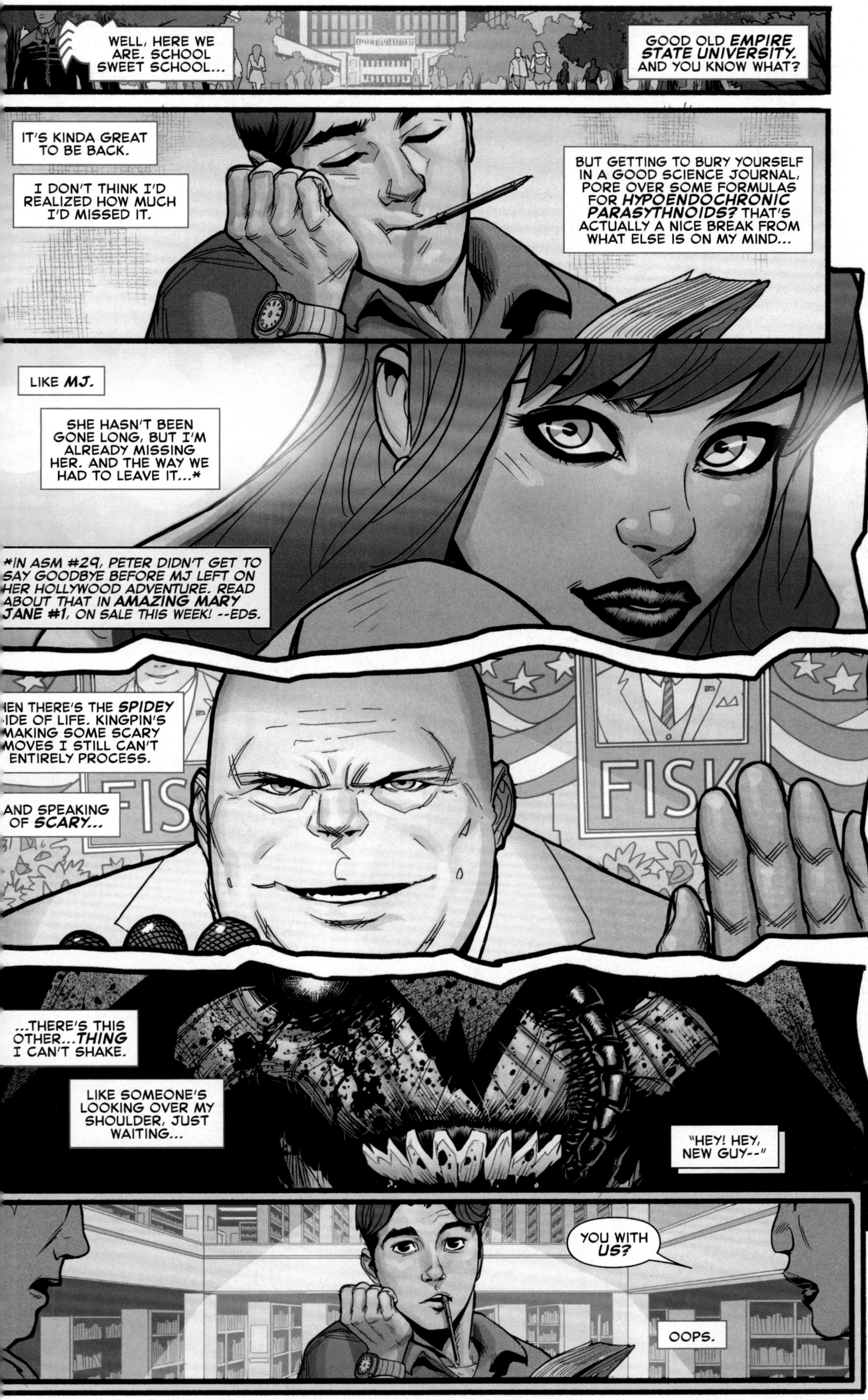
WELL, HERE WE ARE. SCHOOL SWEET SCHOOL...
GOOD OLD EMPIRE STATE UNIVERSITY. AND YOU KNOW WHAT?
IT'S KINDA GREAT TO BE BACK.
I DON'T THINK I'D REALIZED HOW MUCH I'D MISSED IT.
BUT GETTING TO BURY YOURSELF IN A GOOD SCIENCE JOURNAL, PORE OVER SOME FORMULAS FOR HYPOENDOCHRONIC PARASYTHNOIDS? THAT'S ACTUALLY A NICE BREAK FROM WHAT ELSE IS ON MY MIND...
LIKE MJ.
SHE HASN'T BEEN GONE LONG, BUT I'M ALREADY MISSING HER. AND THE WAY WE HAD TO LEAVE IT...*
*IN ASM #29, PETER DIDN'T GET TO SAY GOODBYE BEFORE MJ LEFT ON HER HOLLYWOOD ADVENTURE. READ ABOUT THAT IN AMAZING MARY JANE #1, ON SALE THIS WEEK! --EDS.
HEN THERE'S THE SPIDEY IDE OF LIFE. KINGPIN'S MAKING SOME SCARY MOVES I STILL CAN'T ENTIRELY PROCESS.
FISK
AND SPEAKING OF SCARY...
...THERE'S THIS OTHER...THING I CAN'T SHAKE.
LIKE SOMEONE'S LOOKING OVER MY SHOULDER, JUST WAITING...
"HEY! HEY, NEW GUY--"
YOU WITH US?
OOPS.

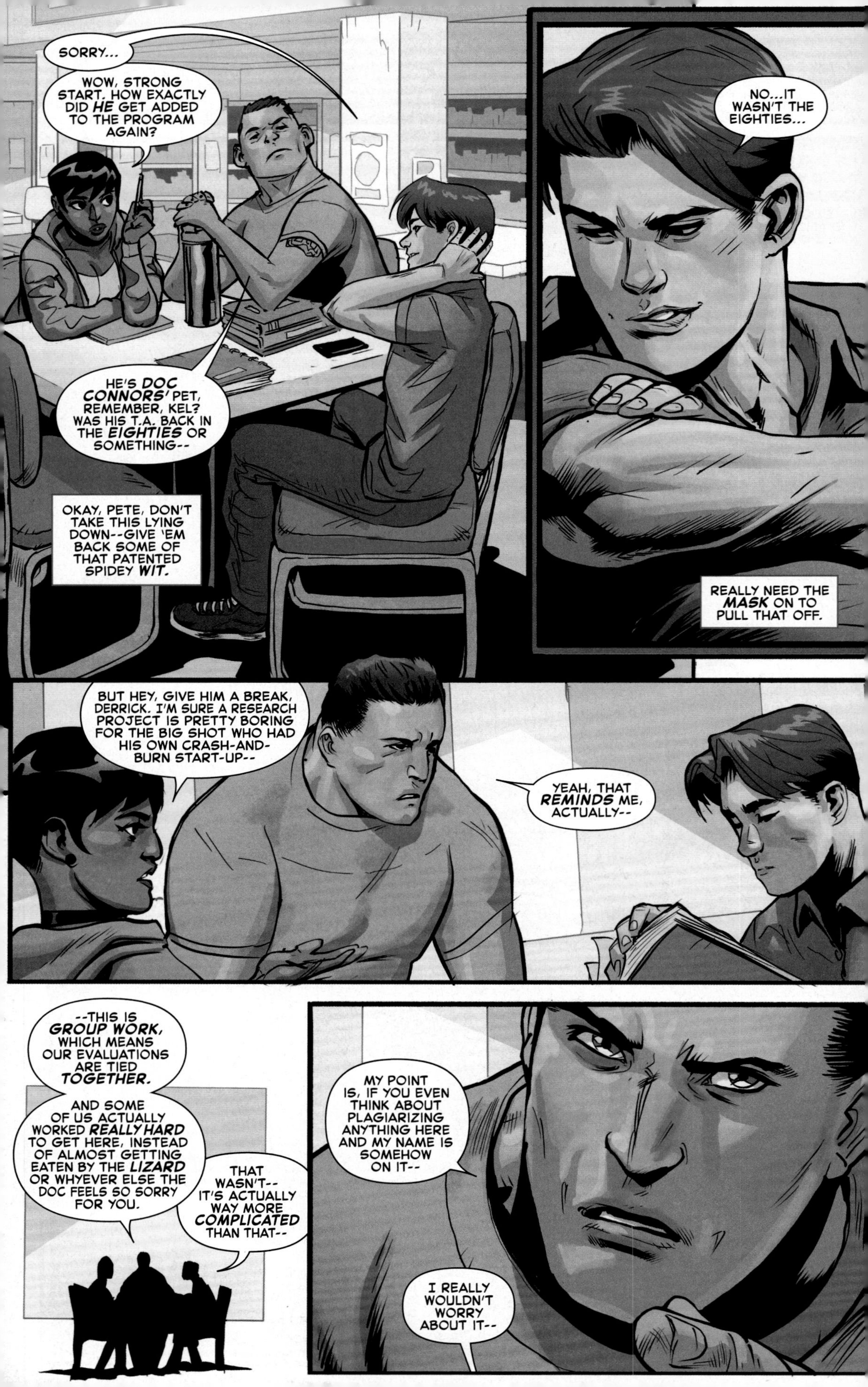
SORRY...
WOW, STRONG START. HOW EXACTLY DID HE GET ADDED TO THE PROGRAM AGAIN?
HE'S DOC CONNORS' PET, REMEMBER, KEL? WAS HIS T.A. BACK IN THE EIGHTIES OR SOMETHING--
OKAY, PETE, DON'T TAKE THIS LYING DOWN--GIVE 'EM BACK SOME OF THAT PATENTED SPIDEY WIT.
NO...IT WASN'T THE EIGHTIES...
REALLY NEED THE MASK ON TO PULL THAT OFF.
BUT HEY, GIVE HIM A BREAK, DERRICK. I'M SURE A RESEARCH PROJECT IS PRETTY BORING FOR THE BIG SHOT WHO HAD HIS OWN CRASH-AND-BURN START-UP--
YEAH, THAT REMINDS ME, ACTUALLY--
--THIS IS GROUP WORK, WHICH MEANS OUR EVALUATIONS ARE TIED TOGETHER.
AND SOME OF US ACTUALLY WORKED REALLY HARD TO GET HERE, INSTEAD OF ALMOST GETTING EATEN BY THE LIZARD OR WHYEVER ELSE THE DOC FEELS SO SORRY FOR YOU.
THAT WASN'T-- IT'S ACTUALLY WAY MORE COMPLICATED THAN THAT--
MY POINT IS, IF YOU EVEN THINK ABOUT PLAGIARIZING ANYTHING HERE AND MY NAME IS SOMEHOW ON IT--
I REALLY WOULDN'T WORRY ABOUT IT--

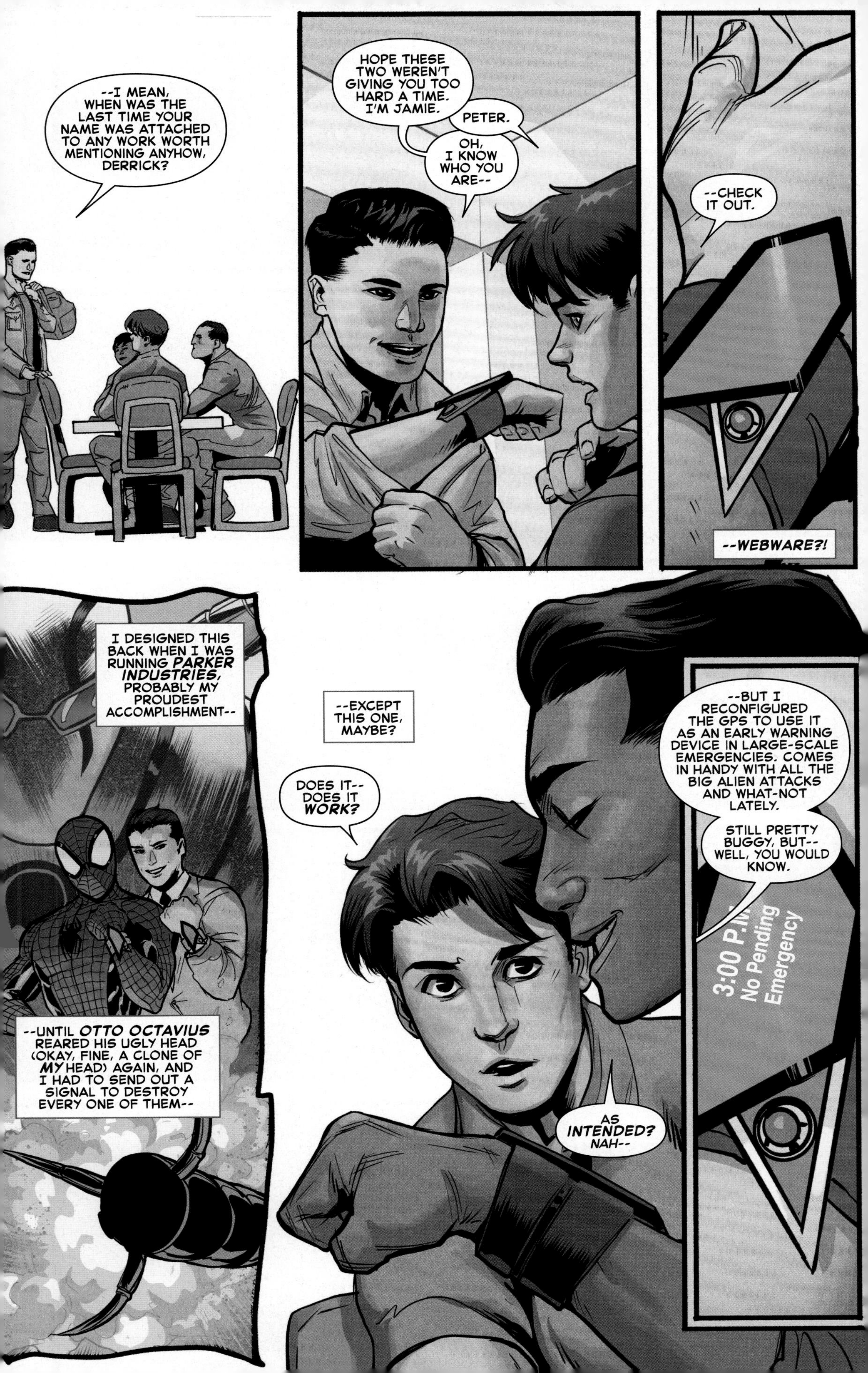
--I MEAN, WHEN WAS THE LAST TIME YOUR NAME WAS ATTACHED TO ANY WORK WORTH MENTIONING ANYHOW, DERRICK?
HOPE THESE TWO WEREN'T GIVING YOU TOO HARD A TIME. I'M JAMIE.
PETER.
OH, I KNOW WHO YOU ARE--
--CHECK IT OUT.
--WEBWARE?!
I DESIGNED THIS BACK WHEN I WAS RUNNING PARKER INDUSTRIES, PROBABLY MY PROUDEST ACCOMPLISHMENT--
--UNTIL OTTO OCTAVIUS REARED HIS UGLY HEAD (OKAY, FINE, A CLONE OF MY HEAD) AGAIN, AND I HAD TO SEND OUT A SIGNAL TO DESTROY EVERY ONE OF THEM--
--EXCEPT THIS ONE, MAYBE?
DOES IT-- DOES IT WORK?
--BUT I RECONFIGURED THE GPS TO USE IT AS AN EARLY WARNING DEVICE IN LARGE-SCALE EMERGENCIES. COMES IN HANDY WITH ALL THE BIG ALIEN ATTACKS AND WHAT-NOT LATELY.
STILL PRETTY BUGGY, BUT-- WELL, YOU WOULD KNOW.
3:00 P.M.
No Pending Emergency
AS INTENDED? NAH--

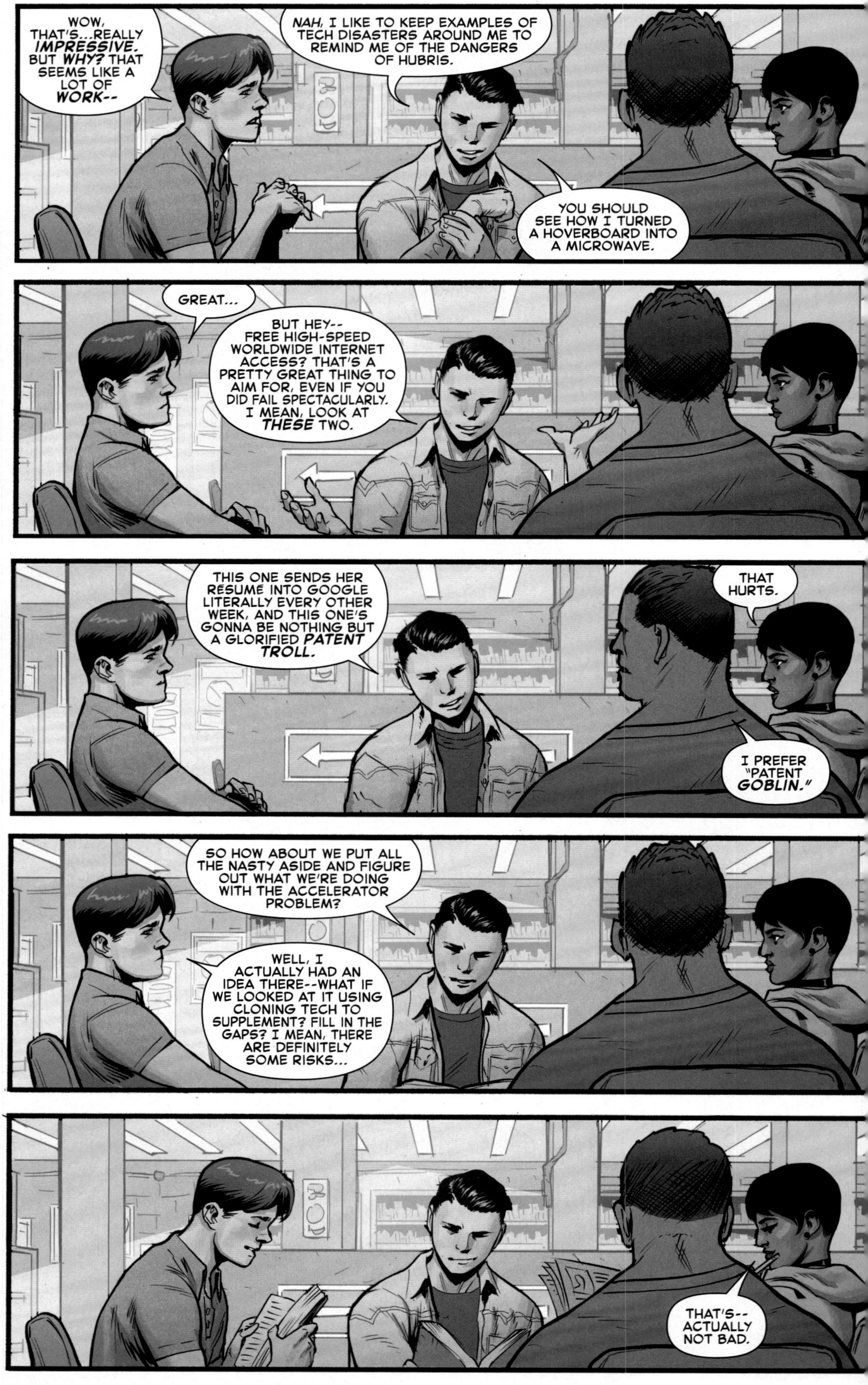
WOW, THAT'S...REALLY IMPRESSIVE. BUT WHY? THAT SEEMS LIKE A LOT OF WORK--
NAH, I LIKE TO KEEP EXAMPLES OF TECH DISASTERS AROUND ME TO REMIND ME OF THE DANGERS OF HUBRIS.
YOU SHOULD SEE HOW I TURNED A HOVERBOARD INTO A MICROWAVE.
GREAT...
BUT HEY-- FREE HIGH-SPEED WORLDWIDE INTERNET ACCESS? THAT'S A PRETTY GREAT THING TO AIM FOR, EVEN IF YOU DID FAIL SPECTACULARLY. I MEAN, LOOK AT THESE TWO.
THIS ONE SENDS HER RÉSUMÉ INTO GOOGLE LITERALLY EVERY OTHER WEEK, AND THIS ONE'S GONNA BE NOTHING BUT A GLORIFIED PATENT TROLL.
THAT HURTS.
I PREFER "PATENT GOBLIN."
SO HOW ABOUT WE PUT ALL THE NASTY ASIDE AND FIGURE OUT WHAT WE'RE DOING WITH THE ACCELERATOR PROBLEM?
WELL, I ACTUALLY HAD AN IDEA THERE--WHAT IF WE LOOKED AT IT USING CLONING TECH TO SUPPLEMENT? FILL IN THE GAPS? I MEAN, THERE ARE DEFINITELY SOME RISKS...
THAT'S-- ACTUALLY NOT BAD.

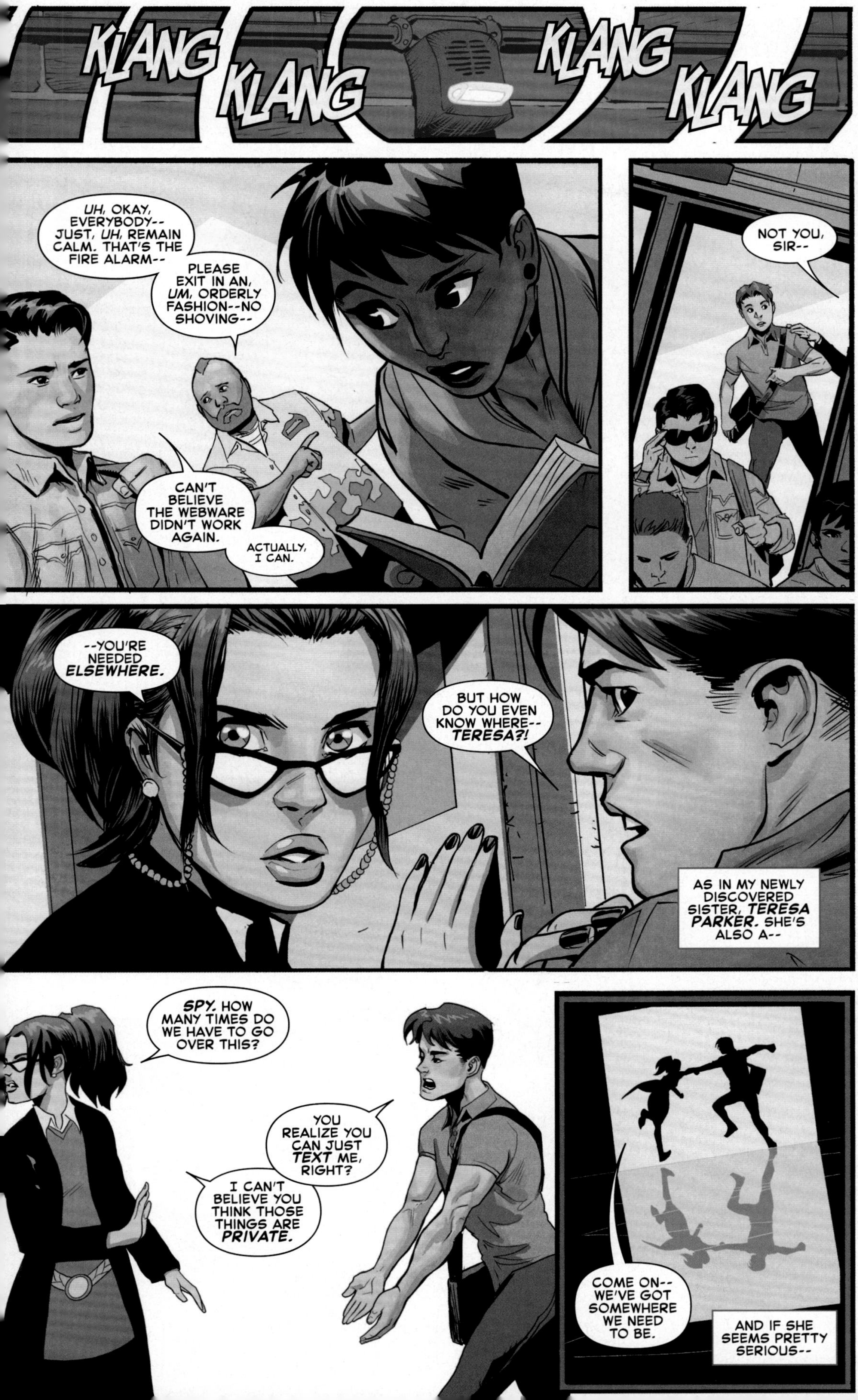
KLANG
KLANG
KLANG
KLANG
UH, OKAY, EVERYBODY--JUST, UH, REMAIN CALM. THAT'S THE FIRE ALARM--
PLEASE EXIT IN AN, UM, ORDERLY FASHION--NO SHOVING--
CAN'T BELIEVE THE WEBWARE DIDN'T WORK AGAIN.
ACTUALLY, I CAN.
NOT YOU, SIR--
--YOU'RE NEEDED ELSEWHERE.
BUT HOW DO YOU EVEN KNOW WHERE--TERESA?!
AS IN MY NEWLY DISCOVERED SISTER, TERESA PARKER. SHE'S ALSO A--
SPY. HOW MANY TIMES DO WE HAVE TO GO OVER THIS?
YOU REALIZE YOU CAN JUST TEXT ME, RIGHT?
I CAN'T BELIEVE YOU THINK THOSE THINGS ARE PRIVATE.
COME ON--WE'VE GOT SOMEWHERE WE NEED TO BE.
AND IF SHE SEEMS PRETTY SERIOUS--

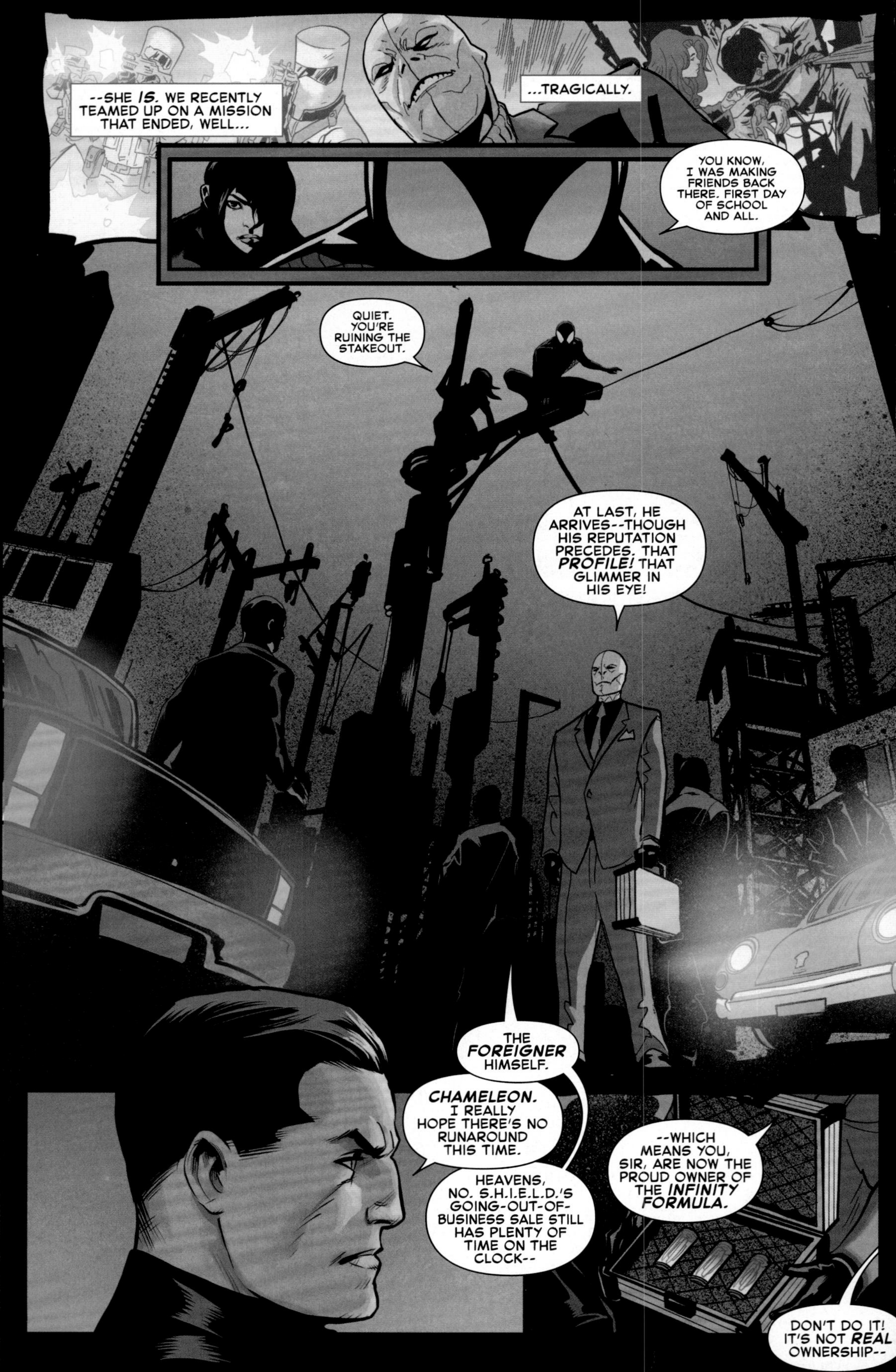
--SHE IS. WE RECENTLY TEAMED UP ON A MISSION THAT ENDED, WELL...
...TRAGICALLY.
YOU KNOW, I WAS MAKING FRIENDS BACK THERE. FIRST DAY OF SCHOOL AND ALL.
QUIET. YOU'RE RUINING THE STAKEOUT.
AT LAST, HE ARRIVES--THOUGH HIS REPUTATION PRECEDES. THAT PROFILE! THAT GLIMMER IN HIS EYE!
THE FOREIGNER HIMSELF.
CHAMELEON. I REALLY HOPE THERE'S NO RUNAROUND THIS TIME.
HEAVENS, NO. S.H.I.E.L.D.'S GOING-OUT-OF-BUSINESS SALE STILL HAS PLENTY OF TIME ON THE CLOCK--
--WHICH MEANS YOU, SIR, ARE NOW THE PROUD OWNER OF THE INFINITY FORMULA.
DON'T DO IT! IT'S NOT REAL OWNERSHIP--

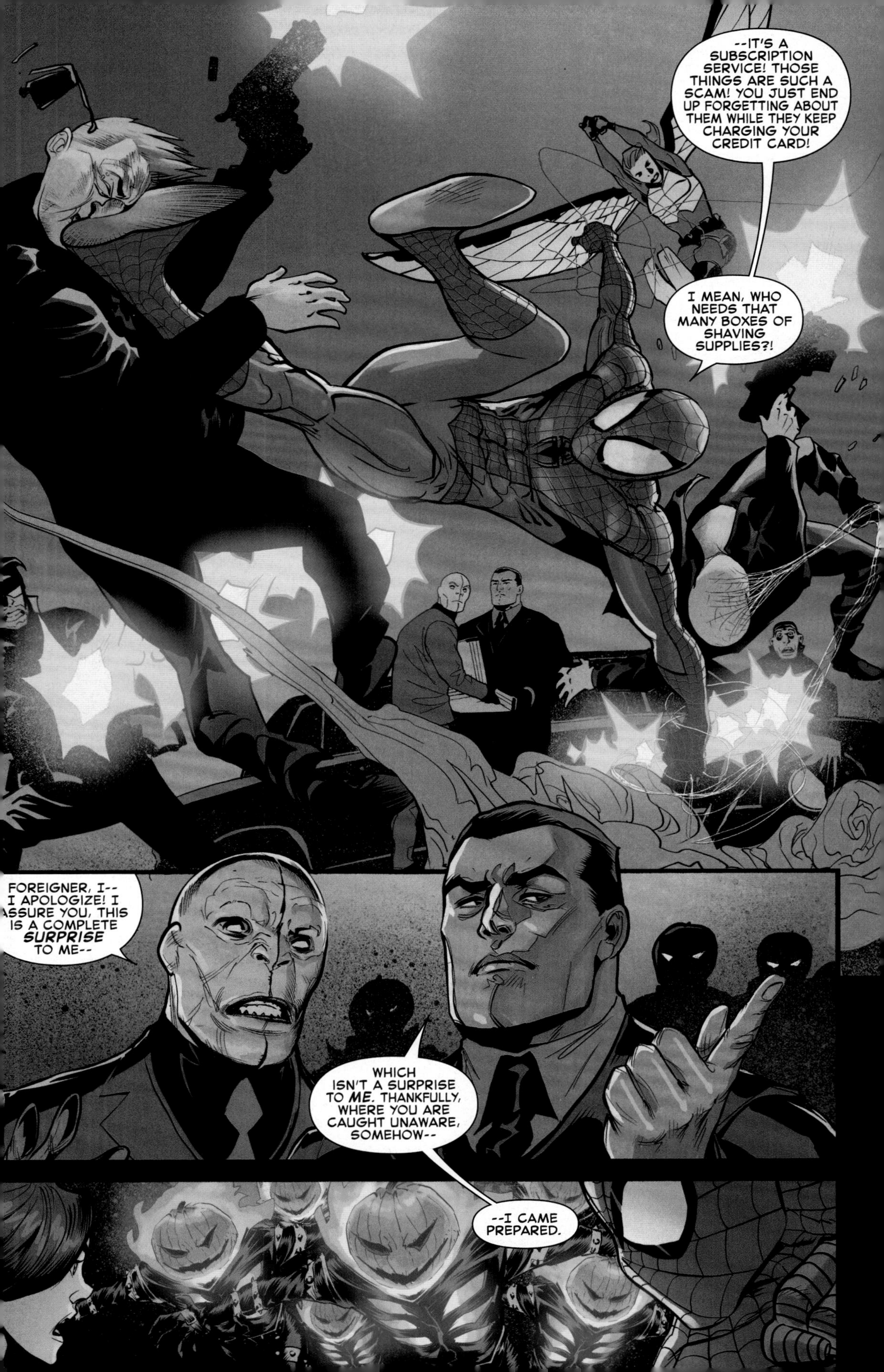
--IT'S A SUBSCRIPTION SERVICE! THOSE THINGS ARE SUCH A SCAM! YOU JUST END UP FORGETTING ABOUT THEM WHILE THEY KEEP CHARGING YOUR CREDIT CARD!
I MEAN, WHO NEEDS THAT MANY BOXES OF SHAVING SUPPLIES?!
FOREIGNER, I-- I APOLOGIZE! I ASSURE YOU, THIS IS A COMPLETE SURPRISE TO ME--
WHICH ISN'T A SURPRISE TO ME. THANKFULLY, WHERE YOU ARE CAUGHT UNAWARE, SOMEHOW--
--I CAME PREPARED.

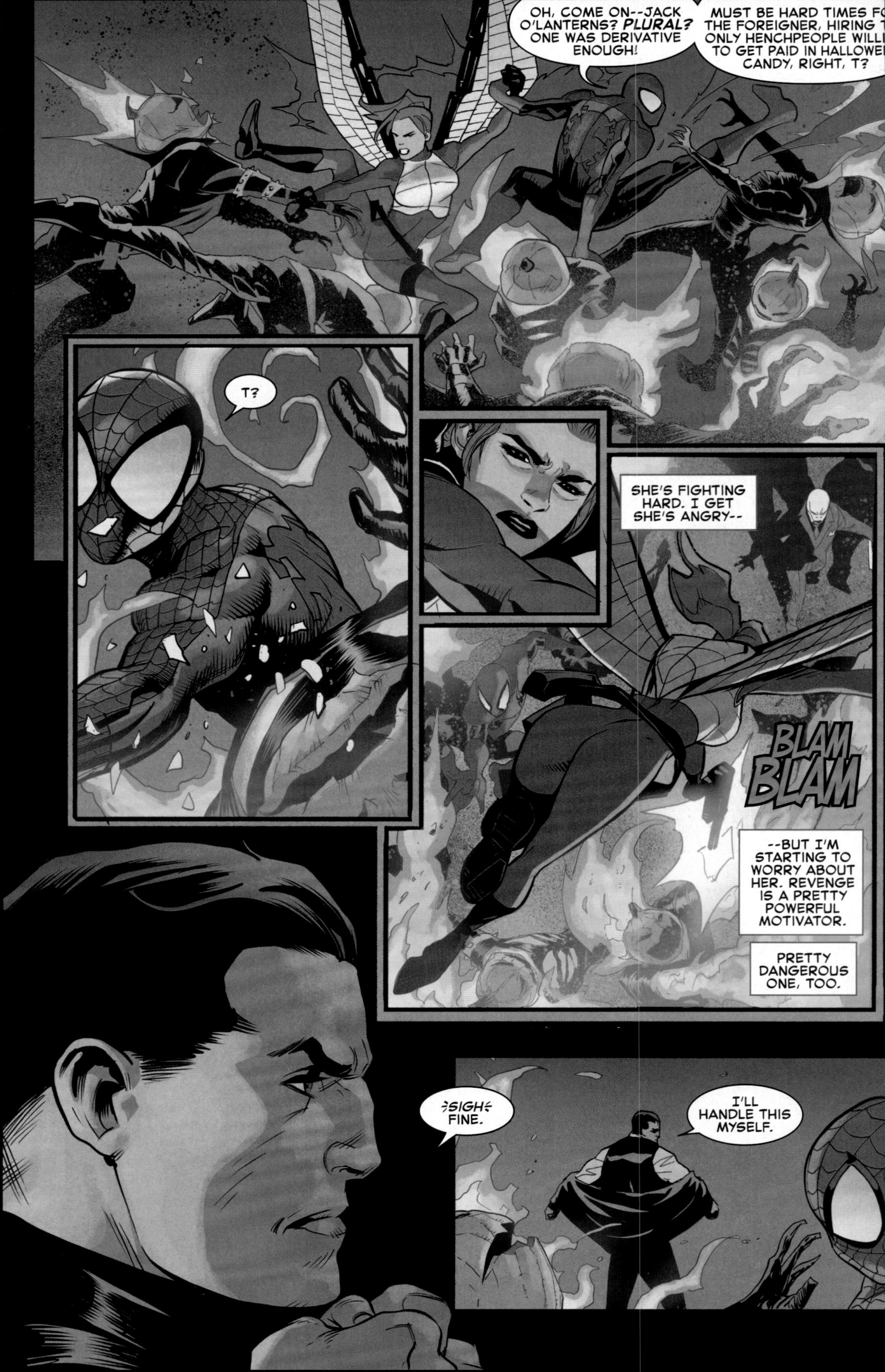
OH, COME ON--JACK O'LANTERNS? PLURAL? ONE WAS DERIVATIVE ENOUGH!
T?
SHE'S FIGHTING HARD. I GET SHE'S ANGRY--
BLAM BLAM
--BUT I'M STARTING TO WORRY ABOUT HER. REVENGE IS A PRETTY POWERFUL MOTIVATOR.
PRETTY DANGEROUS ONE, TOO.
SIGH FINE.
I'LL HANDLE THIS MYSELF.

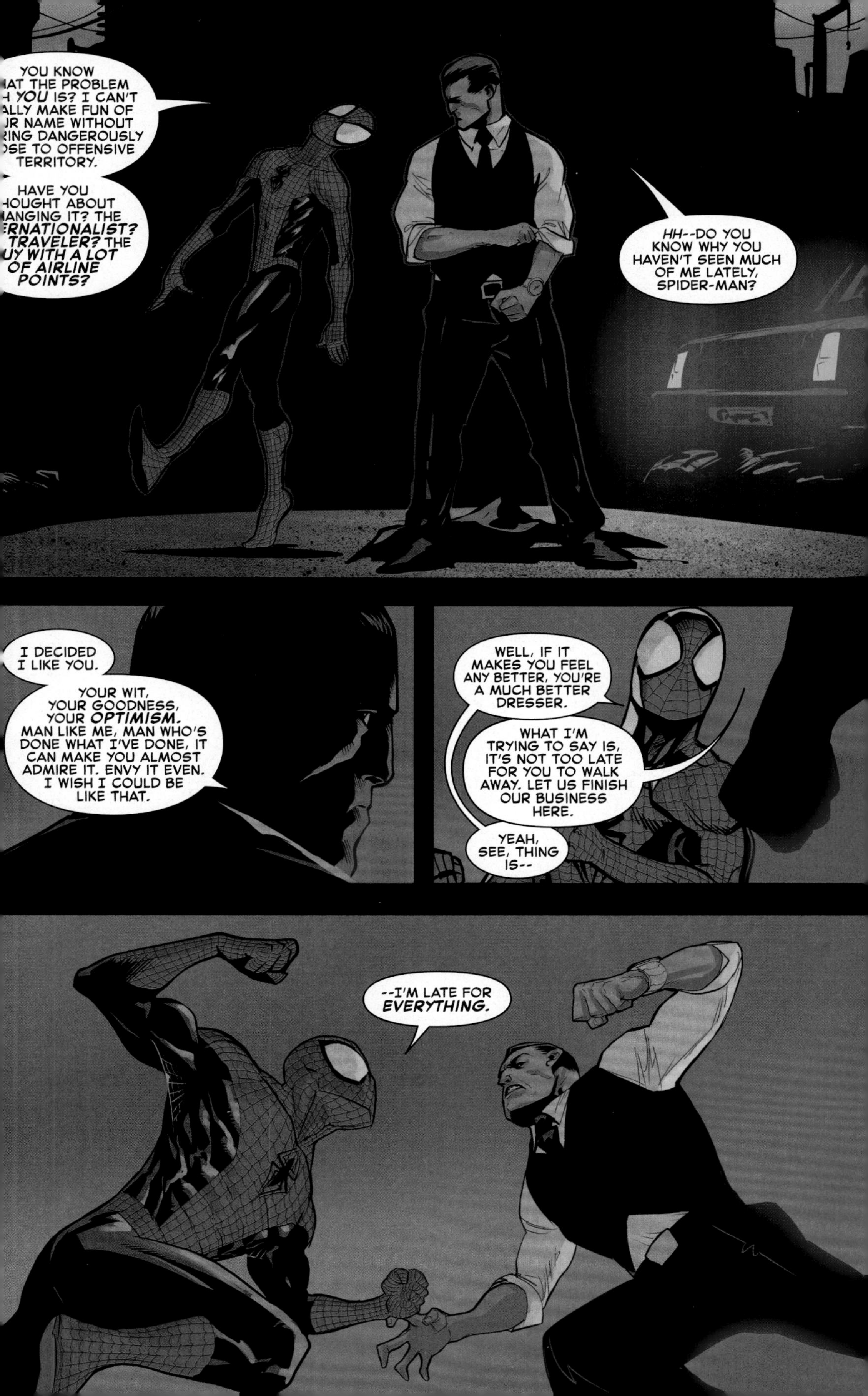

YOU KNOW AT THE PROBLEM H YOU IS? I CAN'T ALLY MAKE FUN OF JR NAME WITHOUT RING DANGEROUSLY OSE TO OFFENSIVE TERRITORY.
HAVE YOU HOUGHT ABOUT ANGING IT? THE ERNATIONALIST? TRAVELER? THE UY WITH A LOT OF AIRLINE POINTS?
HH--DO YOU KNOW WHY YOU HAVEN'T SEEN MUCH OF ME LATELY, SPIDER-MAN?
I DECIDED I LIKE YOU.
YOUR WIT, YOUR GOODNESS, YOUR OPTIMISM. MAN LIKE ME, MAN WHO'S DONE WHAT I'VE DONE, IT CAN MAKE YOU ALMOST ADMIRE IT. ENVY IT EVEN. I WISH I COULD BE LIKE THAT.
WELL, IF IT MAKES YOU FEEL ANY BETTER, YOU'RE A MUCH BETTER DRESSER.
WHAT I'M TRYING TO SAY IS, IT'S NOT TOO LATE FOR YOU TO WALK AWAY. LET US FINISH OUR BUSINESS HERE.
YEAH, SEE, THING IS--
--I'M LATE FOR EVERYTHING.

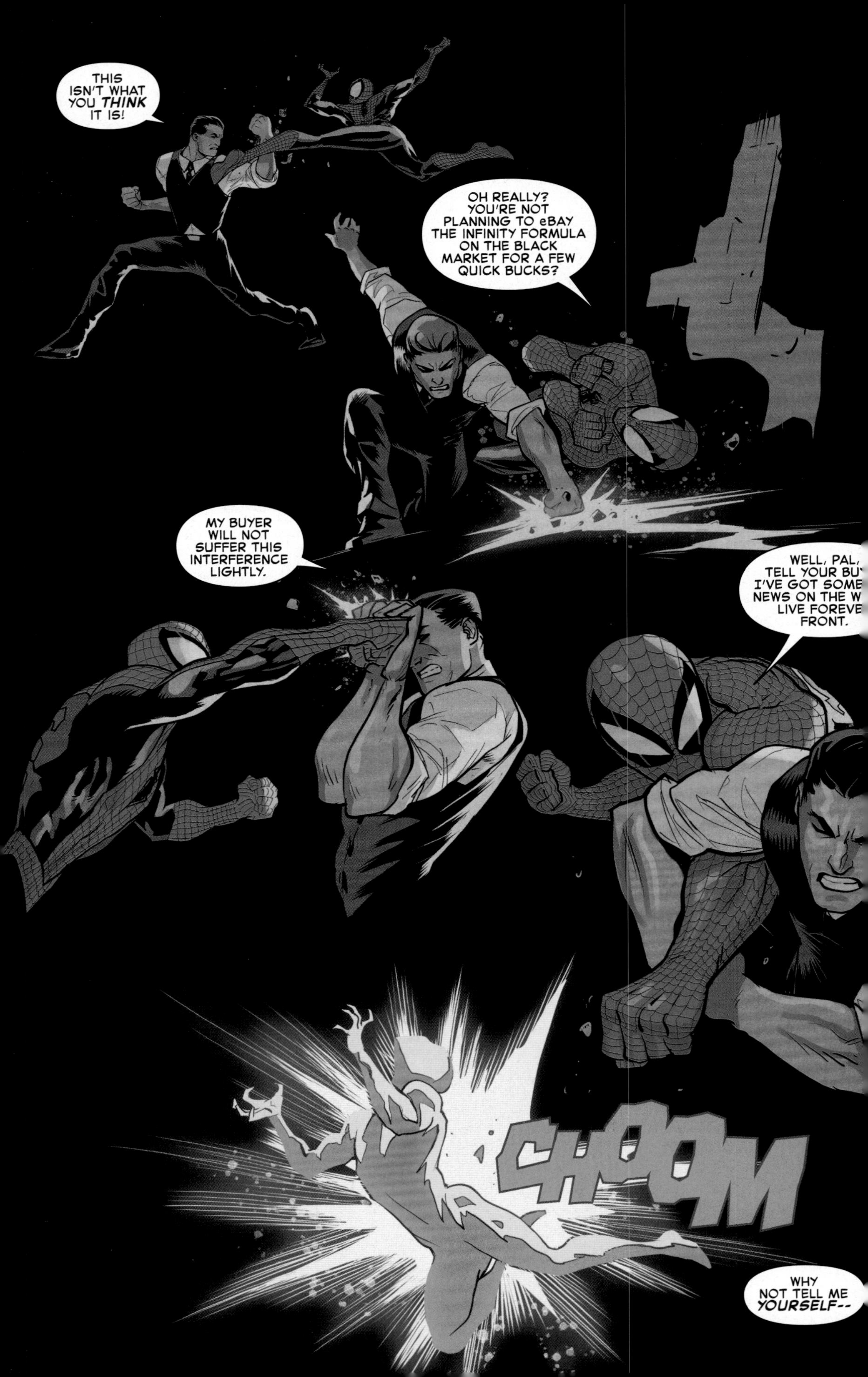
THIS ISN'T WHAT YOU *THINK* IT IS!
OH REALLY? YOU'RE NOT PLANNING TO eBAY THE INFINITY FORMULA ON THE BLACK MARKET FOR A FEW QUICK BUCKS?
MY BUYER WILL NOT SUFFER THIS INTERFERENCE LIGHTLY.
WELL, PAL, TELL YOUR BU
I'VE GOT SOME
NEWS ON THE W
LIVE FOREVE
FRONT.
CHOOOM
WHY NOT TELL ME *YOURSELF--*

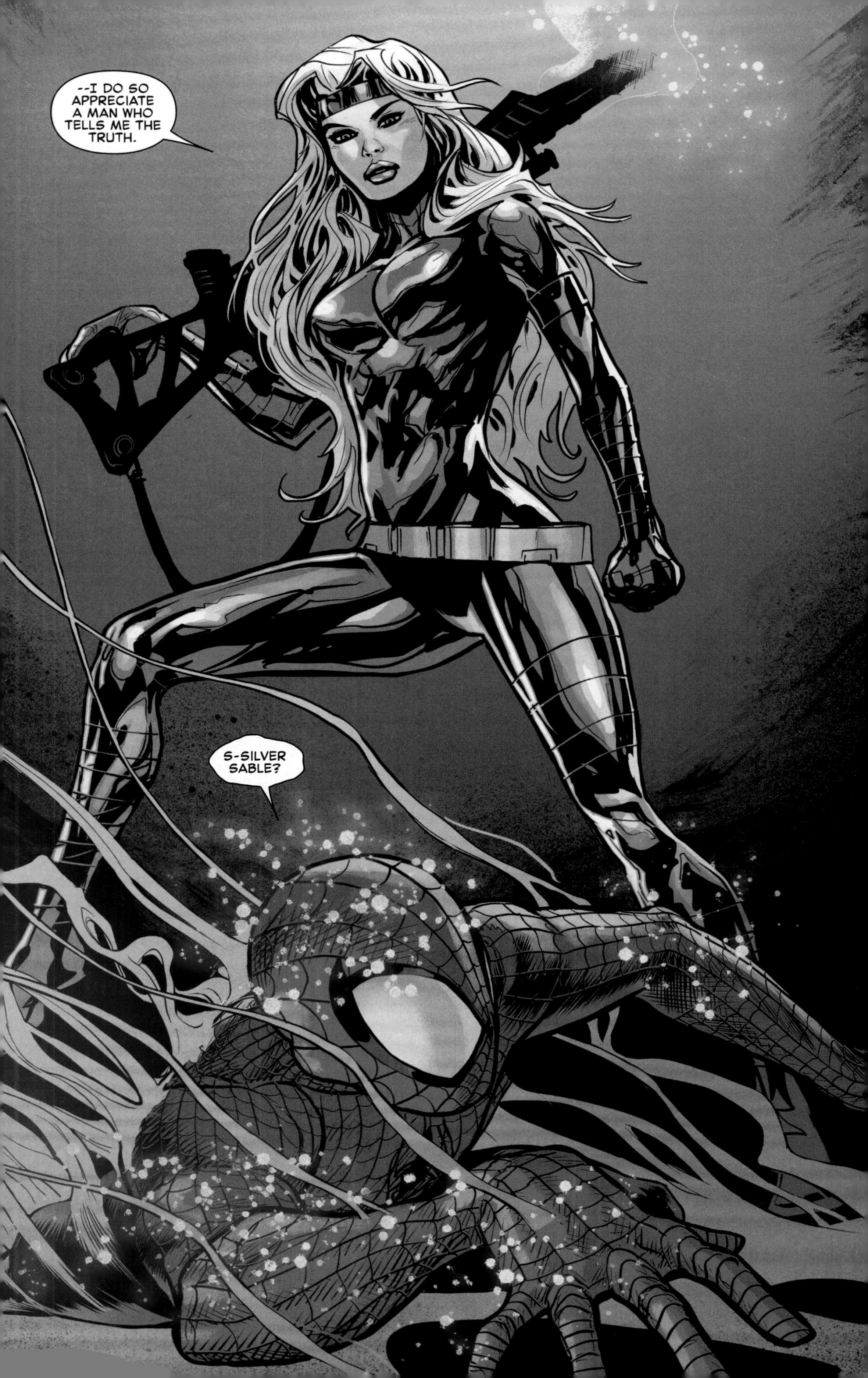
--I DO SO APPRECIATE A MAN WHO TELLS ME THE TRUTH.
S-SILVER SABLE?

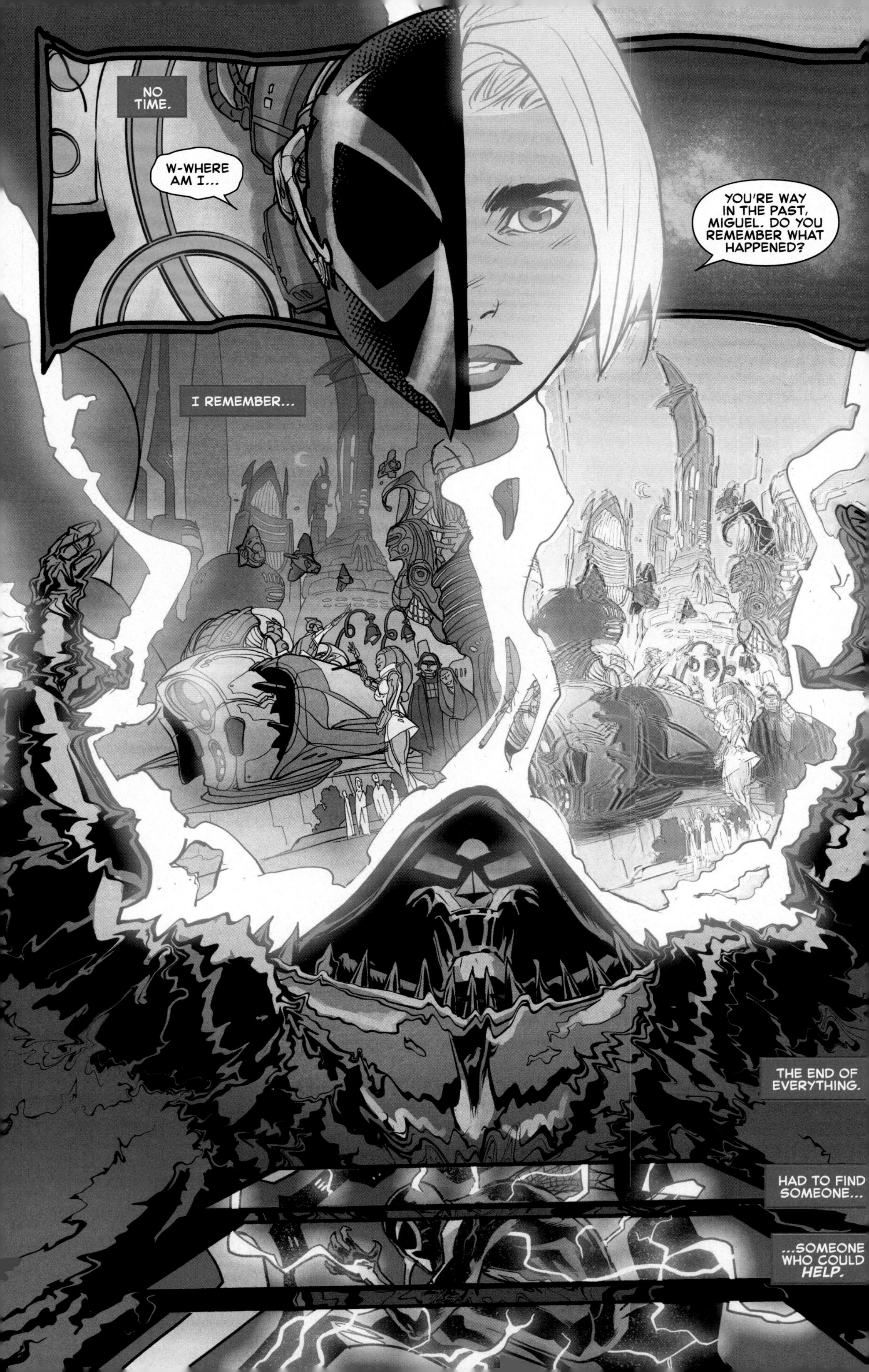
NO TIME.
W-WHERE AM I...
YOU'RE WAY IN THE PAST, MIGUEL. DO YOU REMEMBER WHAT HAPPENED?
I REMEMBER...
THE END OF EVERYTHING.
HAD TO FIND SOMEONE...
...SOMEONE WHO COULD HELP.

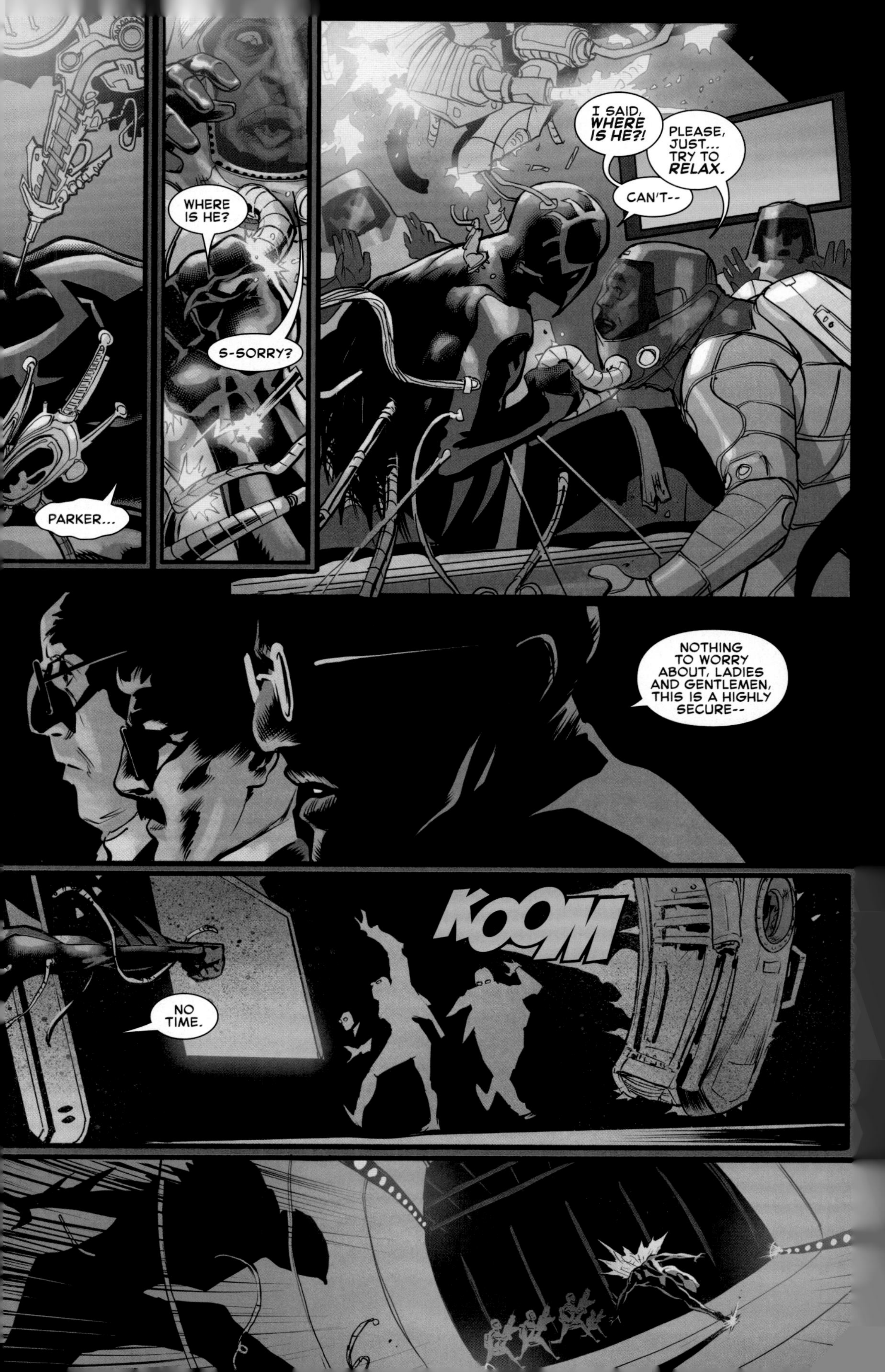

PARKER...
WHERE IS HE?
S-SORRY?
I SAID, WHERE IS HE?!
CAN'T--
PLEASE, JUST... TRY TO RELAX.
NOTHING TO WORRY ABOUT, LADIES AND GENTLEMEN, THIS IS A HIGHLY SECURE--
NO TIME.
KOOM

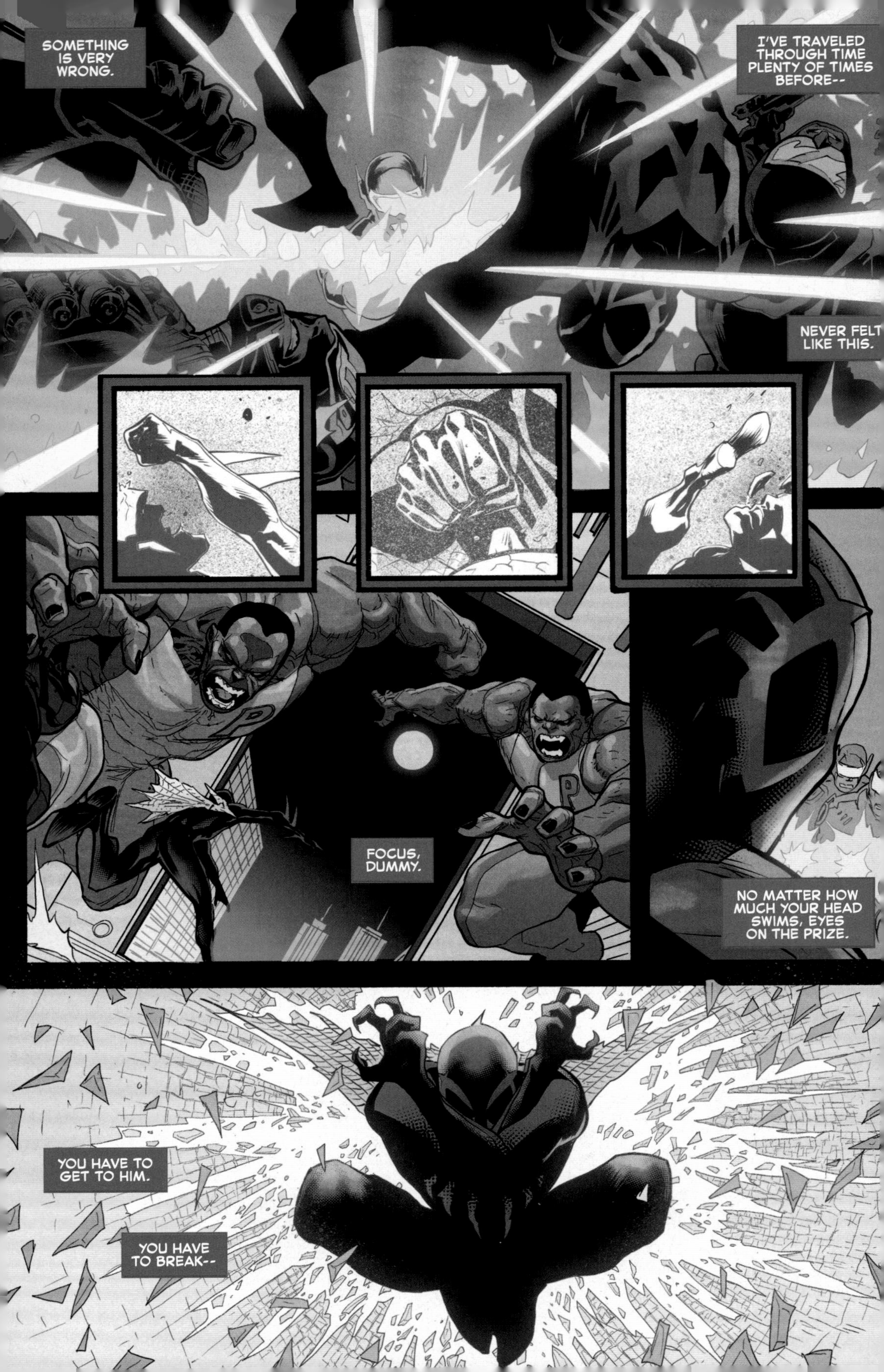
SOMETHING IS VERY WRONG.
I'VE TRAVELED THROUGH TIME PLENTY OF TIMES BEFORE--
NEVER FELT LIKE THIS.
FOCUS, DUMMY.
NO MATTER HOW MUCH YOUR HEAD SWIMS, EYES ON THE PRIZE.
YOU HAVE TO GET TO HIM.
YOU HAVE TO BREAK--

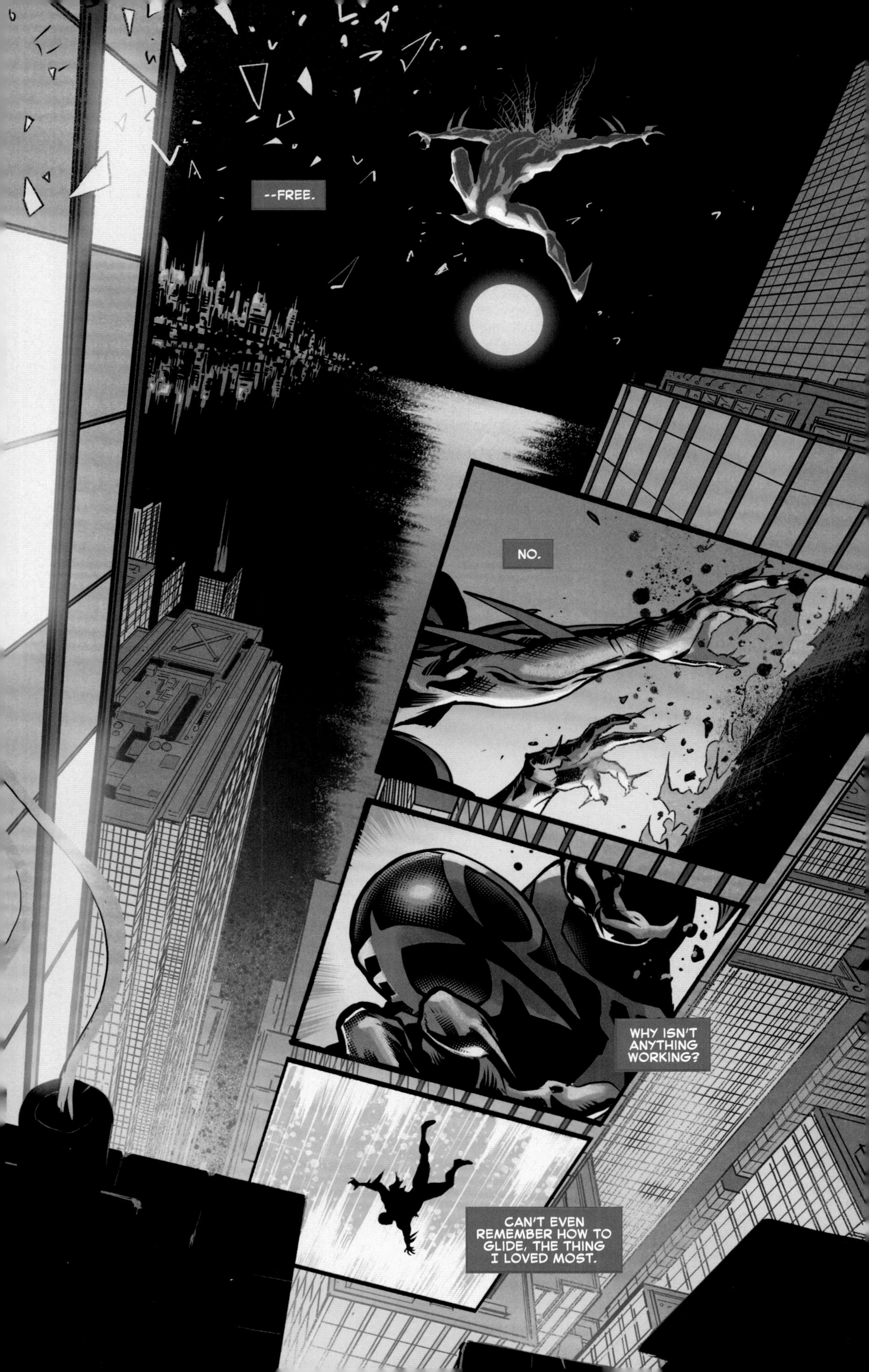
--FREE.
NO.
WHY ISN'T ANYTHING WORKING?
CAN'T EVEN REMEMBER HOW TO GLIDE, THE THING I LOVED MOST.

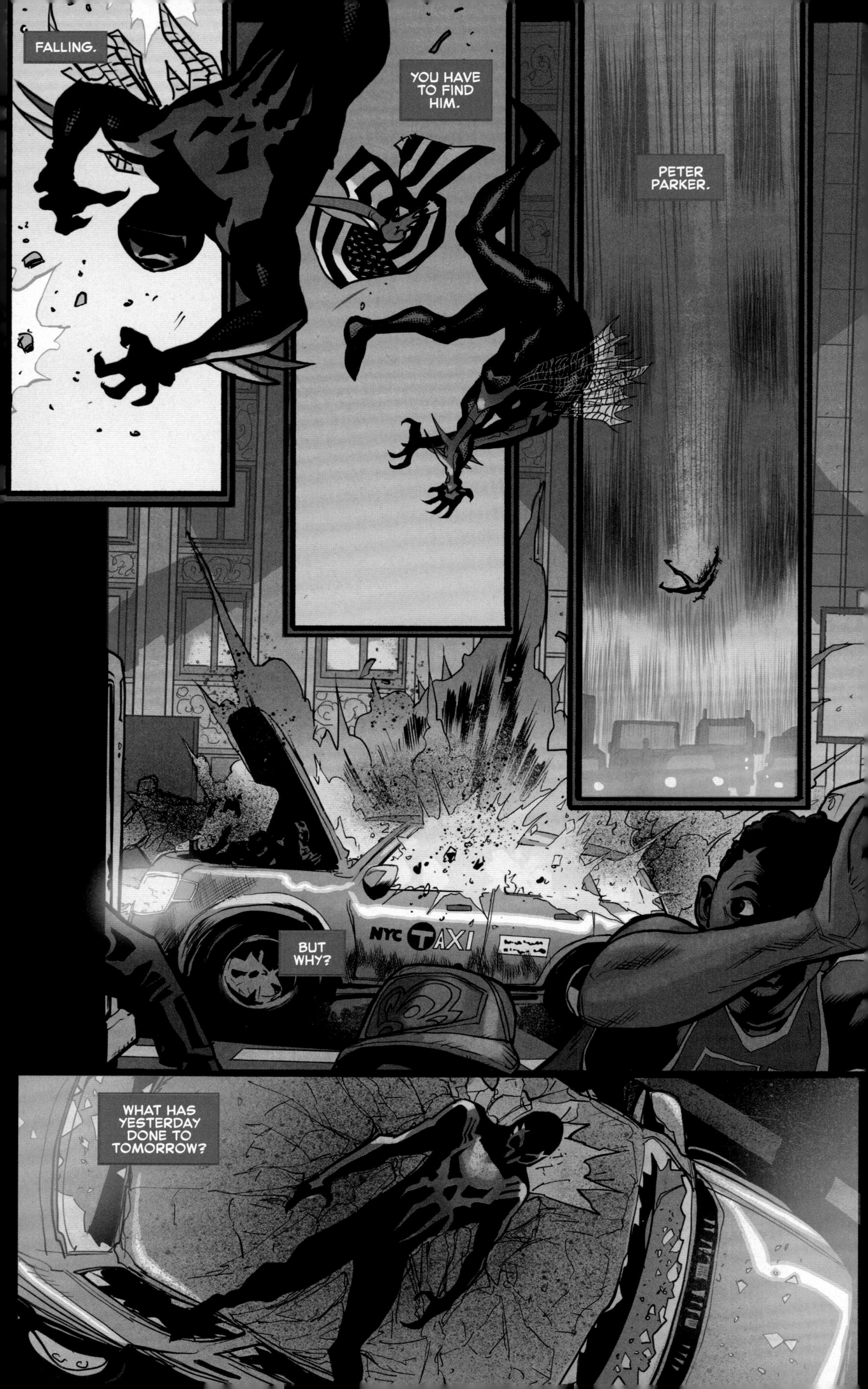
FALLING.
YOU HAVE TO FIND HIM.
PETER PARKER.
NYC TAXI
BUT WHY?
WHAT HAS YESTERDAY DONE TO TOMORROW?

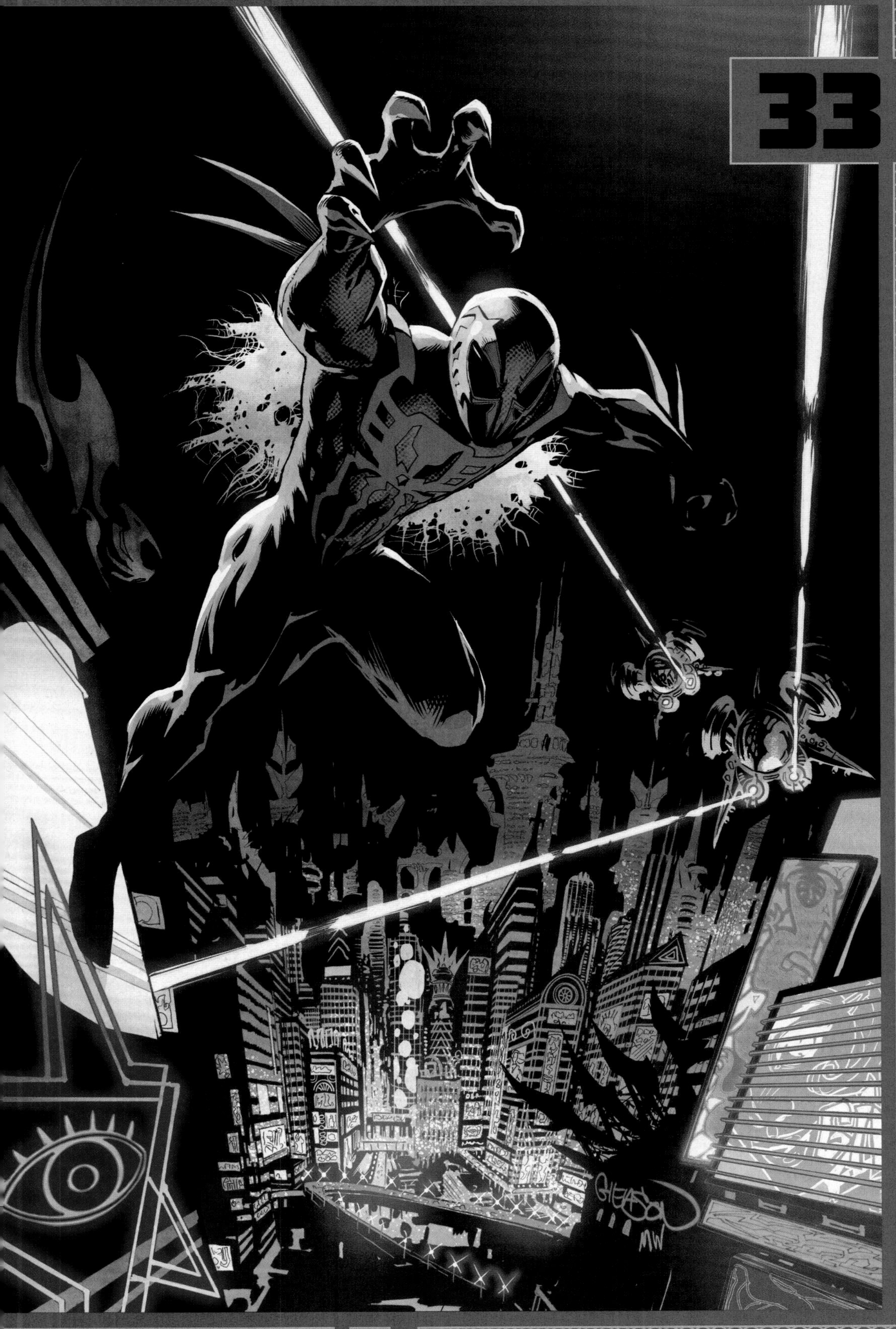

33

POINT BLANK

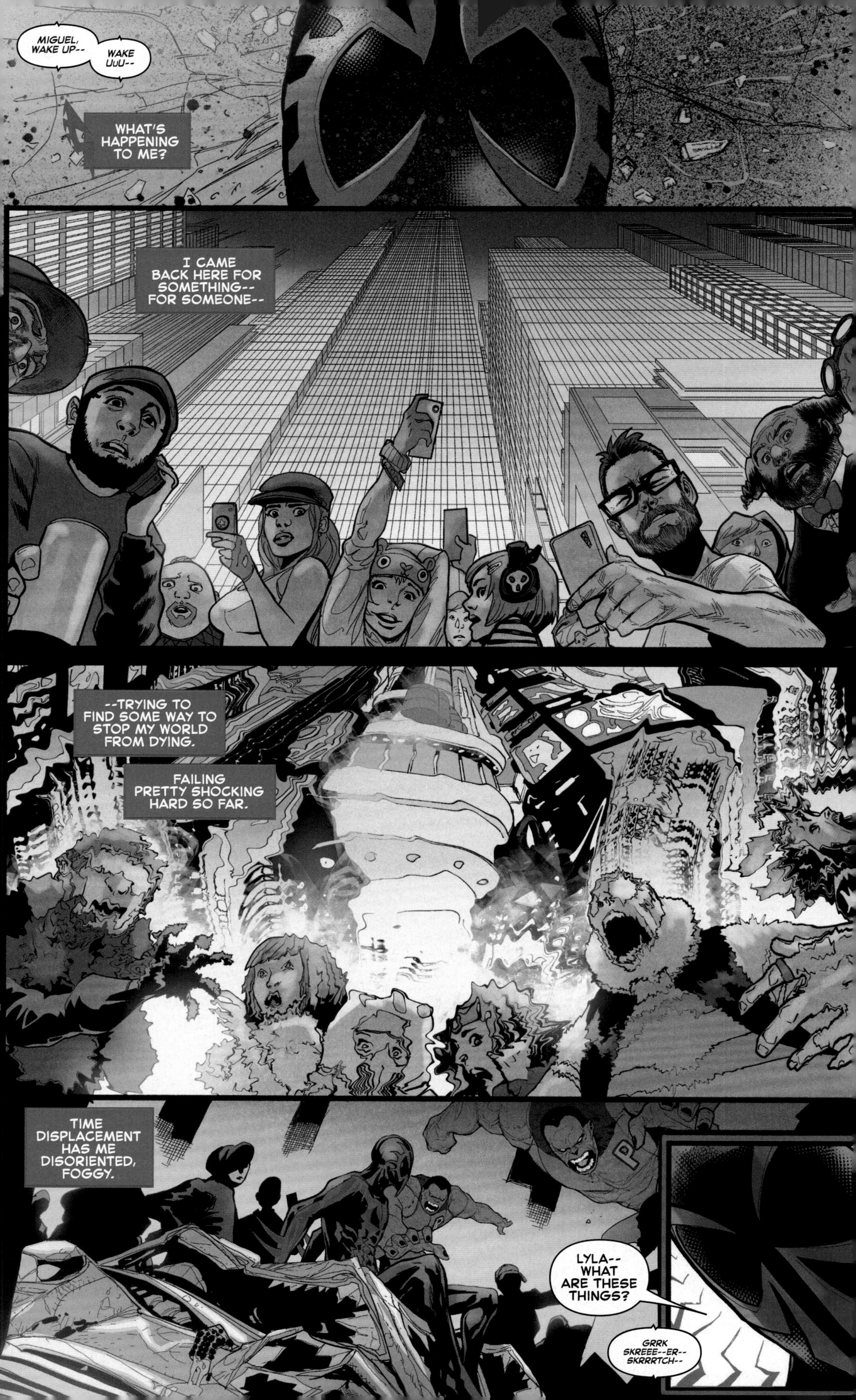
MIGUEL, WAKE UP--
WAKE UUU--
WHAT'S HAPPENING TO ME?
I CAME BACK HERE FOR SOMETHING-- FOR SOMEONE--
--TRYING TO FIND SOME WAY TO STOP MY WORLD FROM DYING.
FAILING PRETTY SHOCKING HARD SO FAR.
TIME DISPLACEMENT HAS ME DISORIENTED, FOGGY.
LYLA-- WHAT ARE THESE THINGS?
GRRK SKREEE--ER-- SKRRRTCH--

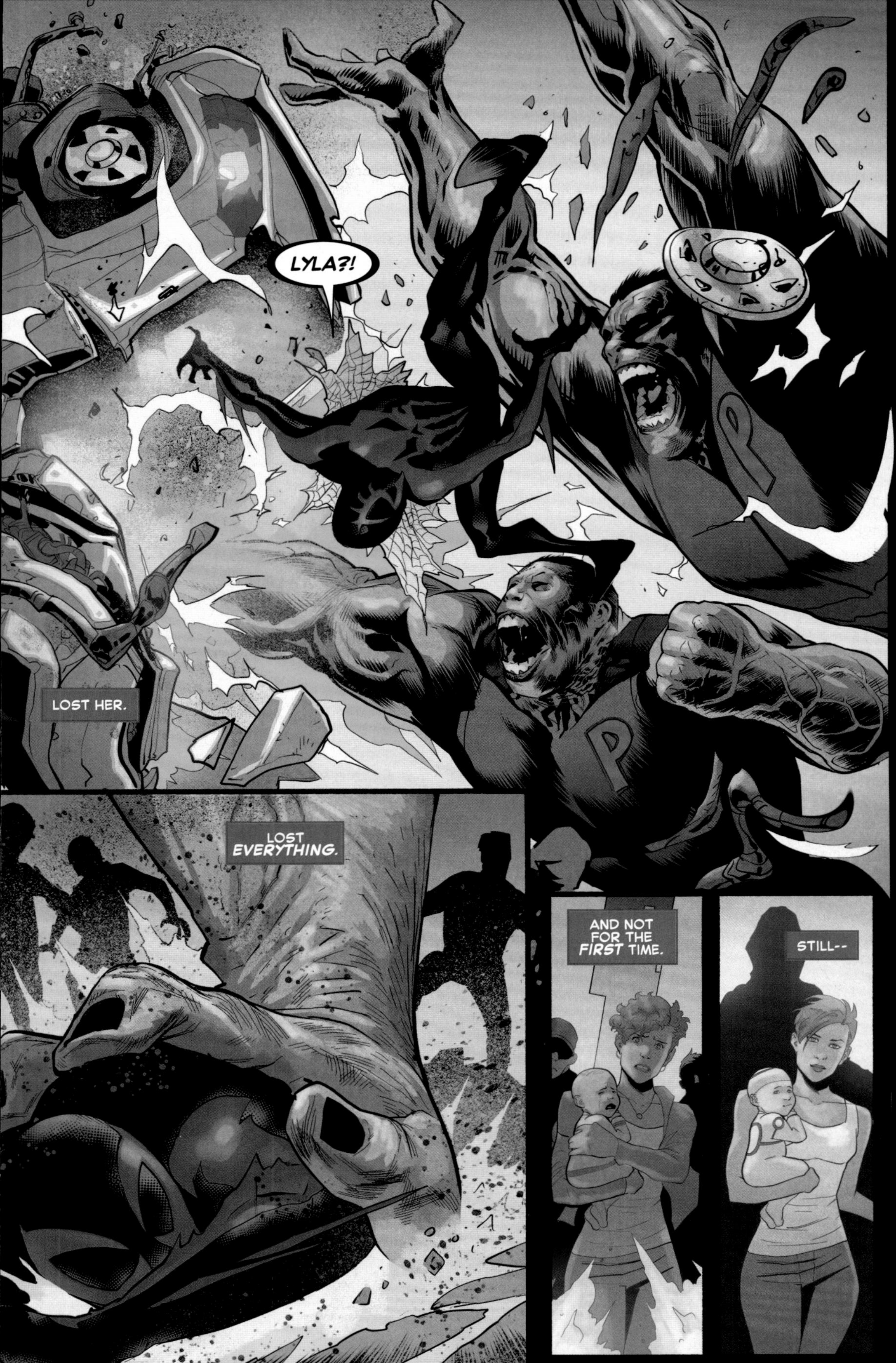
LYLA?!
LOST HER.
LOST EVERYTHING.
AND NOT FOR THE FIRST TIME.
STILL--

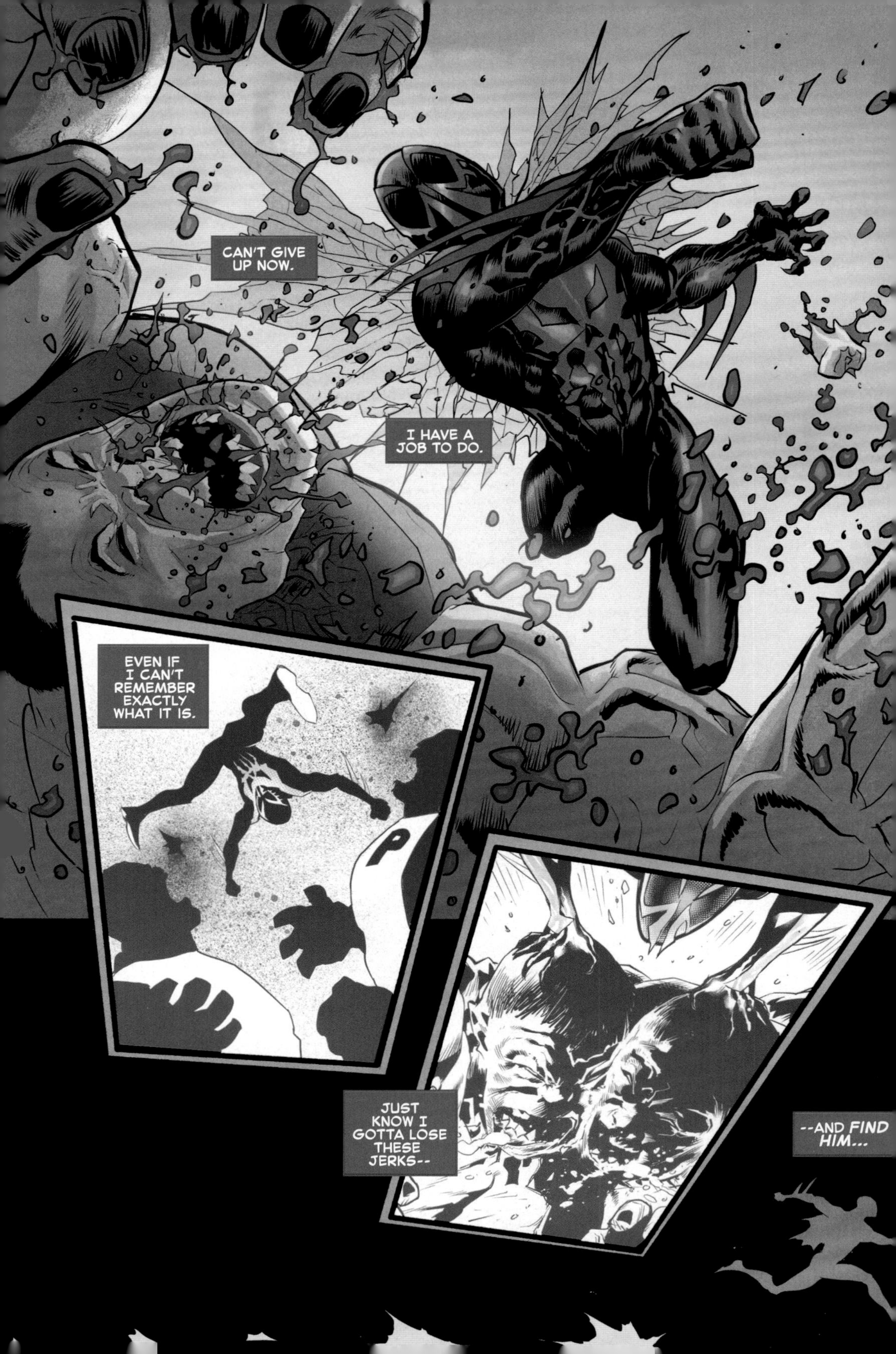
CAN'T GIVE UP NOW.
I HAVE A JOB TO DO.
EVEN IF I CAN'T REMEMBER EXACTLY WHAT IT IS.
JUST KNOW I GOTTA LOSE THESE JERKS--
--AND FIND HIM...

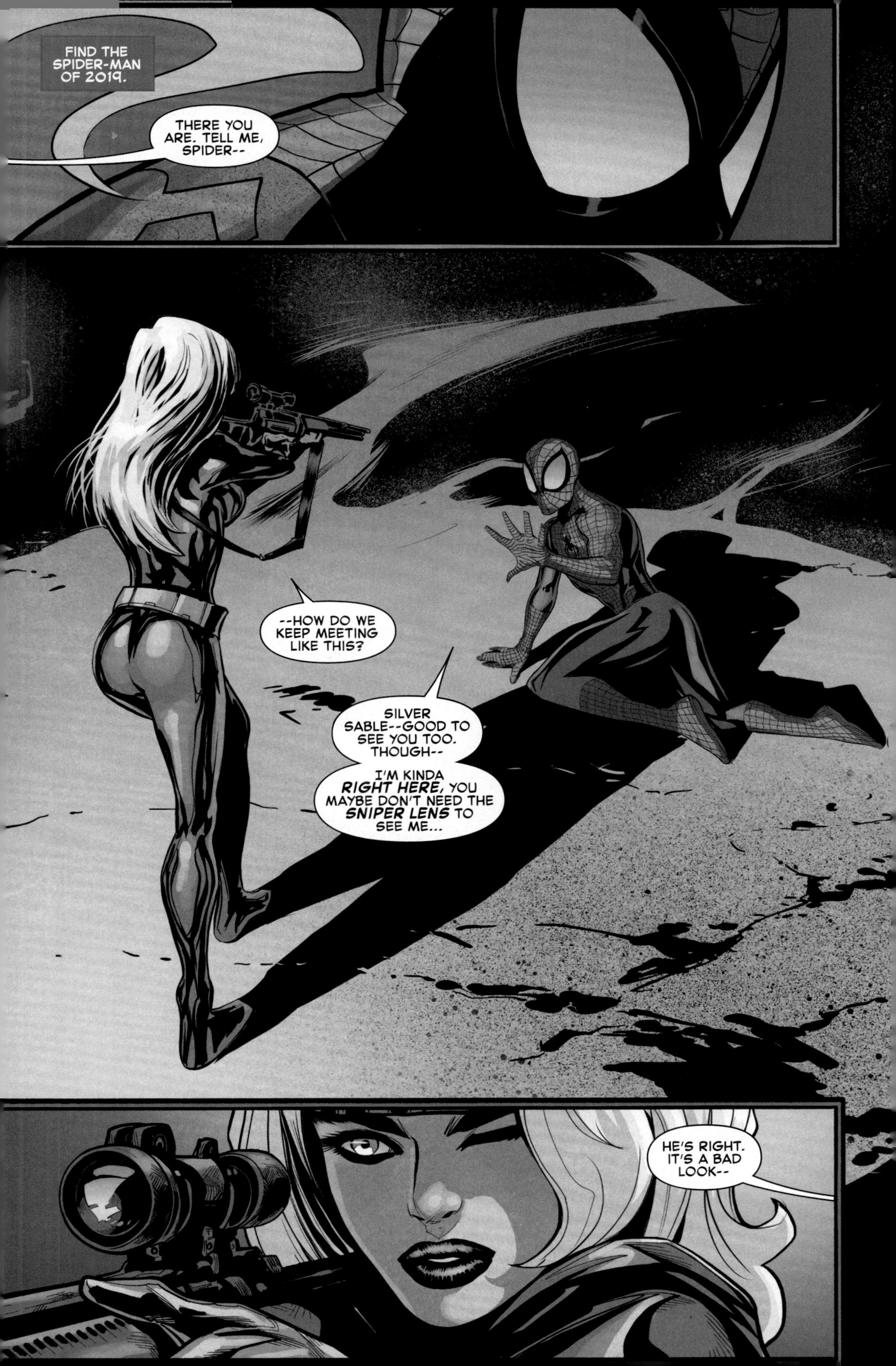
FIND THE SPIDER-MAN OF 2019.
THERE YOU ARE. TELL ME, SPIDER--
--HOW DO WE KEEP MEETING LIKE THIS?
SILVER SABLE--GOOD TO SEE YOU TOO. THOUGH--
I'M KINDA RIGHT HERE, YOU MAYBE DON'T NEED THE SNIPER LENS TO SEE ME...
HE'S RIGHT. IT'S A BAD LOOK--

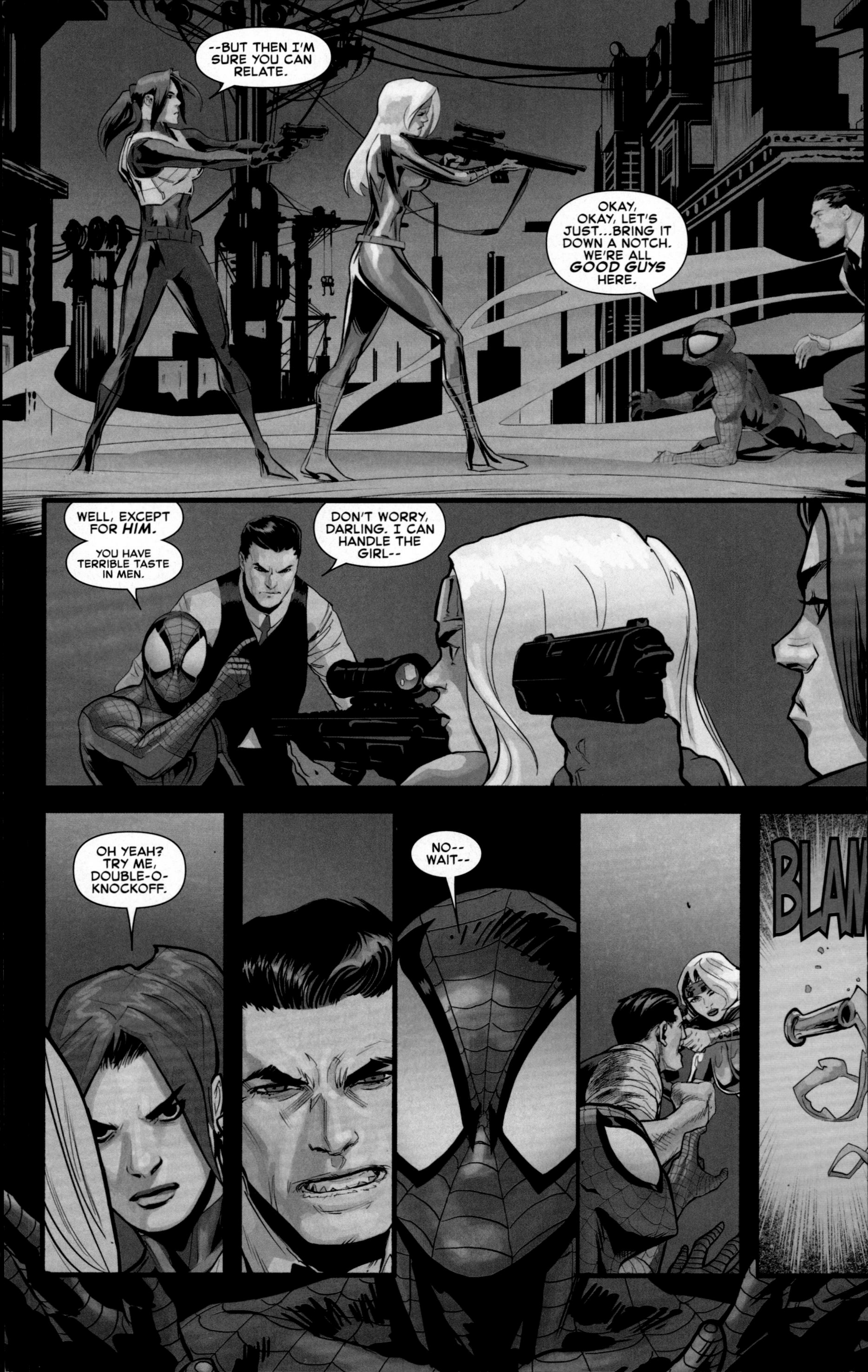
--BUT THEN I'M SURE YOU CAN RELATE.
OKAY, OKAY, LET'S JUST...BRING IT DOWN A NOTCH. WE'RE ALL GOOD GUYS HERE.
WELL, EXCEPT FOR HIM.
YOU HAVE TERRIBLE TASTE IN MEN.
DON'T WORRY, DARLING. I CAN HANDLE THE GIRL--
OH YEAH? TRY ME, DOUBLE-O-KNOCKOFF.
NO-- WAIT--
BLAM

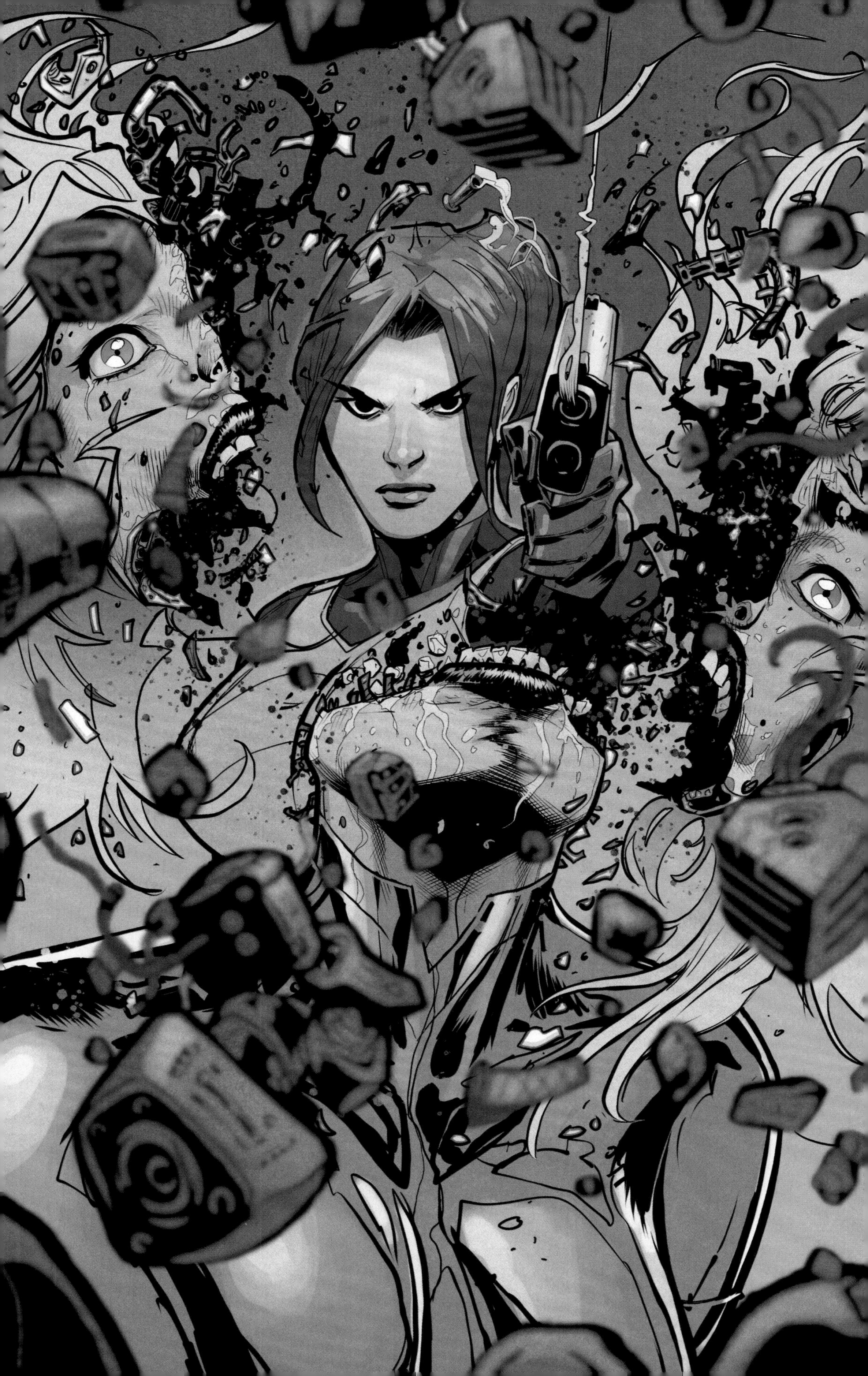

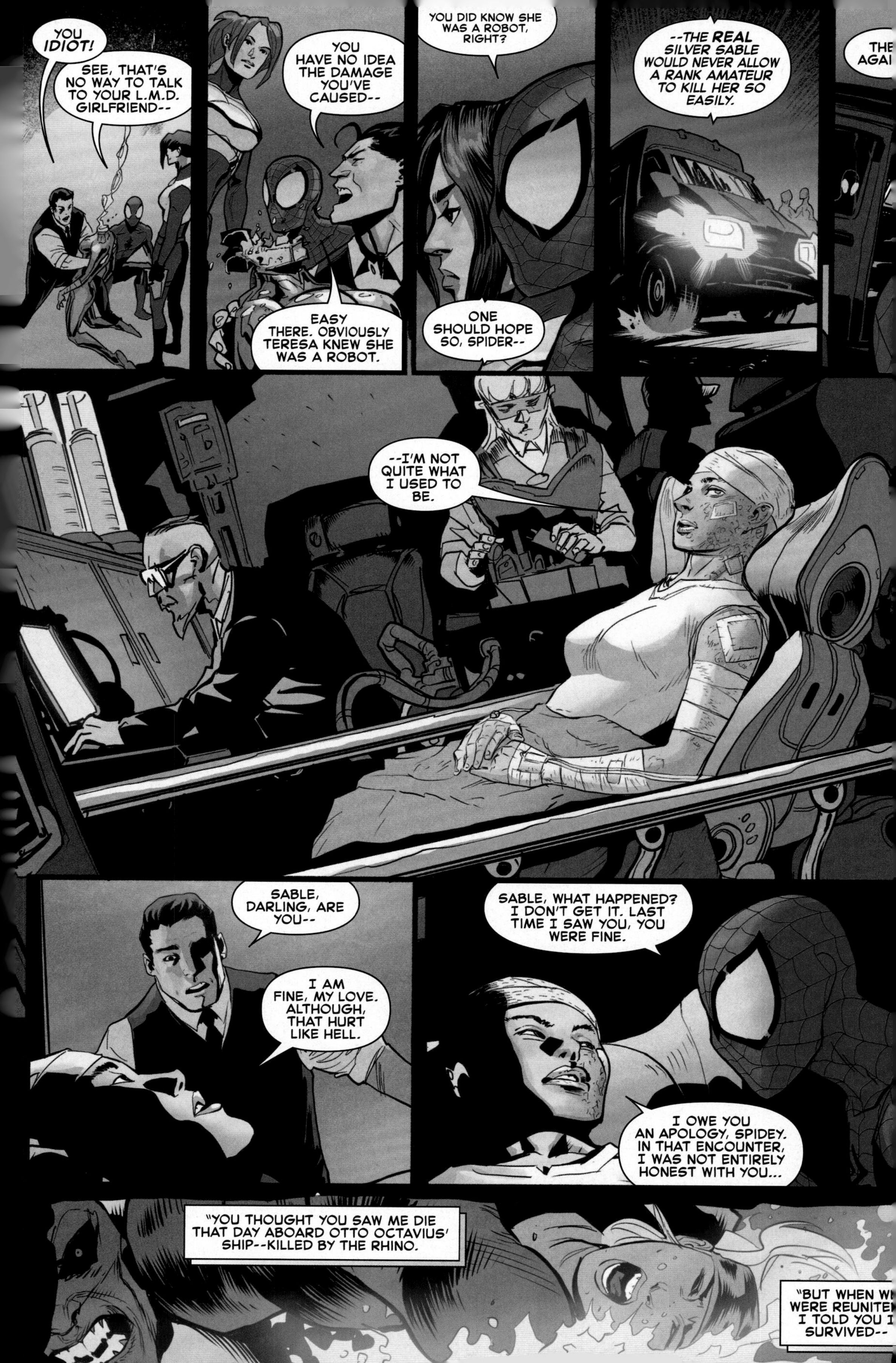
YOU IDIOT!
SEE, THAT'S NO WAY TO TALK TO YOUR L.M.D. GIRLFRIEND--
YOU HAVE NO IDEA THE DAMAGE YOU'VE CAUSED--
EASY THERE. OBVIOUSLY TERESA KNEW SHE WAS A ROBOT.
YOU DID KNOW SHE WAS A ROBOT, RIGHT?
ONE SHOULD HOPE SO, SPIDER--
--THE REAL SILVER SABLE WOULD NEVER ALLOW A RANK AMATEUR TO KILL HER SO EASILY.
--I'M NOT QUITE WHAT I USED TO BE.
SABLE, DARLING, ARE YOU--
I AM FINE, MY LOVE. ALTHOUGH, THAT HURT LIKE HELL.
SABLE, WHAT HAPPENED? I DON'T GET IT. LAST TIME I SAW YOU, YOU WERE FINE.
I OWE YOU AN APOLOGY, SPIDEY. IN THAT ENCOUNTER, I WAS NOT ENTIRELY HONEST WITH YOU...
"YOU THOUGHT YOU SAW ME DIE THAT DAY ABOARD OTTO OCTAVIUS' SHIP--KILLED BY THE RHINO.

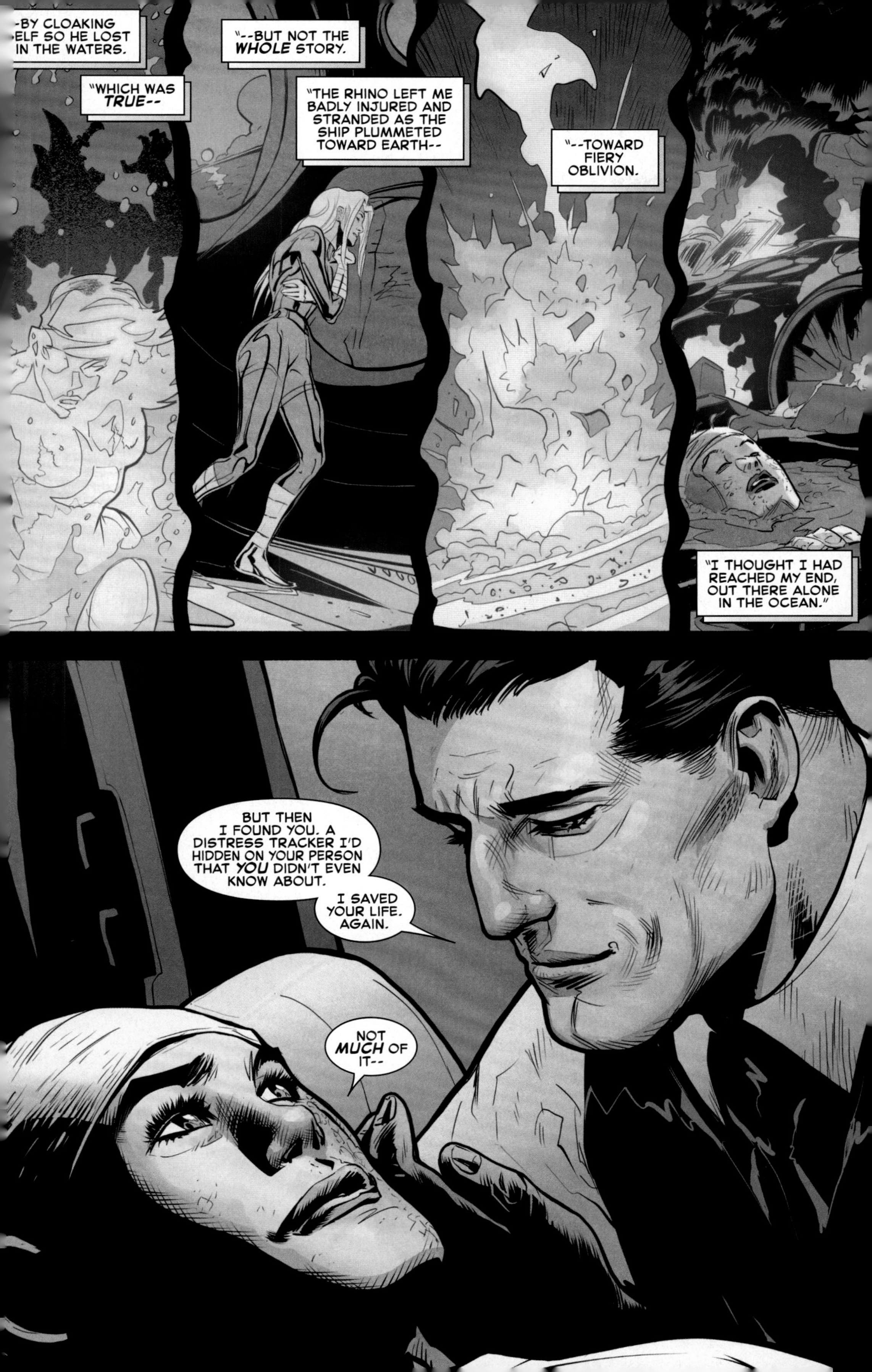
-BY CLOAKING
ELF SO HE LOST
IN THE WATERS.
"WHICH WAS TRUE--
"--BUT NOT THE WHOLE STORY.
"THE RHINO LEFT ME BADLY INJURED AND STRANDED AS THE SHIP PLUMMETED TOWARD EARTH--
"--TOWARD FIERY OBLIVION.
"I THOUGHT I HAD REACHED MY END, OUT THERE ALONE IN THE OCEAN."
BUT THEN I FOUND YOU. A DISTRESS TRACKER I'D HIDDEN ON YOUR PERSON THAT YOU DIDN'T EVEN KNOW ABOUT.
I SAVED YOUR LIFE. AGAIN.
NOT MUCH OF IT--

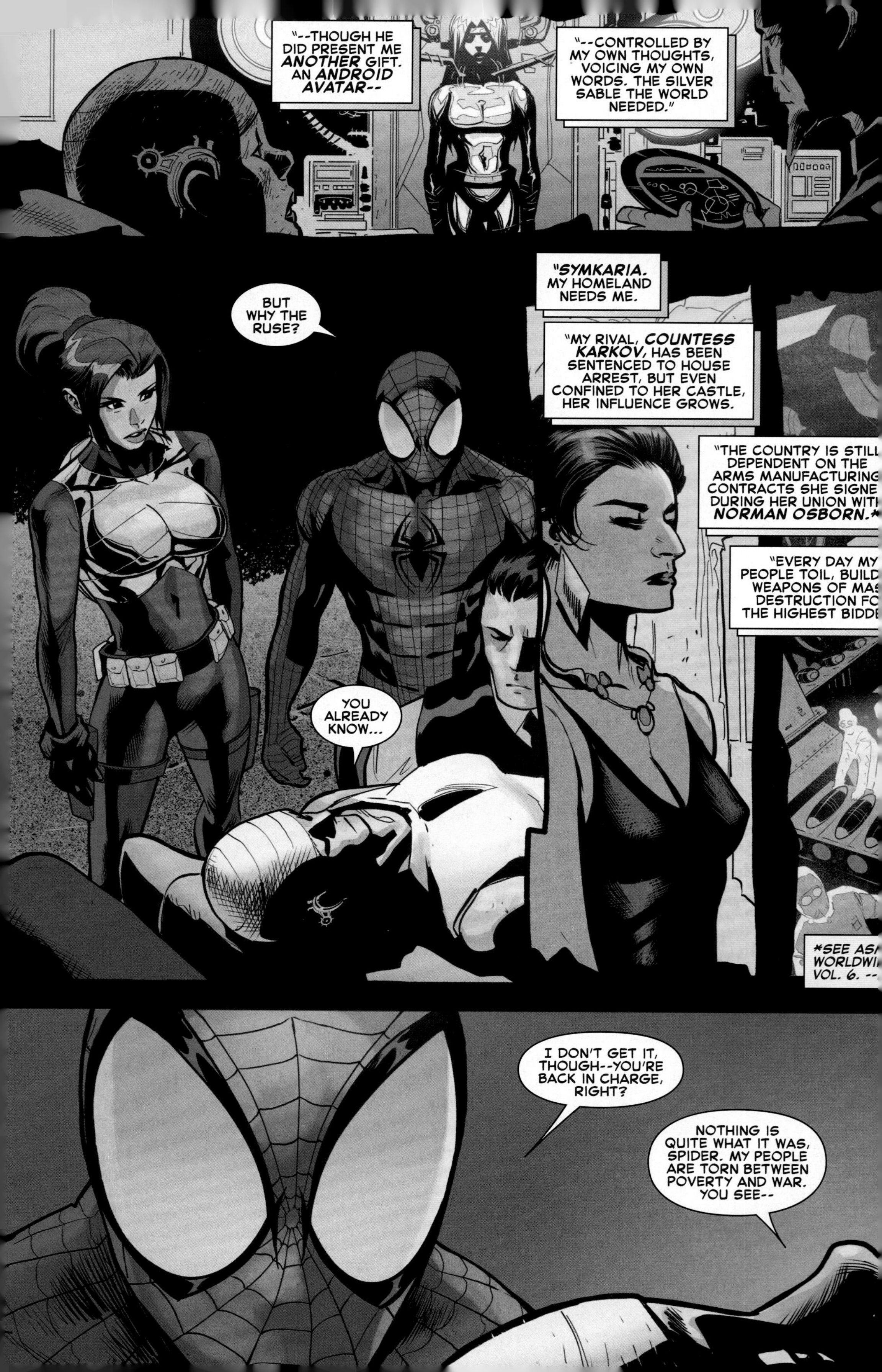
"--THOUGH HE DID PRESENT ME ANOTHER GIFT. AN ANDROID AVATAR--
"--CONTROLLED BY MY OWN THOUGHTS, VOICING MY OWN WORDS. THE SILVER SABLE THE WORLD NEEDED."
BUT WHY THE RUSE?
"SYMKARIA. MY HOMELAND NEEDS ME.
"MY RIVAL, COUNTESS KARKOV, HAS BEEN SENTENCED TO HOUSE ARREST, BUT EVEN CONFINED TO HER CASTLE, HER INFLUENCE GROWS.
"THE COUNTRY IS STILL DEPENDENT ON THE ARMS MANUFACTURING CONTRACTS SHE SIGNE DURING HER UNION WITH NORMAN OSBORN.*
"EVERY DAY MY PEOPLE TOIL, BUILD WEAPONS OF MAS DESTRUCTION FO THE HIGHEST BIDDE
YOU ALREADY KNOW...
*SEE ASI WORLDWI VOL. 6. --
I DON'T GET IT, THOUGH--YOU'RE BACK IN CHARGE, RIGHT?
NOTHING IS QUITE WHAT IT WAS, SPIDER. MY PEOPLE ARE TORN BETWEEN POVERTY AND WAR. YOU SEE--

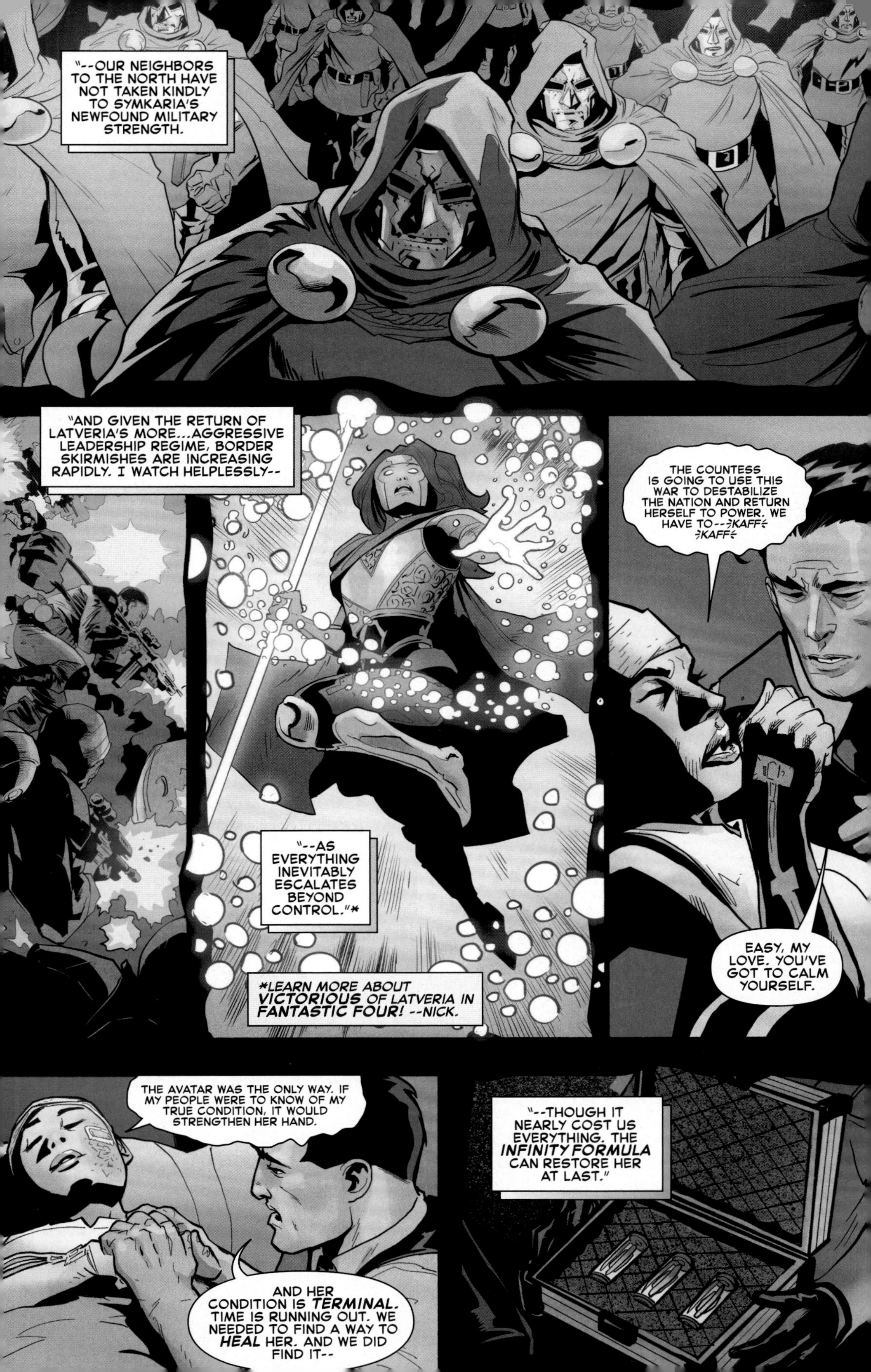
"--OUR NEIGHBORS TO THE NORTH HAVE NOT TAKEN KINDLY TO SYMKARIA'S NEWFOUND MILITARY STRENGTH.
"AND GIVEN THE RETURN OF LATVERIA'S MORE...AGGRESSIVE LEADERSHIP REGIME, BORDER SKIRMISHES ARE INCREASING RAPIDLY. I WATCH HELPLESSLY--
"--AS EVERYTHING INEVITABLY ESCALATES BEYOND CONTROL."*
*LEARN MORE ABOUT VICTORIOUS OF LATVERIA IN FANTASTIC FOUR! --NICK.
THE COUNTESS IS GOING TO USE THIS WAR TO DESTABILIZE THE NATION AND RETURN HERSELF TO POWER. WE HAVE TO-- KAFF KAFF
EASY, MY LOVE. YOU'VE GOT TO CALM YOURSELF.
THE AVATAR WAS THE ONLY WAY. IF MY PEOPLE WERE TO KNOW OF MY TRUE CONDITION, IT WOULD STRENGTHEN HER HAND.
AND HER CONDITION IS TERMINAL. TIME IS RUNNING OUT. WE NEEDED TO FIND A WAY TO HEAL HER. AND WE DID FIND IT--
"--THOUGH IT NEARLY COST US EVERYTHING. THE INFINITY FORMULA CAN RESTORE HER AT LAST."

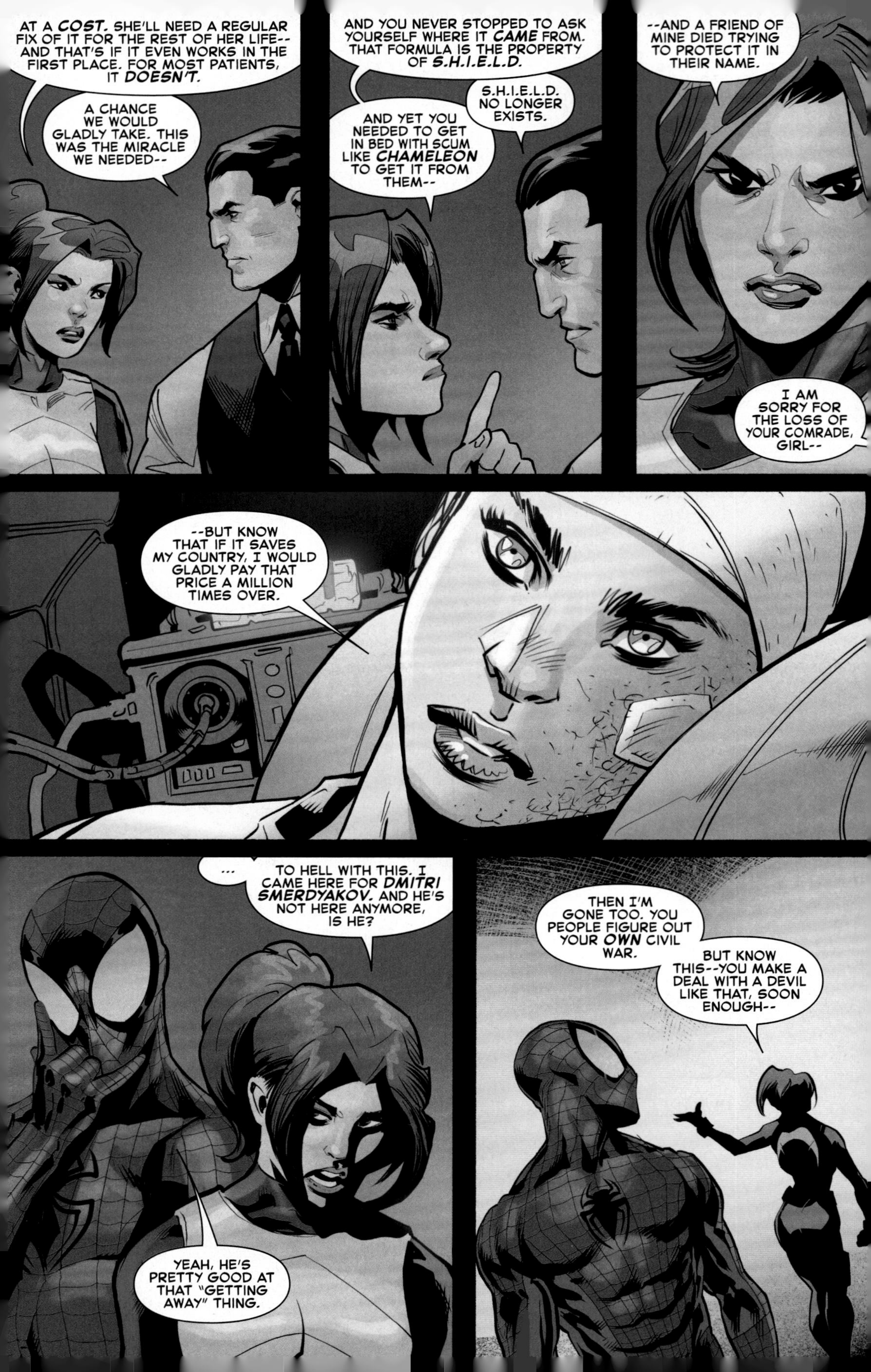
AT A COST. SHE'LL NEED A REGULAR FIX OF IT FOR THE REST OF HER LIFE--AND THAT'S IF IT EVEN WORKS IN THE FIRST PLACE. FOR MOST PATIENTS, IT DOESN'T.
A CHANCE WE WOULD GLADLY TAKE. THIS WAS THE MIRACLE WE NEEDED--
AND YOU NEVER STOPPED TO ASK YOURSELF WHERE IT CAME FROM. THAT FORMULA IS THE PROPERTY OF S.H.I.E.L.D.
S.H.I.E.L.D. NO LONGER EXISTS.
AND YET YOU NEEDED TO GET IN BED WITH SCUM LIKE CHAMELEON TO GET IT FROM THEM--
--AND A FRIEND OF MINE DIED TRYING TO PROTECT IT IN THEIR NAME.
I AM SORRY FOR THE LOSS OF YOUR COMRADE, GIRL--
--BUT KNOW THAT IF IT SAVES MY COUNTRY, I WOULD GLADLY PAY THAT PRICE A MILLION TIMES OVER.
...
TO HELL WITH THIS. I CAME HERE FOR DMITRI SMERDYAKOV. AND HE'S NOT HERE ANYMORE, IS HE?
YEAH, HE'S PRETTY GOOD AT THAT "GETTING AWAY" THING.
THEN I'M GONE TOO. YOU PEOPLE FIGURE OUT YOUR OWN CIVIL WAR.
BUT KNOW THIS--YOU MAKE A DEAL WITH A DEVIL LIKE THAT, SOON ENOUGH--

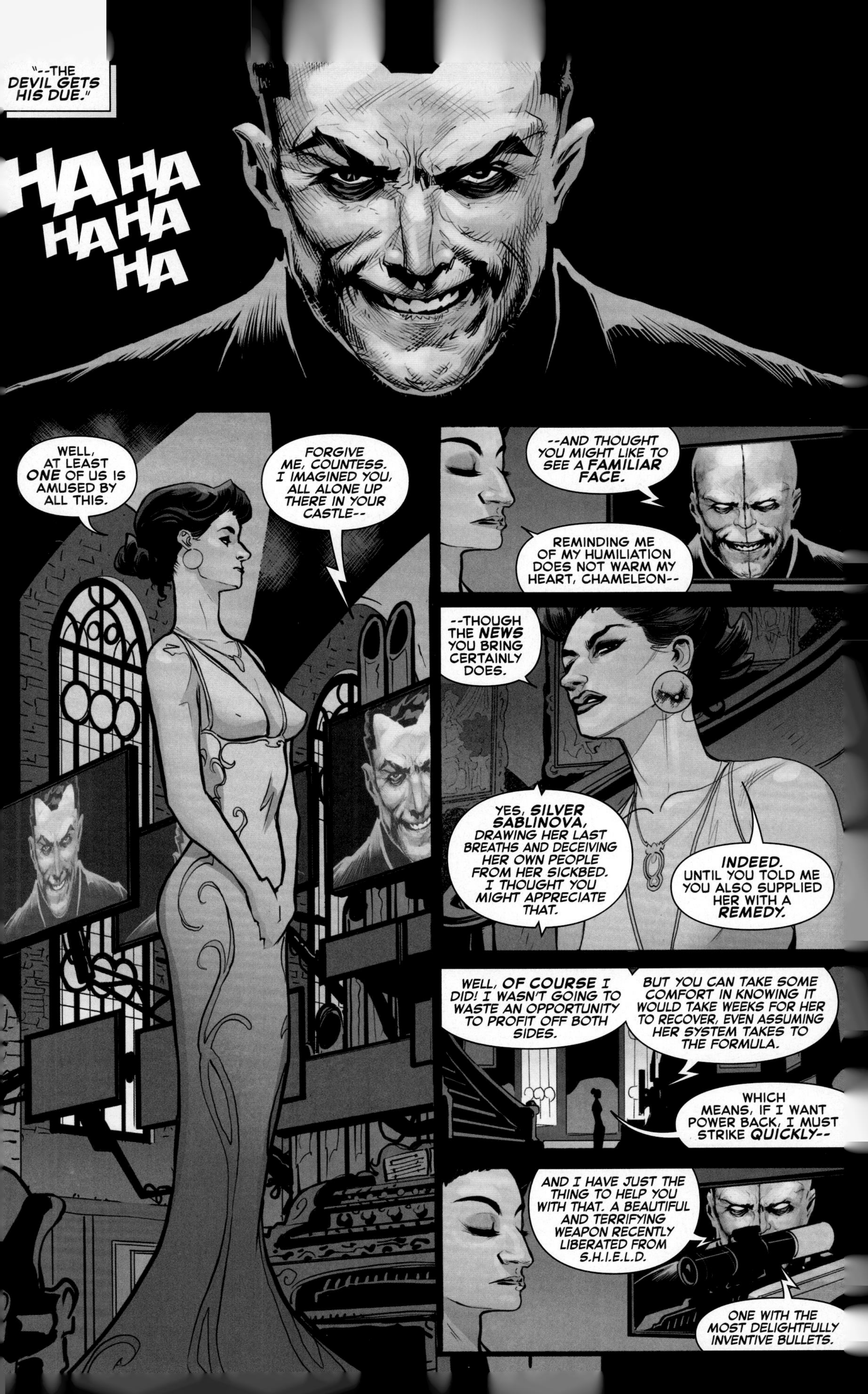
"--THE DEVIL GETS HIS DUE."
HAHA HAHA HA
WELL, AT LEAST ONE OF US IS AMUSED BY ALL THIS.
FORGIVE ME, COUNTESS. I IMAGINED YOU, ALL ALONE UP THERE IN YOUR CASTLE--
--AND THOUGHT YOU MIGHT LIKE TO SEE A FAMILIAR FACE.
REMINDING ME OF MY HUMILIATION DOES NOT WARM MY HEART, CHAMELEON--
--THOUGH THE NEWS YOU BRING CERTAINLY DOES.
YES, SILVER SABLINOVA, DRAWING HER LAST BREATHS AND DECEIVING HER OWN PEOPLE FROM HER SICKBED. I THOUGHT YOU MIGHT APPRECIATE THAT.
INDEED. UNTIL YOU TOLD ME YOU ALSO SUPPLIED HER WITH A REMEDY.
WELL, OF COURSE I DID! I WASN'T GOING TO WASTE AN OPPORTUNITY TO PROFIT OFF BOTH SIDES.
BUT YOU CAN TAKE SOME COMFORT IN KNOWING IT WOULD TAKE WEEKS FOR HER TO RECOVER, EVEN ASSUMING HER SYSTEM TAKES TO THE FORMULA.
WHICH MEANS, IF I WANT POWER BACK, I MUST STRIKE QUICKLY--
AND I HAVE JUST THE THING TO HELP YOU WITH THAT. A BEAUTIFUL AND TERRIFYING WEAPON RECENTLY LIBERATED FROM S.H.I.E.L.D.
ONE WITH THE MOST DELIGHTFULLY INVENTIVE BULLETS.

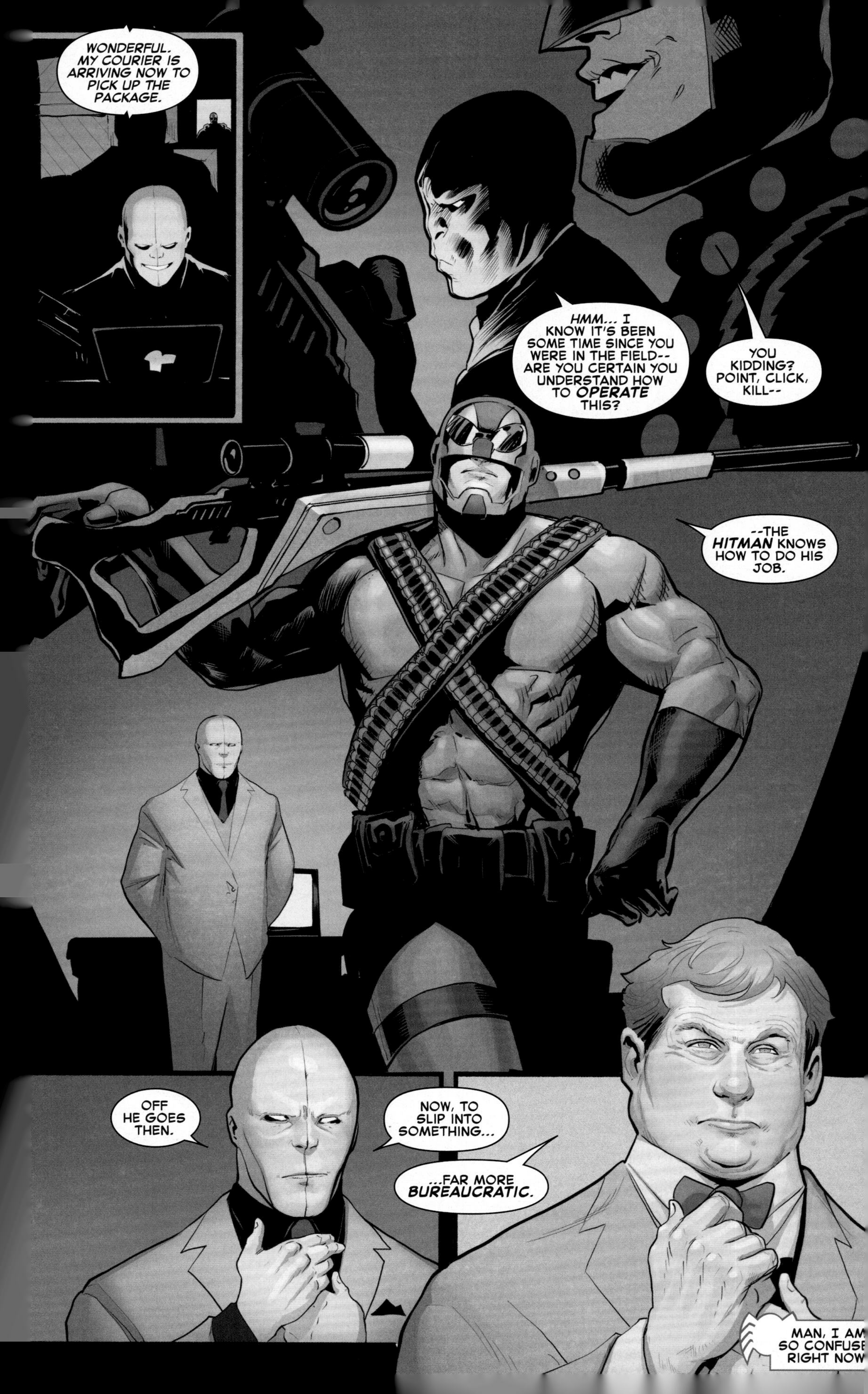
WONDERFUL. MY COURIER IS ARRIVING NOW TO PICK UP THE PACKAGE.
HMM... I KNOW IT'S BEEN SOME TIME SINCE YOU WERE IN THE FIELD--ARE YOU CERTAIN YOU UNDERSTAND HOW TO OPERATE THIS?
YOU KIDDING? POINT, CLICK, KILL--
--THE HITMAN KNOWS HOW TO DO HIS JOB.
OFF HE GOES THEN.
NOW, TO SLIP INTO SOMETHING...
...FAR MORE BUREAUCRATIC.
MAN, I AM SO CONFUSE RIGHT NOW

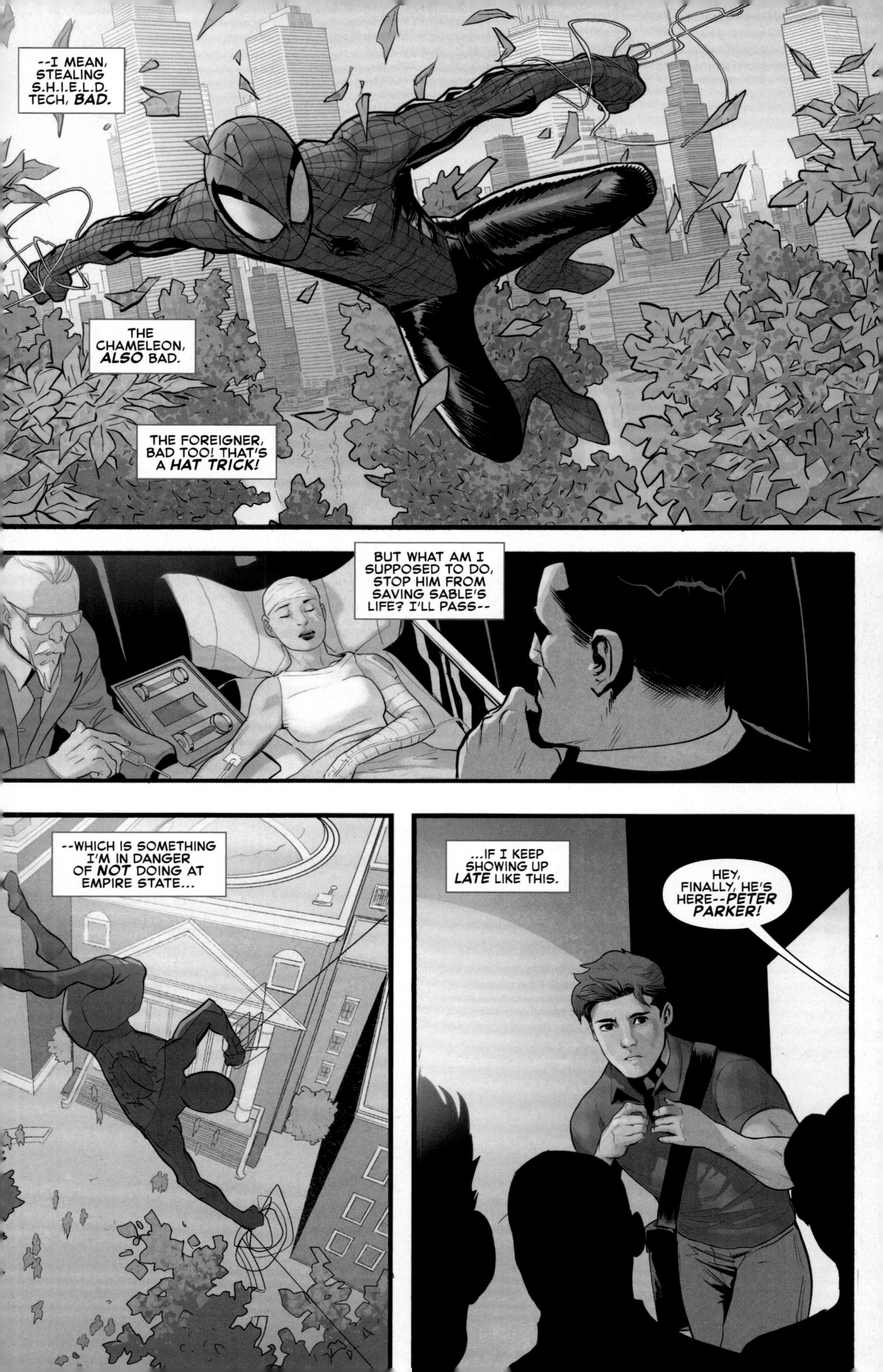
--I MEAN, STEALING S.H.I.E.L.D. TECH, BAD.
THE CHAMELEON, ALSO BAD.
THE FOREIGNER, BAD TOO! THAT'S A HAT TRICK!
BUT WHAT AM I SUPPOSED TO DO, STOP HIM FROM SAVING SABLE'S LIFE? I'LL PASS--
--WHICH IS SOMETHING I'M IN DANGER OF NOT DOING AT EMPIRE STATE...
...IF I KEEP SHOWING UP LATE LIKE THIS.
HEY, FINALLY, HE'S HERE--PETER PARKER!

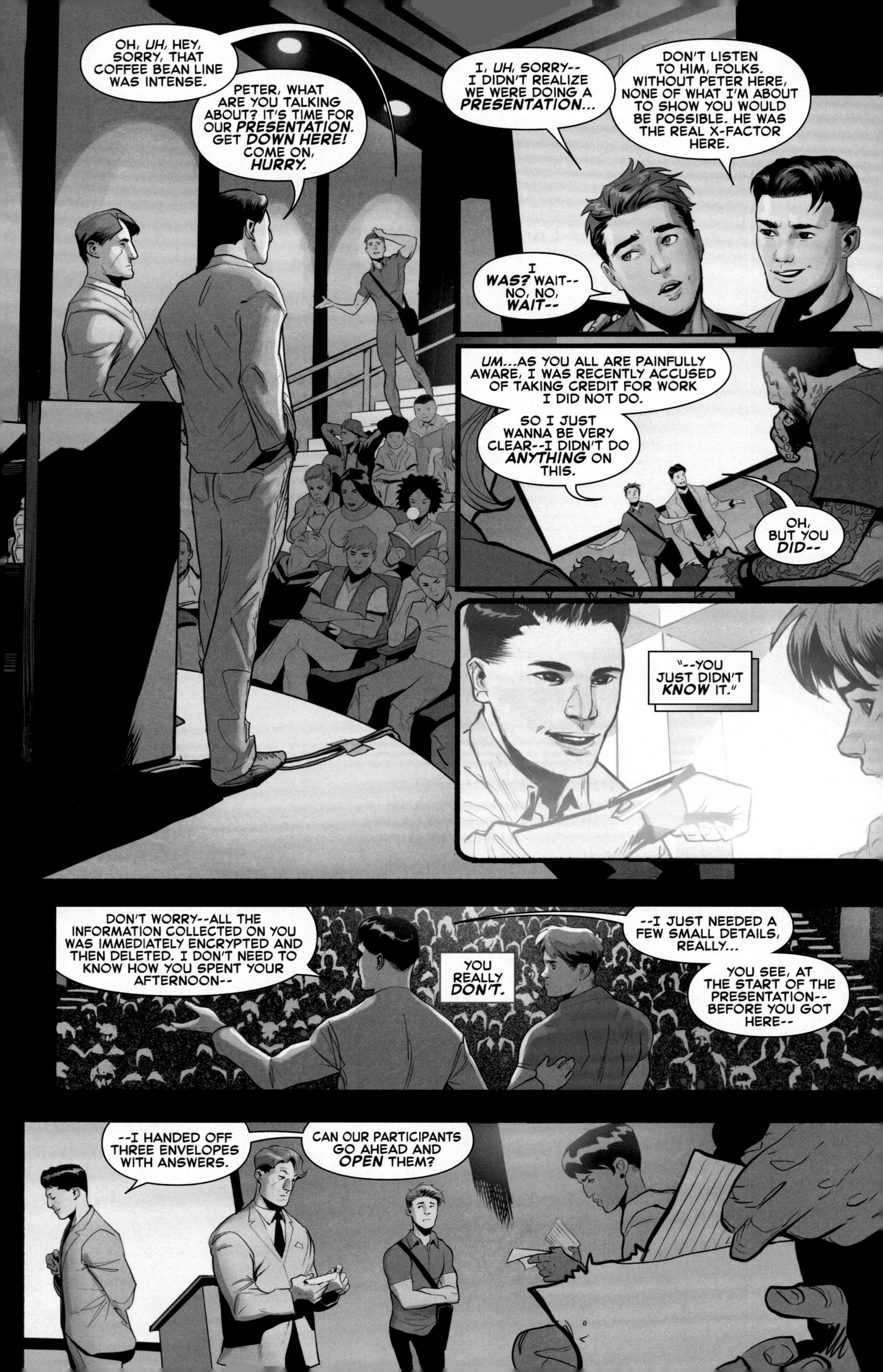

OH, UH, HEY, SORRY, THAT COFFEE BEAN LINE WAS INTENSE.
PETER, WHAT ARE YOU TALKING ABOUT? IT'S TIME FOR OUR PRESENTATION. GET DOWN HERE! COME ON, HURRY.
I, UH, SORRY-- I DIDN'T REALIZE WE WERE DOING A PRESENTATION...
DON'T LISTEN TO HIM, FOLKS. WITHOUT PETER HERE, NONE OF WHAT I'M ABOUT TO SHOW YOU WOULD BE POSSIBLE. HE WAS THE REAL X-FACTOR HERE.
I WAS? WAIT-- NO, NO, WAIT--
UM...AS YOU ALL ARE PAINFULLY AWARE, I WAS RECENTLY ACCUSED OF TAKING CREDIT FOR WORK I DID NOT DO.
SO I JUST WANNA BE VERY CLEAR--I DIDN'T DO ANYTHING ON THIS.
OH, BUT YOU DID--
"--YOU JUST DIDN'T KNOW IT."
DON'T WORRY--ALL THE INFORMATION COLLECTED ON YOU WAS IMMEDIATELY ENCRYPTED AND THEN DELETED. I DON'T NEED TO KNOW HOW YOU SPENT YOUR AFTERNOON--
YOU REALLY DON'T.
--I JUST NEEDED A FEW SMALL DETAILS, REALLY...
YOU SEE, AT THE START OF THE PRESENTATION-- BEFORE YOU GOT HERE--
--I HANDED OFF THREE ENVELOPES WITH ANSWERS.
CAN OUR PARTICIPANTS GO AHEAD AND OPEN THEM?

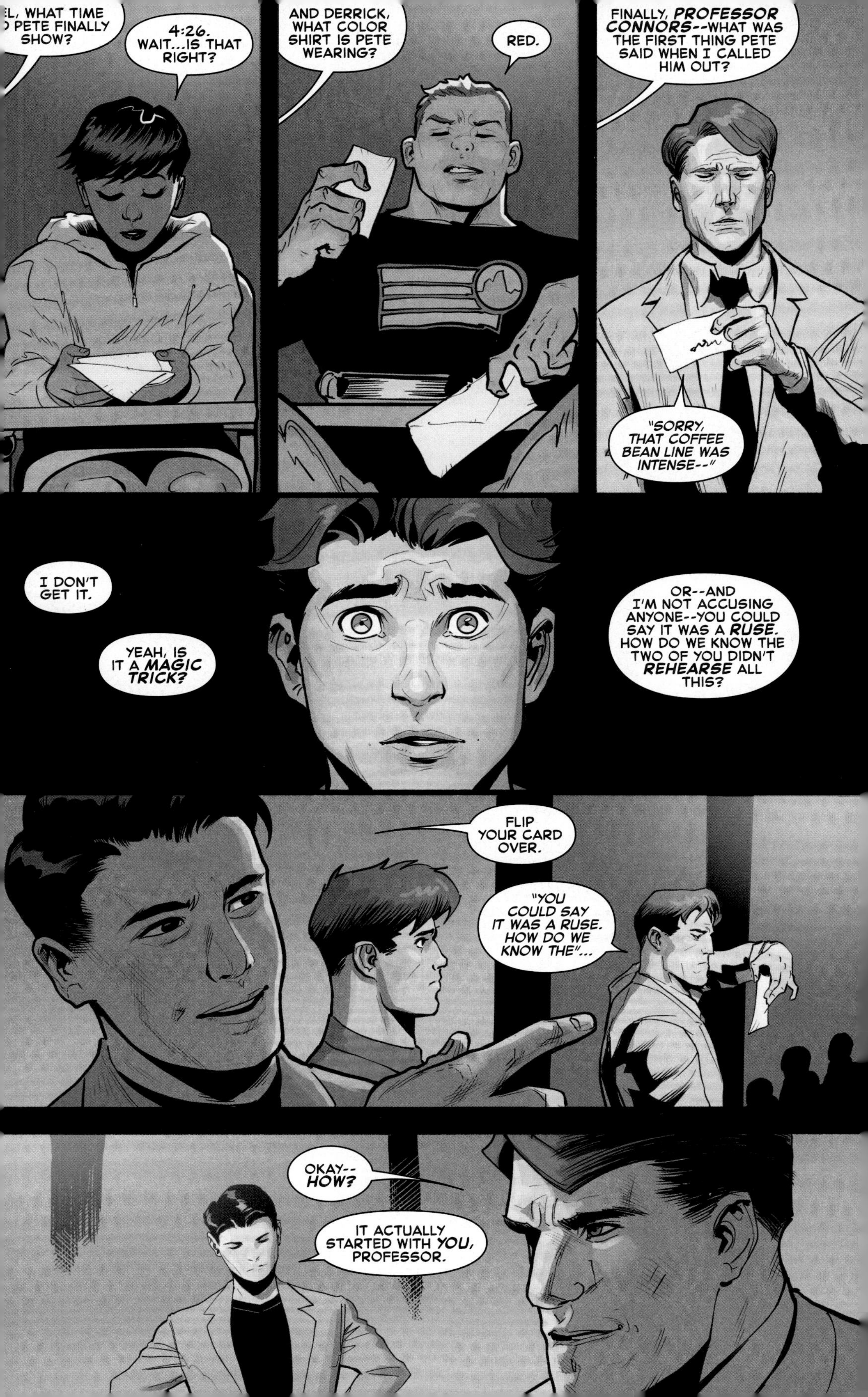
EL, WHAT TIME
D PETE FINALLY SHOW?
4:26. WAIT...IS THAT RIGHT?
AND DERRICK, WHAT COLOR SHIRT IS PETE WEARING?
RED.
FINALLY, PROFESSOR CONNORS--WHAT WAS THE FIRST THING PETE SAID WHEN I CALLED HIM OUT?
"SORRY, THAT COFFEE BEAN LINE WAS INTENSE--"
I DON'T GET IT.
YEAH, IS IT A MAGIC TRICK?
OR--AND I'M NOT ACCUSING ANYONE--YOU COULD SAY IT WAS A RUSE. HOW DO WE KNOW THE TWO OF YOU DIDN'T REHEARSE ALL THIS?
FLIP YOUR CARD OVER.
"YOU COULD SAY IT WAS A RUSE. HOW DO WE KNOW THE"...
OKAY-- HOW?
IT ACTUALLY STARTED WITH YOU, PROFESSOR.

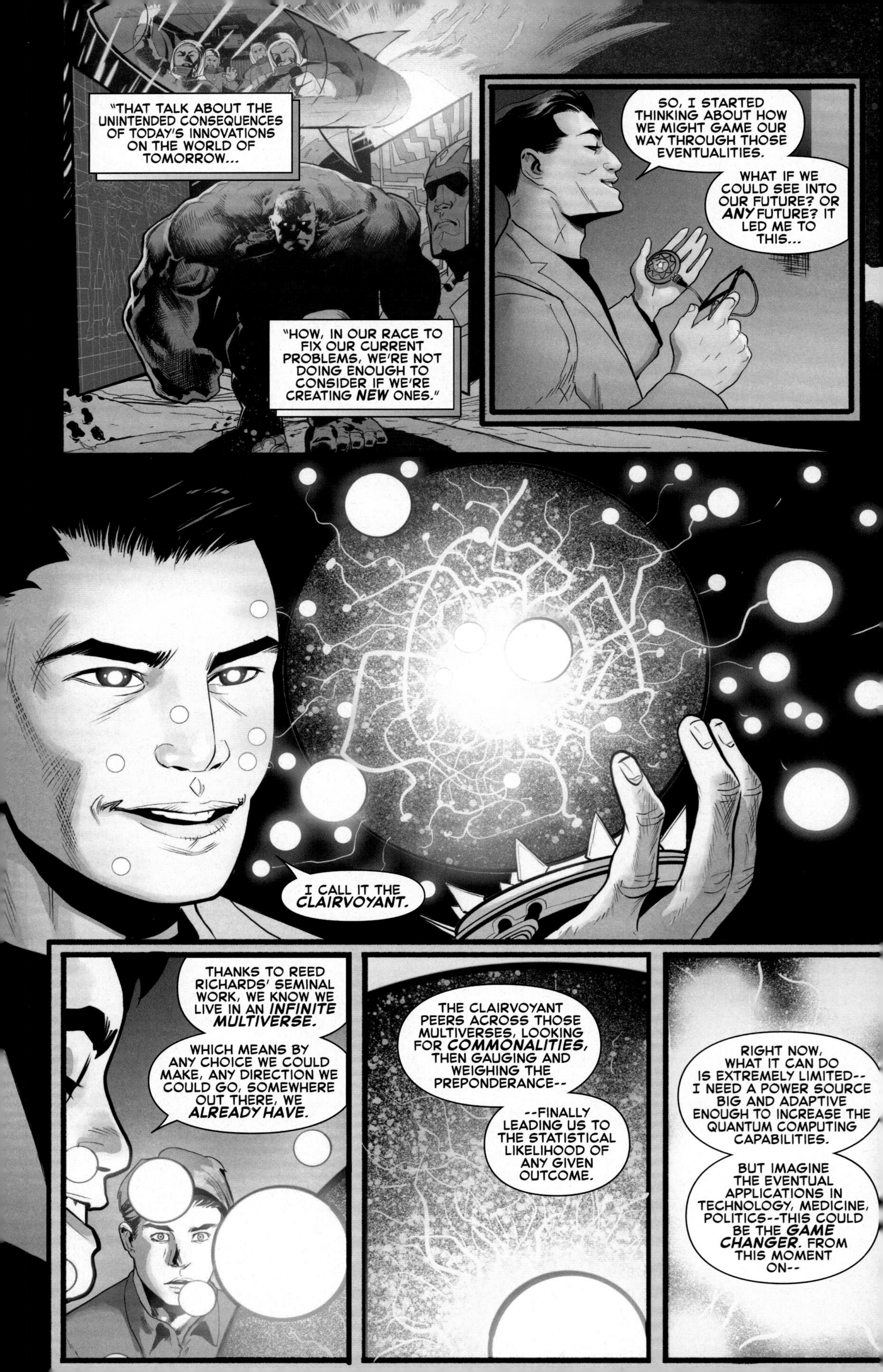
"THAT TALK ABOUT THE UNINTENDED CONSEQUENCES OF TODAY'S INNOVATIONS ON THE WORLD OF TOMORROW...
"HOW, IN OUR RACE TO FIX OUR CURRENT PROBLEMS, WE'RE NOT DOING ENOUGH TO CONSIDER IF WE'RE CREATING NEW ONES."
SO, I STARTED THINKING ABOUT HOW WE MIGHT GAME OUR WAY THROUGH THOSE EVENTUALITIES.
WHAT IF WE COULD SEE INTO OUR FUTURE? OR ANY FUTURE? IT LED ME TO THIS...
I CALL IT THE CLAIRVOYANT.
THANKS TO REED RICHARDS' SEMINAL WORK, WE KNOW WE LIVE IN AN INFINITE MULTIVERSE.
WHICH MEANS BY ANY CHOICE WE COULD MAKE, ANY DIRECTION WE COULD GO, SOMEWHERE OUT THERE, WE ALREADY HAVE.
THE CLAIRVOYANT PEERS ACROSS THOSE MULTIVERSES, LOOKING FOR COMMONALITIES, THEN GAUGING AND WEIGHING THE PREPONDERANCE--
--FINALLY LEADING US TO THE STATISTICAL LIKELIHOOD OF ANY GIVEN OUTCOME.
RIGHT NOW, WHAT IT CAN DO IS EXTREMELY LIMITED-- I NEED A POWER SOURCE BIG AND ADAPTIVE ENOUGH TO INCREASE THE QUANTUM COMPUTING CAPABILITIES.
BUT IMAGINE THE EVENTUAL APPLICATIONS IN TECHNOLOGY, MEDICINE, POLITICS--THIS COULD BE THE GAME CHANGER. FROM THIS MOMENT ON--

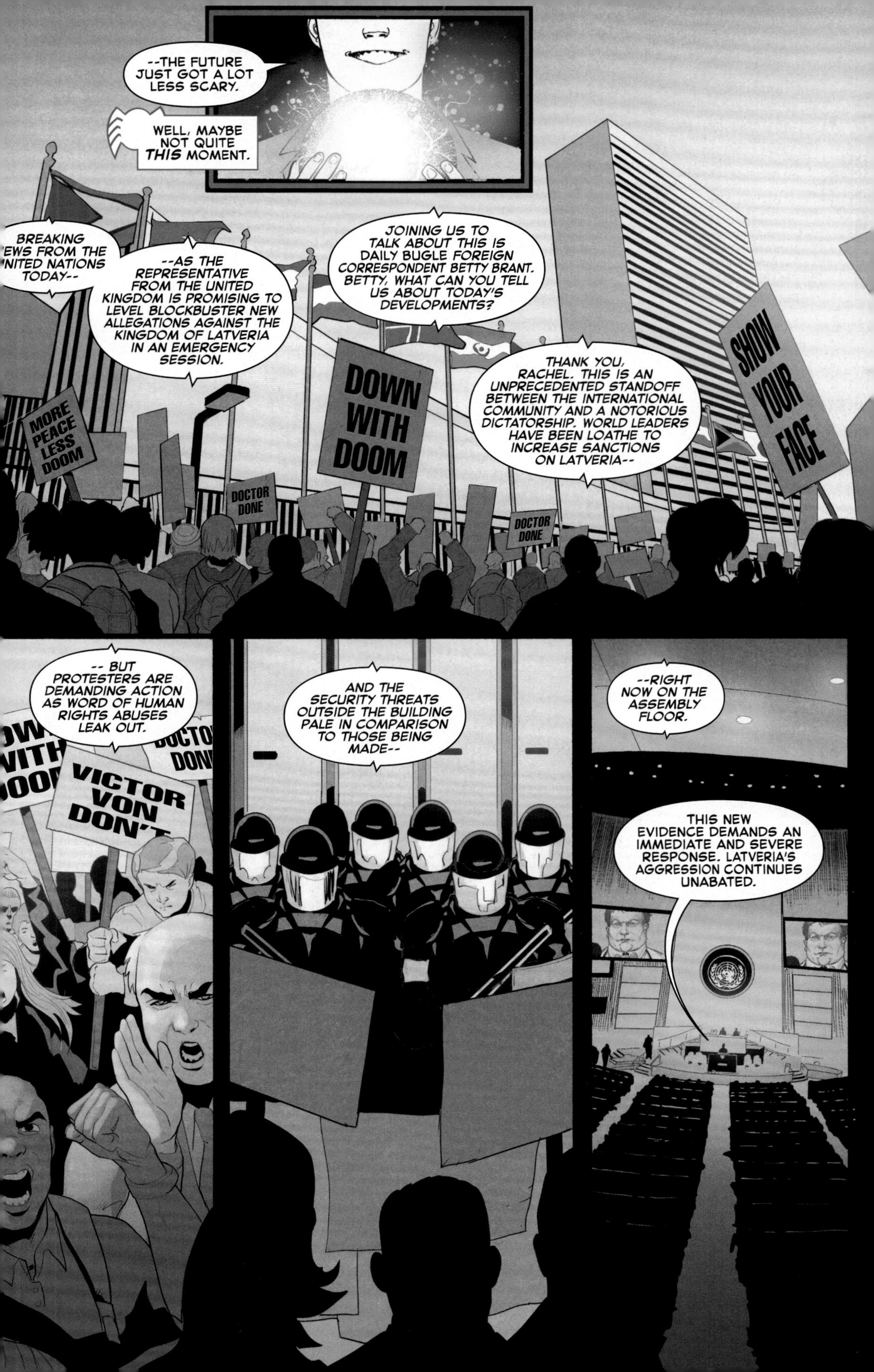
--THE FUTURE JUST GOT A LOT LESS SCARY.
WELL, MAYBE NOT QUITE THIS MOMENT.
BREAKING EWS FROM THE NITED NATIONS TODAY--
--AS THE REPRESENTATIVE FROM THE UNITED KINGDOM IS PROMISING TO LEVEL BLOCKBUSTER NEW ALLEGATIONS AGAINST THE KINGDOM OF LATVERIA IN AN EMERGENCY SESSION.
JOINING US TO TALK ABOUT THIS IS DAILY BUGLE FOREIGN CORRESPONDENT BETTY BRANT. BETTY, WHAT CAN YOU TELL US ABOUT TODAY'S DEVELOPMENTS?
THANK YOU, RACHEL. THIS IS AN UNPRECEDENTED STANDOFF BETWEEN THE INTERNATIONAL COMMUNITY AND A NOTORIOUS DICTATORSHIP. WORLD LEADERS HAVE BEEN LOATHE TO INCREASE SANCTIONS ON LATVERIA--
MORE PEACE LESS DOOM
DOWN WITH DOOM
SHOW YOUR FACE
DOCTOR DONE
DOCTOR DONE
-- BUT PROTESTERS ARE DEMANDING ACTION AS WORD OF HUMAN RIGHTS ABUSES LEAK OUT.
VICTOR VON DON'T
AND THE SECURITY THREATS OUTSIDE THE BUILDING PALE IN COMPARISON TO THOSE BEING MADE--
--RIGHT NOW ON THE ASSEMBLY FLOOR.
THIS NEW EVIDENCE DEMANDS AN IMMEDIATE AND SEVERE RESPONSE. LATVERIA'S AGGRESSION CONTINUES UNABATED.

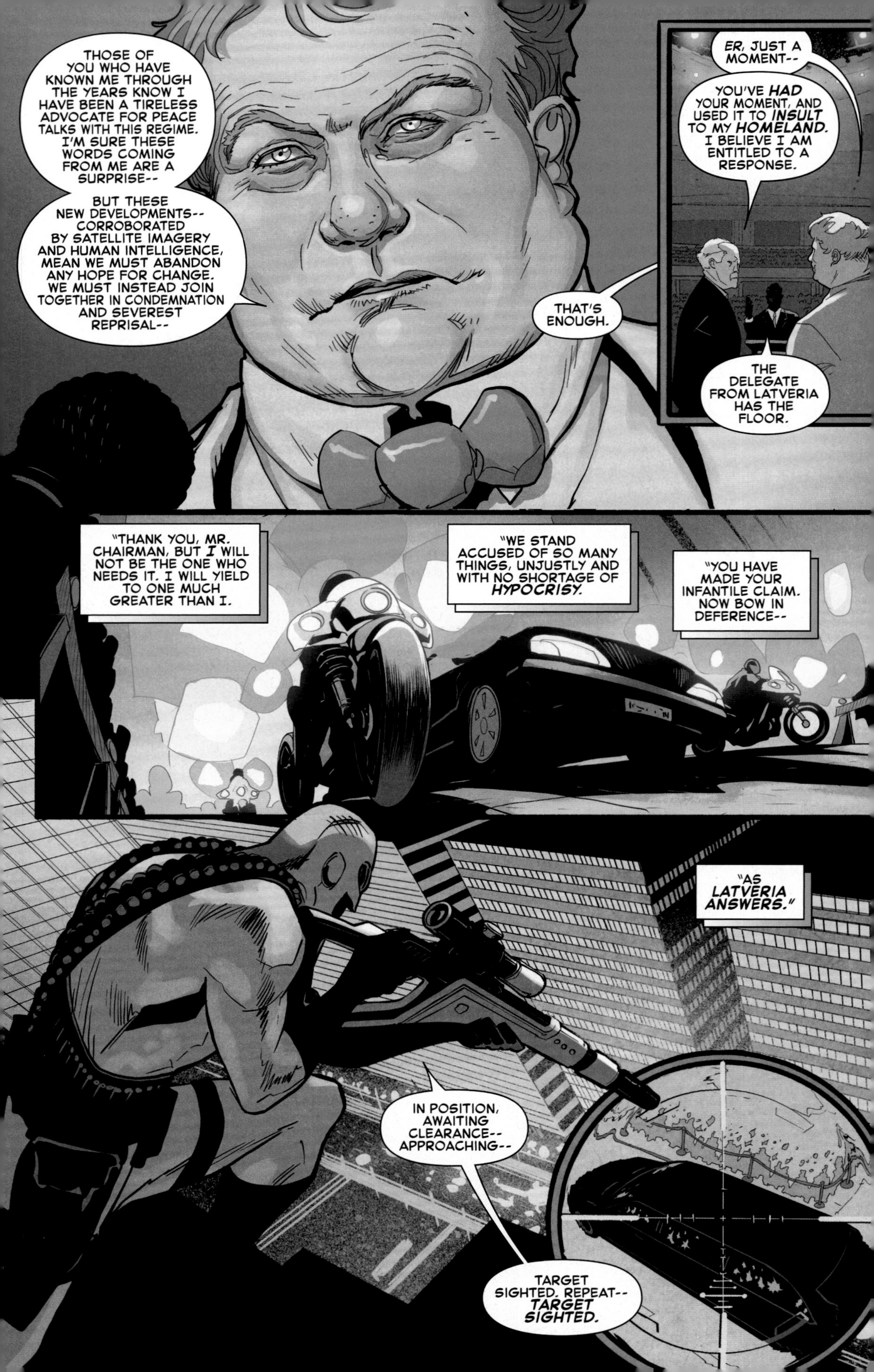
THOSE OF YOU WHO HAVE KNOWN ME THROUGH THE YEARS KNOW I HAVE BEEN A TIRELESS ADVOCATE FOR PEACE TALKS WITH THIS REGIME. I'M SURE THESE WORDS COMING FROM ME ARE A SURPRISE--
BUT THESE NEW DEVELOPMENTS--CORROBORATED BY SATELLITE IMAGERY AND HUMAN INTELLIGENCE, MEAN WE MUST ABANDON ANY HOPE FOR CHANGE. WE MUST INSTEAD JOIN TOGETHER IN CONDEMNATION AND SEVEREST REPRISAL--
THAT'S ENOUGH.
ER, JUST A MOMENT--
YOU'VE HAD YOUR MOMENT, AND USED IT TO INSULT TO MY HOMELAND. I BELIEVE I AM ENTITLED TO A RESPONSE.
THE DELEGATE FROM LATVERIA HAS THE FLOOR.
"THANK YOU, MR. CHAIRMAN, BUT I WILL NOT BE THE ONE WHO NEEDS IT. I WILL YIELD TO ONE MUCH GREATER THAN I.
"WE STAND ACCUSED OF SO MANY THINGS, UNJUSTLY AND WITH NO SHORTAGE OF HYPOCRISY.
"YOU HAVE MADE YOUR INFANTILE CLAIM. NOW BOW IN DEFERENCE--
"AS LATVERIA ANSWERS."
IN POSITION, AWAITING CLEARANCE--APPROACHING--
TARGET SIGHTED. REPEAT--TARGET SIGHTED.

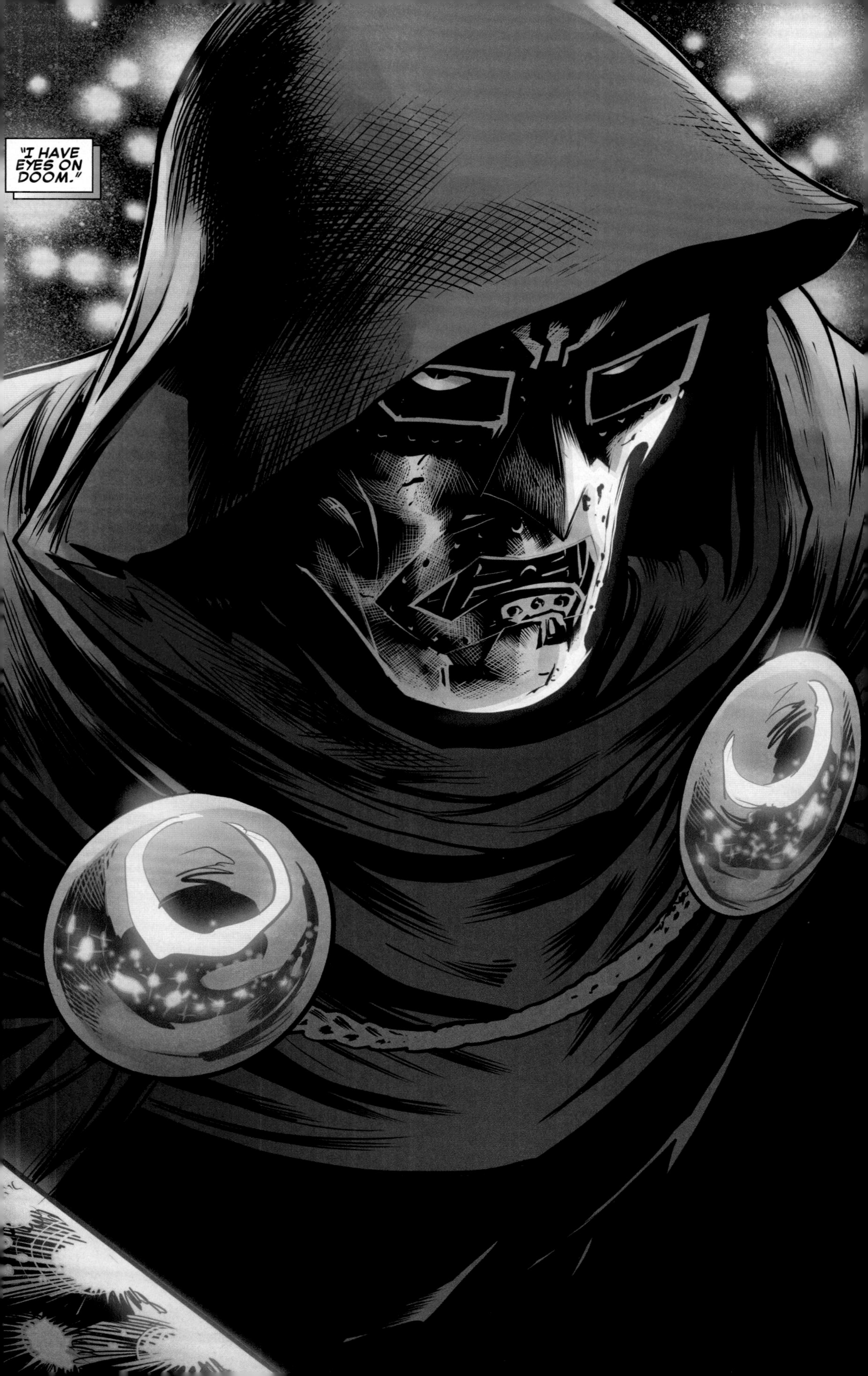
"I HAVE EYES ON DOOM."

34

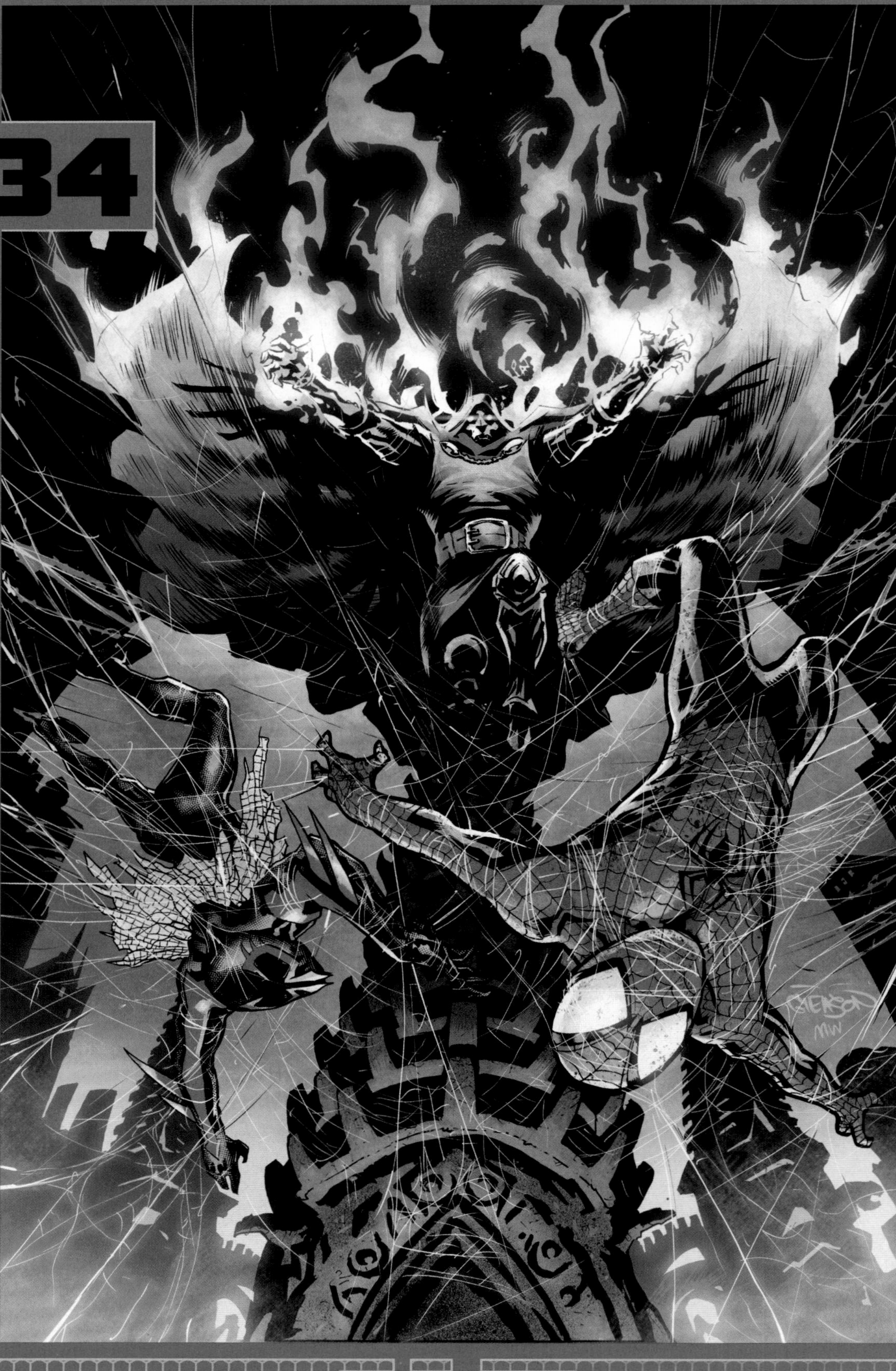

TARGET: DOOM

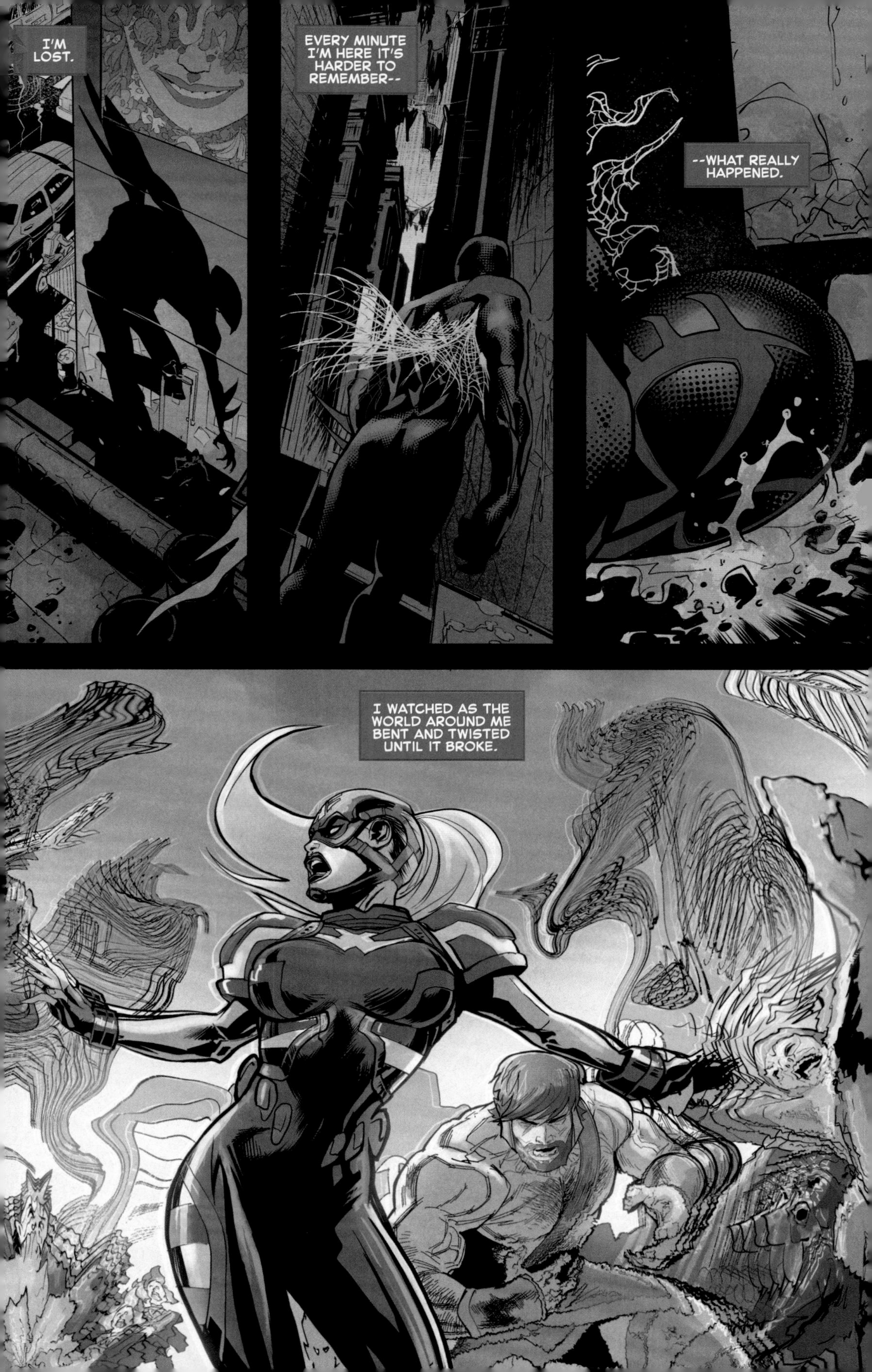
I'M LOST.
EVERY MINUTE I'M HERE IT'S HARDER TO REMEMBER--
--WHAT REALLY HAPPENED.
I WATCHED AS THE WORLD AROUND ME BENT AND TWISTED UNTIL IT BROKE.

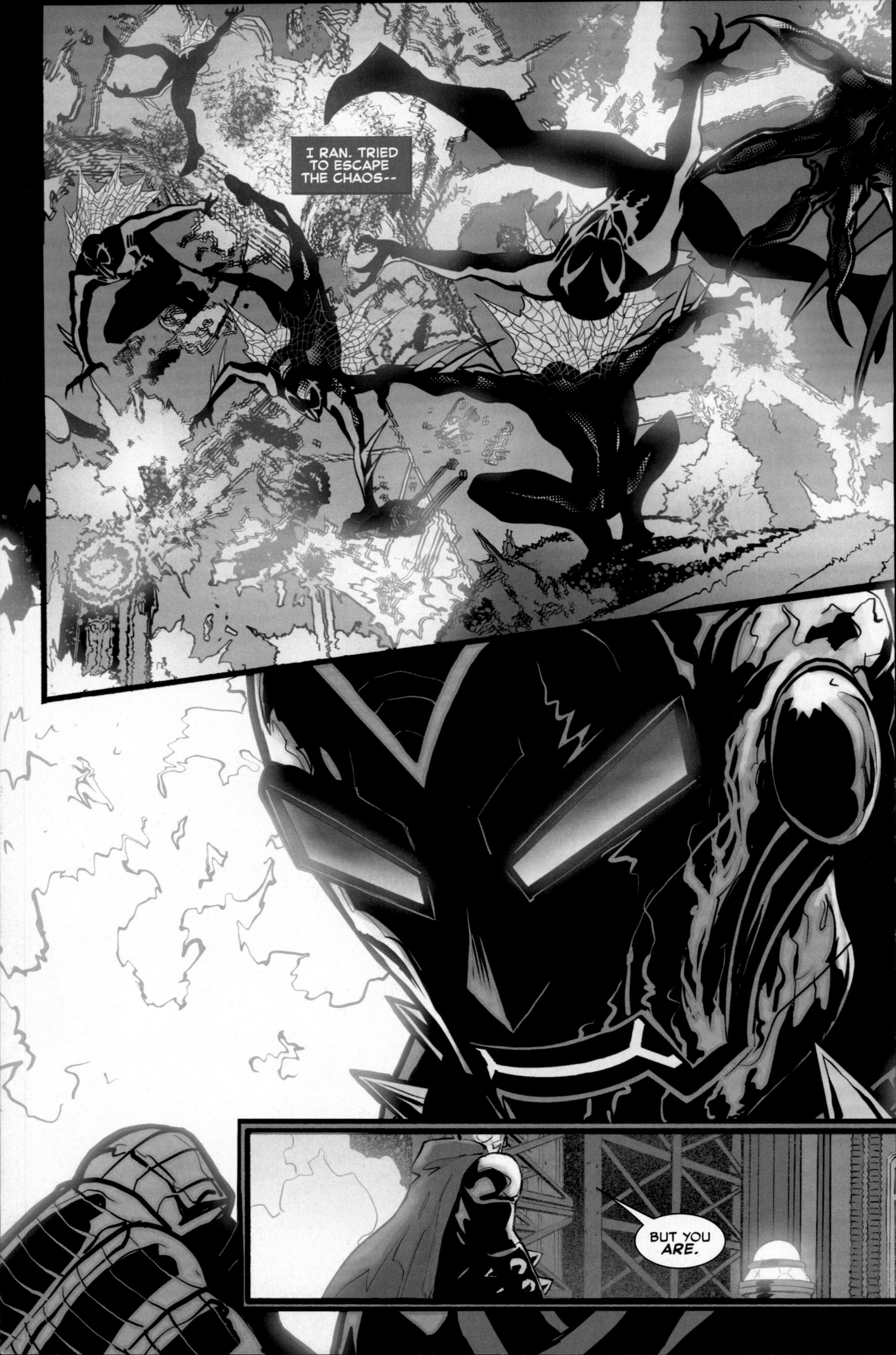

I RAN. TRIED TO ESCAPE THE CHAOS--
BUT YOU ARE.

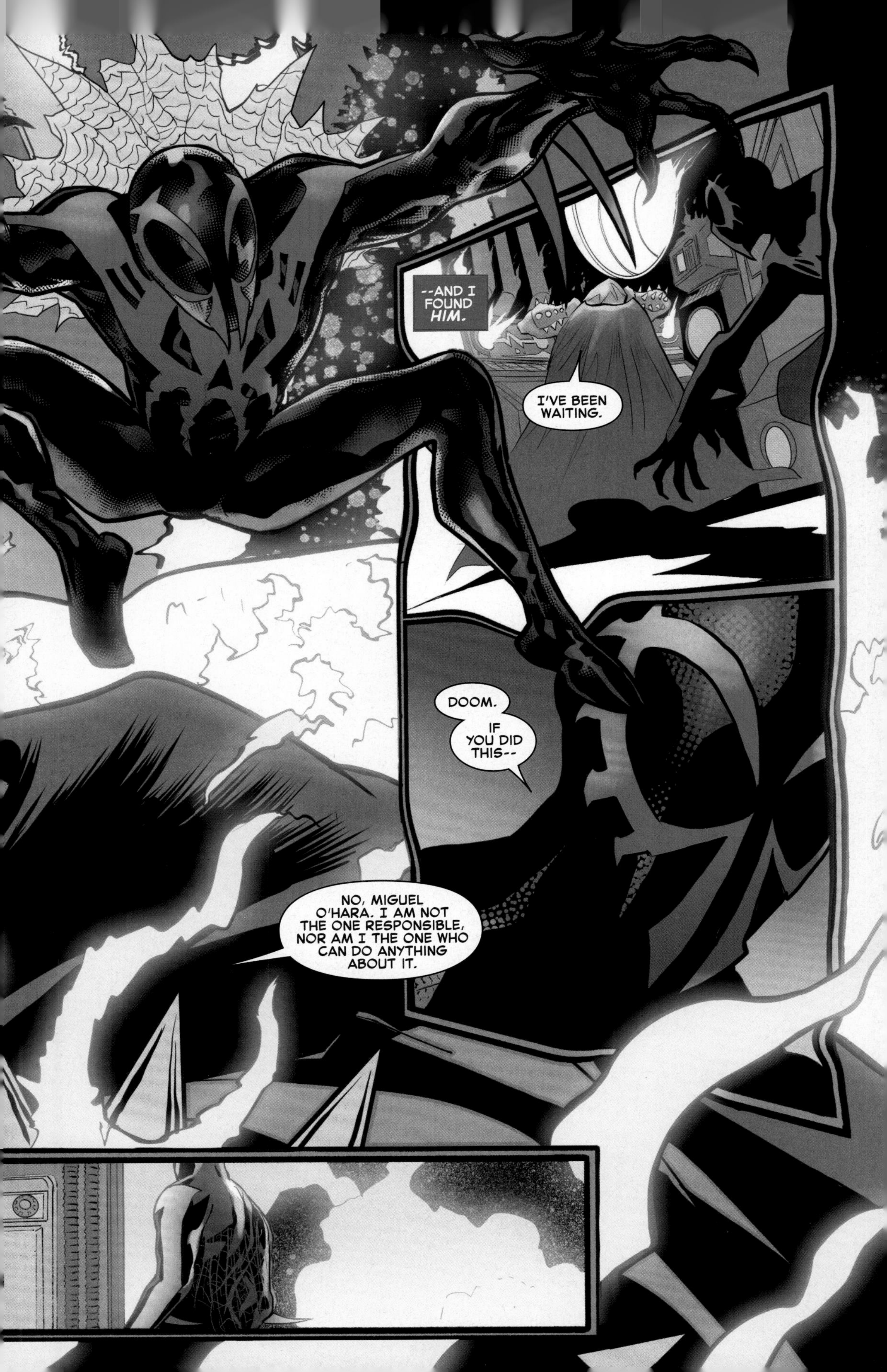
--AND I FOUND HIM.
I'VE BEEN WAITING.
DOOM. IF YOU DID THIS--
NO, MIGUEL O'HARA. I AM NOT THE ONE RESPONSIBLE, NOR AM I THE ONE WHO CAN DO ANYTHING ABOUT IT.

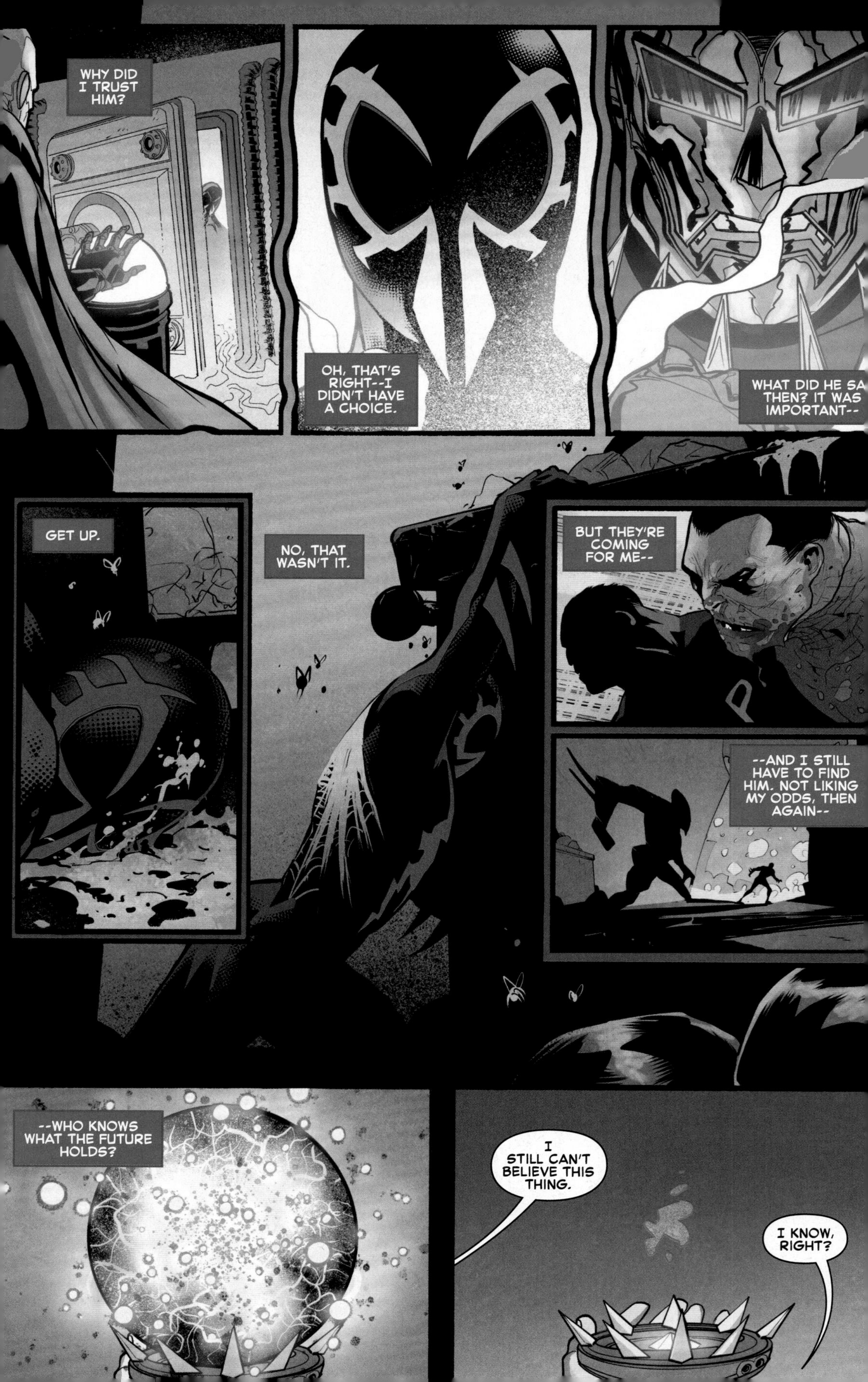

WHY DID I TRUST HIM?
OH, THAT'S RIGHT--I DIDN'T HAVE A CHOICE.
WHAT DID HE SA THEN? IT WAS IMPORTANT--
GET UP.
NO, THAT WASN'T IT.
BUT THEY'RE COMING FOR ME--
--AND I STILL HAVE TO FIND HIM. NOT LIKING MY ODDS, THEN AGAIN--
--WHO KNOWS WHAT THE FUTURE HOLDS?
I STILL CAN'T BELIEVE THIS THING.
I KNOW, RIGHT?

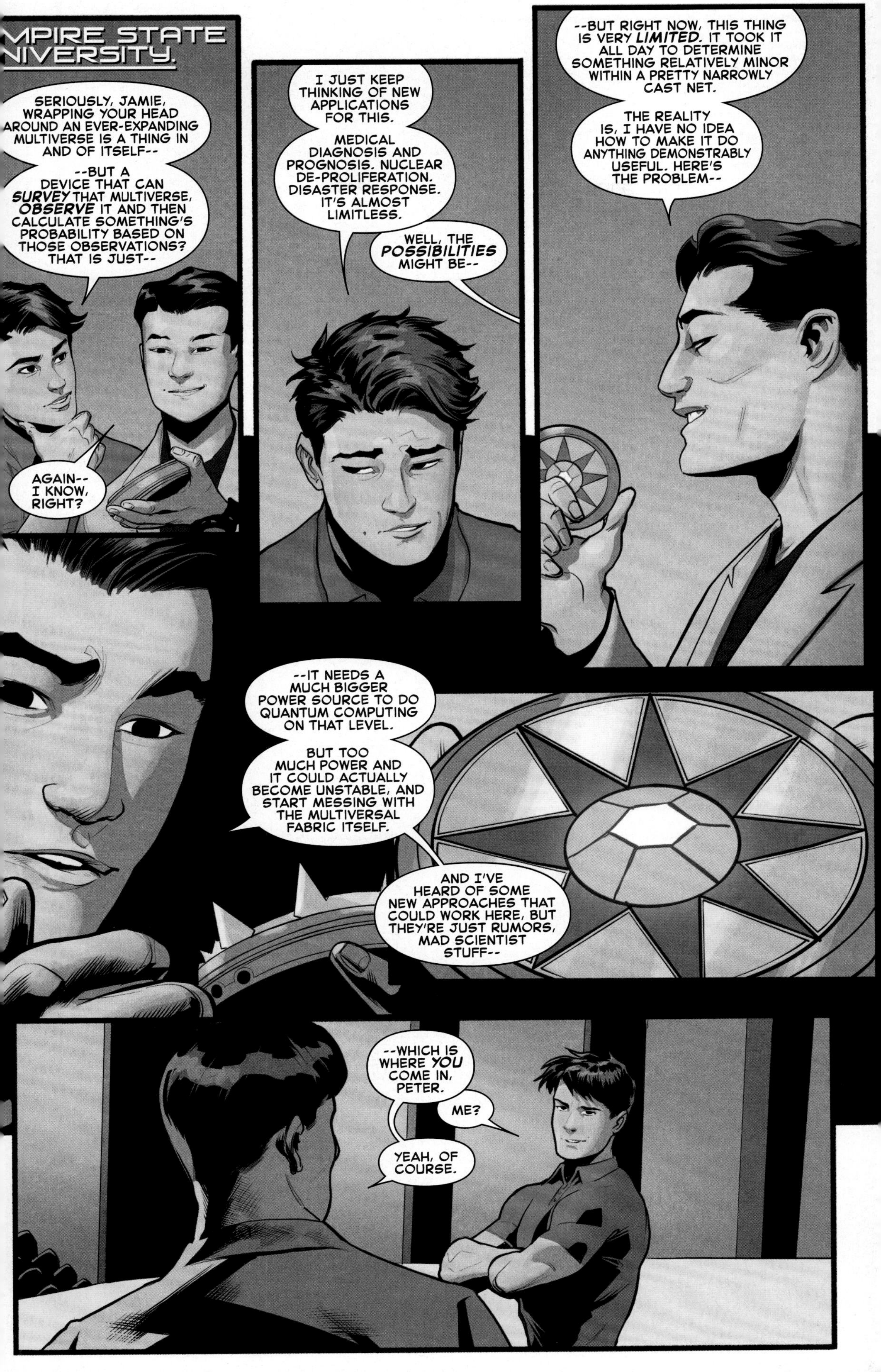

MPIRE STATE NIVERSITY.
SERIOUSLY, JAMIE, WRAPPING YOUR HEAD AROUND AN EVER-EXPANDING MULTIVERSE IS A THING IN AND OF ITSELF--
--BUT A DEVICE THAT CAN SURVEY THAT MULTIVERSE, OBSERVE IT AND THEN CALCULATE SOMETHING'S PROBABILITY BASED ON THOSE OBSERVATIONS? THAT IS JUST--
AGAIN-- I KNOW, RIGHT?
I JUST KEEP THINKING OF NEW APPLICATIONS FOR THIS.
MEDICAL DIAGNOSIS AND PROGNOSIS. NUCLEAR DE-PROLIFERATION. DISASTER RESPONSE. IT'S ALMOST LIMITLESS.
WELL, THE POSSIBILITIES MIGHT BE--
--BUT RIGHT NOW, THIS THING IS VERY LIMITED. IT TOOK IT ALL DAY TO DETERMINE SOMETHING RELATIVELY MINOR WITHIN A PRETTY NARROWLY CAST NET.
THE REALITY IS, I HAVE NO IDEA HOW TO MAKE IT DO ANYTHING DEMONSTRABLY USEFUL. HERE'S THE PROBLEM--
--IT NEEDS A MUCH BIGGER POWER SOURCE TO DO QUANTUM COMPUTING ON THAT LEVEL.
BUT TOO MUCH POWER AND IT COULD ACTUALLY BECOME UNSTABLE, AND START MESSING WITH THE MULTIVERSAL FABRIC ITSELF.
AND I'VE HEARD OF SOME NEW APPROACHES THAT COULD WORK HERE, BUT THEY'RE JUST RUMORS, MAD SCIENTIST STUFF--
--WHICH IS WHERE YOU COME IN, PETER.
ME?
YEAH, OF COURSE.

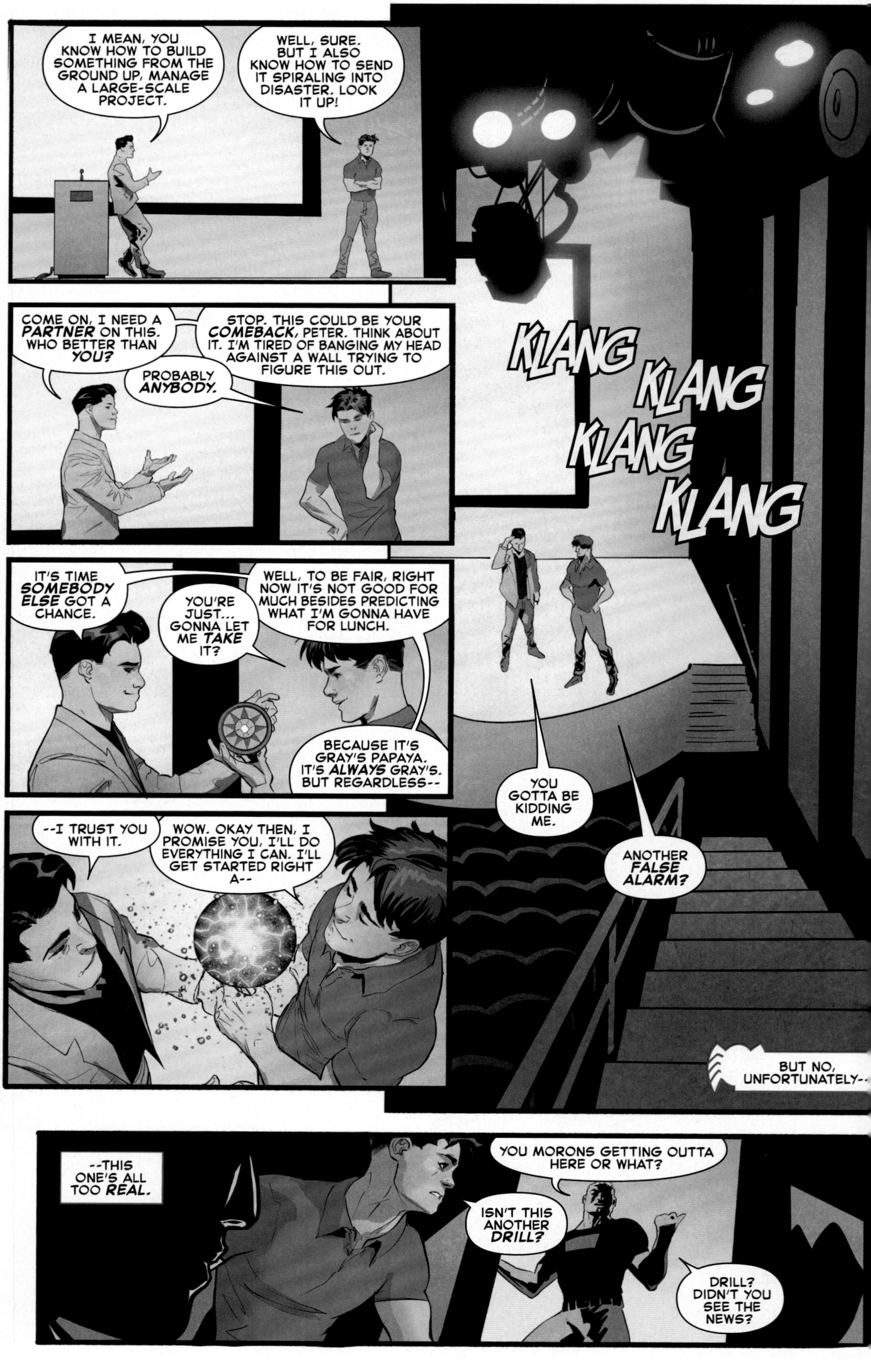

I MEAN, YOU KNOW HOW TO BUILD SOMETHING FROM THE GROUND UP, MANAGE A LARGE-SCALE PROJECT.
WELL, SURE. BUT I ALSO KNOW HOW TO SEND IT SPIRALING INTO DISASTER. LOOK IT UP!
COME ON, I NEED A PARTNER ON THIS. WHO BETTER THAN YOU?
PROBABLY ANYBODY.
STOP. THIS COULD BE YOUR COMEBACK, PETER. THINK ABOUT IT. I'M TIRED OF BANGING MY HEAD AGAINST A WALL TRYING TO FIGURE THIS OUT.
IT'S TIME SOMEBODY ELSE GOT A CHANCE.
YOU'RE JUST... GONNA LET ME TAKE IT?
WELL, TO BE FAIR, RIGHT NOW IT'S NOT GOOD FOR MUCH BESIDES PREDICTING WHAT I'M GONNA HAVE FOR LUNCH.
BECAUSE IT'S GRAY'S PAPAYA. IT'S ALWAYS GRAY'S. BUT REGARDLESS--
--I TRUST YOU WITH IT.
WOW. OKAY THEN, I PROMISE YOU, I'LL DO EVERYTHING I CAN. I'LL GET STARTED RIGHT A--
KLANG KLANG KLANG KLANG
YOU GOTTA BE KIDDING ME.
ANOTHER FALSE ALARM?
BUT NO, UNFORTUNATELY--
--THIS ONE'S ALL TOO REAL.
YOU MORONS GETTING OUTTA HERE OR WHAT?
ISN'T THIS ANOTHER DRILL?
DRILL? DIDN'T YOU SEE THE NEWS?

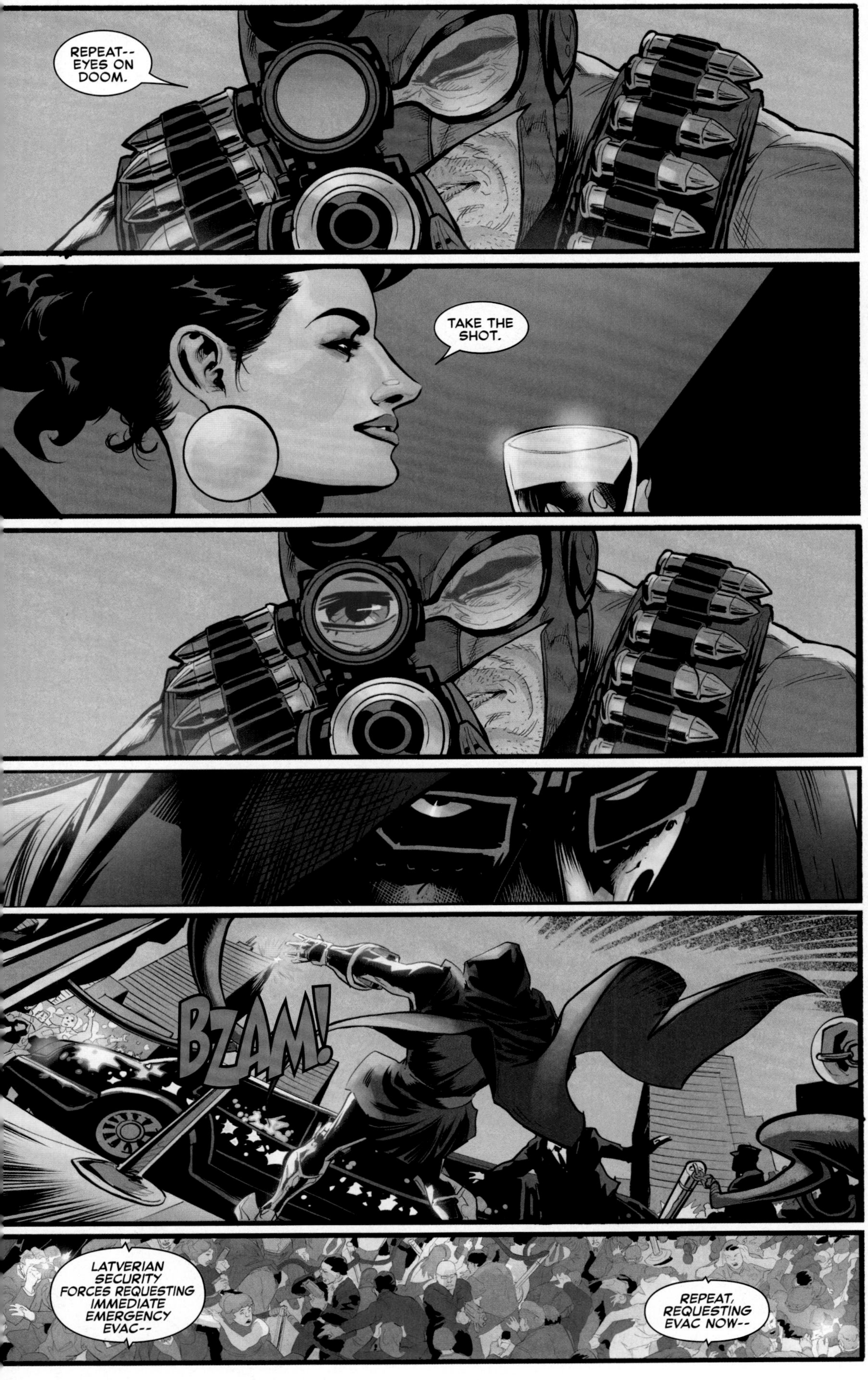
REPEAT--
EYES ON
DOOM.
TAKE THE
SHOT.
BZAM!
LATVERIAN
SECURITY
FORCES REQUESTING
IMMEDIATE
EMERGENCY
EVAC--
REPEAT,
REQUESTING
EVAC NOW--

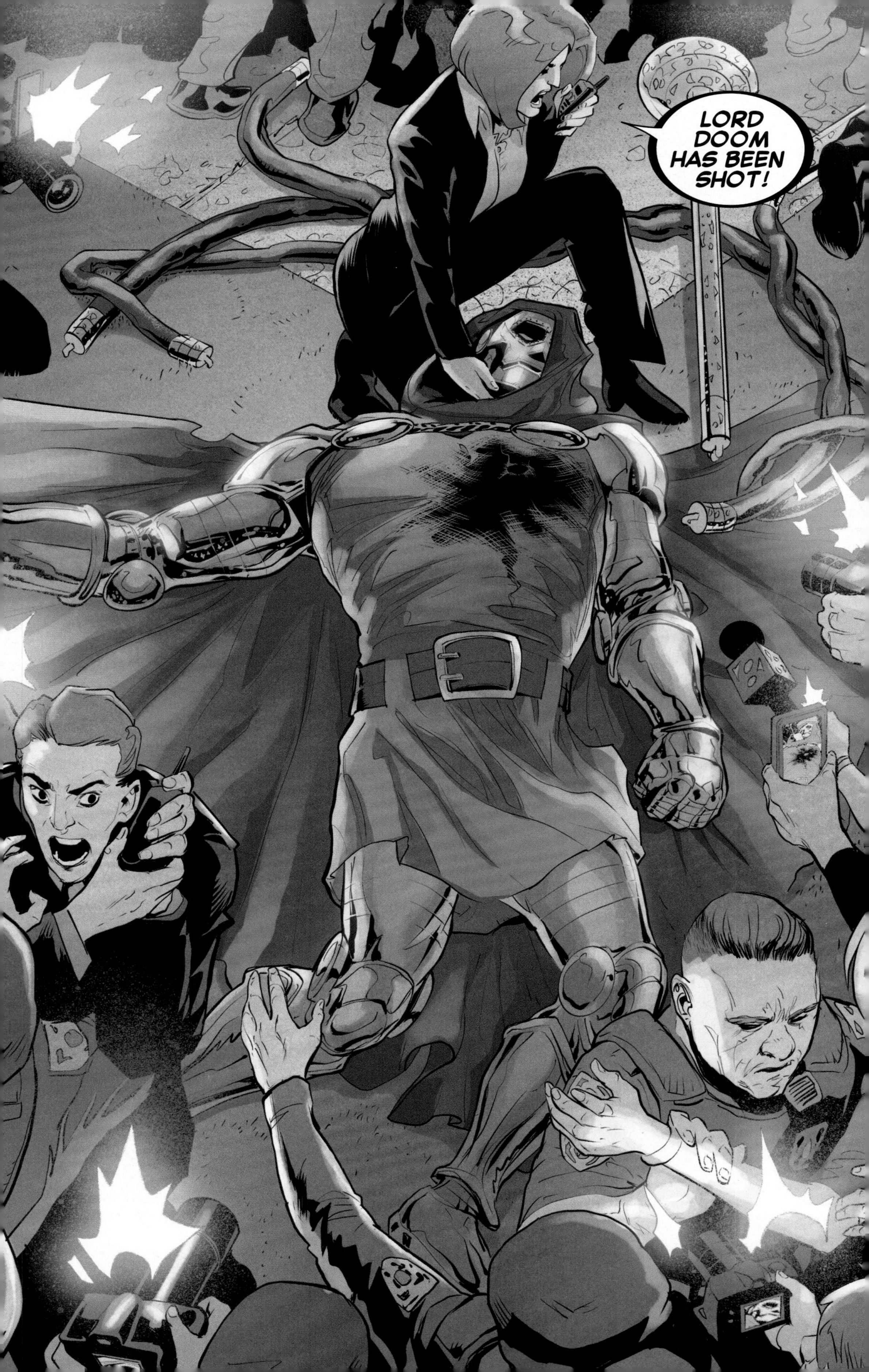
LORD DOOM HAS BEEN SHOT!

HA HA HA HA HA HA

WELL, I'M GLAD **ONE** OF US IS AMUSED BY ALL THIS, COUNTESS.

NOT USUALLY THE RESPONSE ONE EXPECTS WHEN IT COMES TO THE DEMISE OF A HEAD OF STATE.

H RELAX, AMELEON. U DID YOUR RT AND DID IT WELL.

I KNEW DOOM OULDN'T E ABLE TO SIST SUCH A DIRECT HALLENGE.

HM. PERHAPS. I MUST ADMIT, HOWEVER, SEEING YOUR DREAMS REALIZED, I WORRY YOU MIGHT BE... WHAT DO THE AMERICANS CALL IT?

THE DOG WHO CAUGHT THE CAR.

I ADMIRED THE AMBITION OF YOUR PLAN, BUT IF I'D KNOWN YOU WERE ACTUALLY GOING TO BE SUCCESSFUL, I MIGHT HAVE THOUGHT TWICE--

--LATVERIA IS A POWERFUL ENEMY TO MAKE. AND THIS WILL MOST CERTAINLY ESCALATE FROM HERE.

WELL, YOU COULD ALWAYS REFUSE PAYMENT.

DON'T BE GAUCHE.

THEN I SUGGEST YOU GET **COMFORTABLE**, CHAMELEON.

THE ROOFTOP, THE SNIPER, THE BULLET IN ALL ITS UNIQUE GLORY--THAT WAS MERELY A **PREAMBLE.**

THE BEST IS YET TO COME.

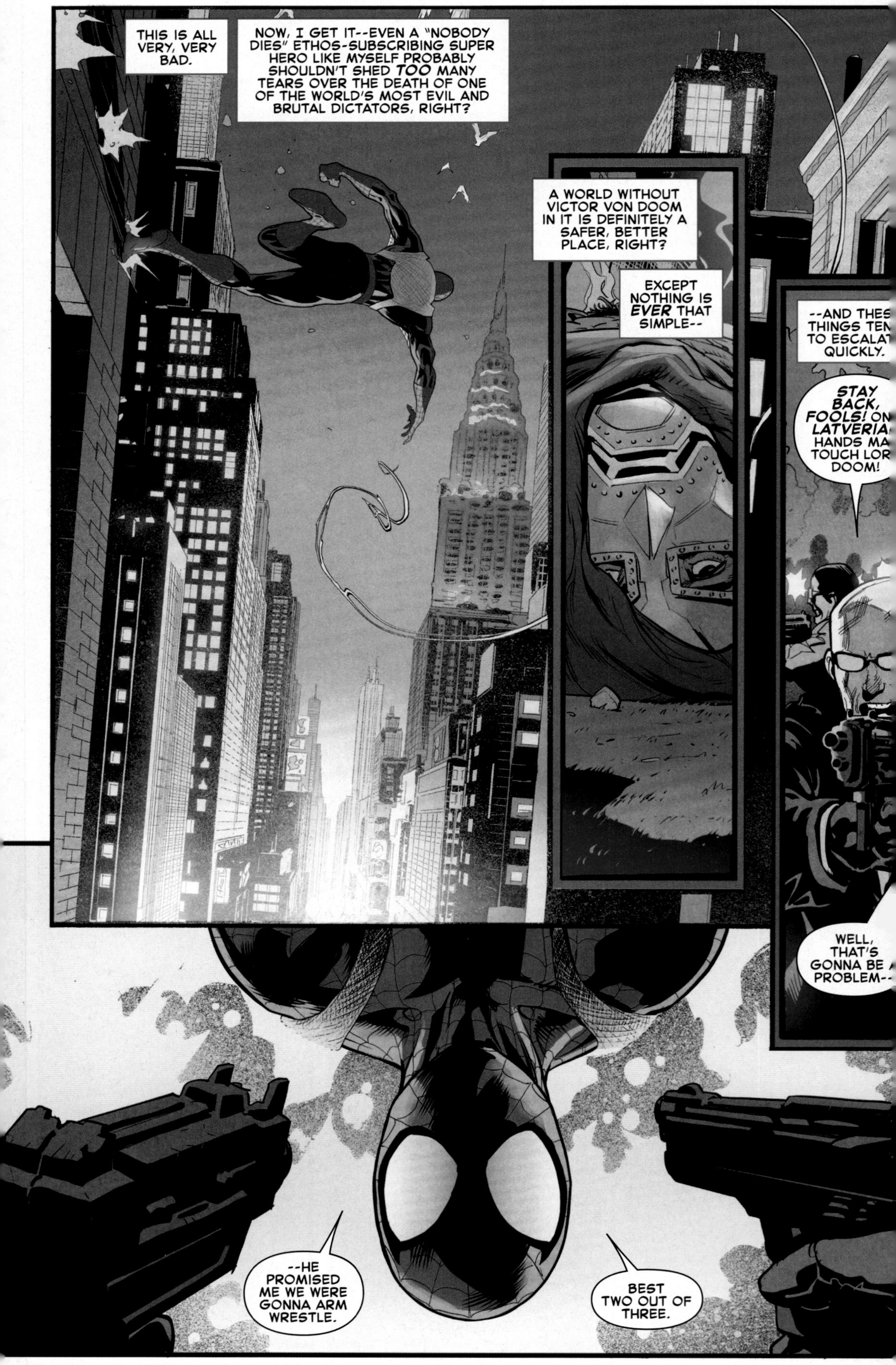
THIS IS ALL VERY, VERY BAD.
NOW, I GET IT--EVEN A "NOBODY DIES" ETHOS-SUBSCRIBING SUPER HERO LIKE MYSELF PROBABLY SHOULDN'T SHED TOO MANY TEARS OVER THE DEATH OF ONE OF THE WORLD'S MOST EVIL AND BRUTAL DICTATORS, RIGHT?
A WORLD WITHOUT VICTOR VON DOOM IN IT IS DEFINITELY A SAFER, BETTER PLACE, RIGHT?
EXCEPT NOTHING IS EVER THAT SIMPLE--
--AND THES THINGS TEN TO ESCALAT QUICKLY.
STAY BACK, FOOLS! ON LATVERIA HANDS MA TOUCH LOR DOOM!
WELL, THAT'S GONNA BE PROBLEM--
--HE PROMISED ME WE WERE GONNA ARM WRESTLE.
BEST TWO OUT OF THREE.

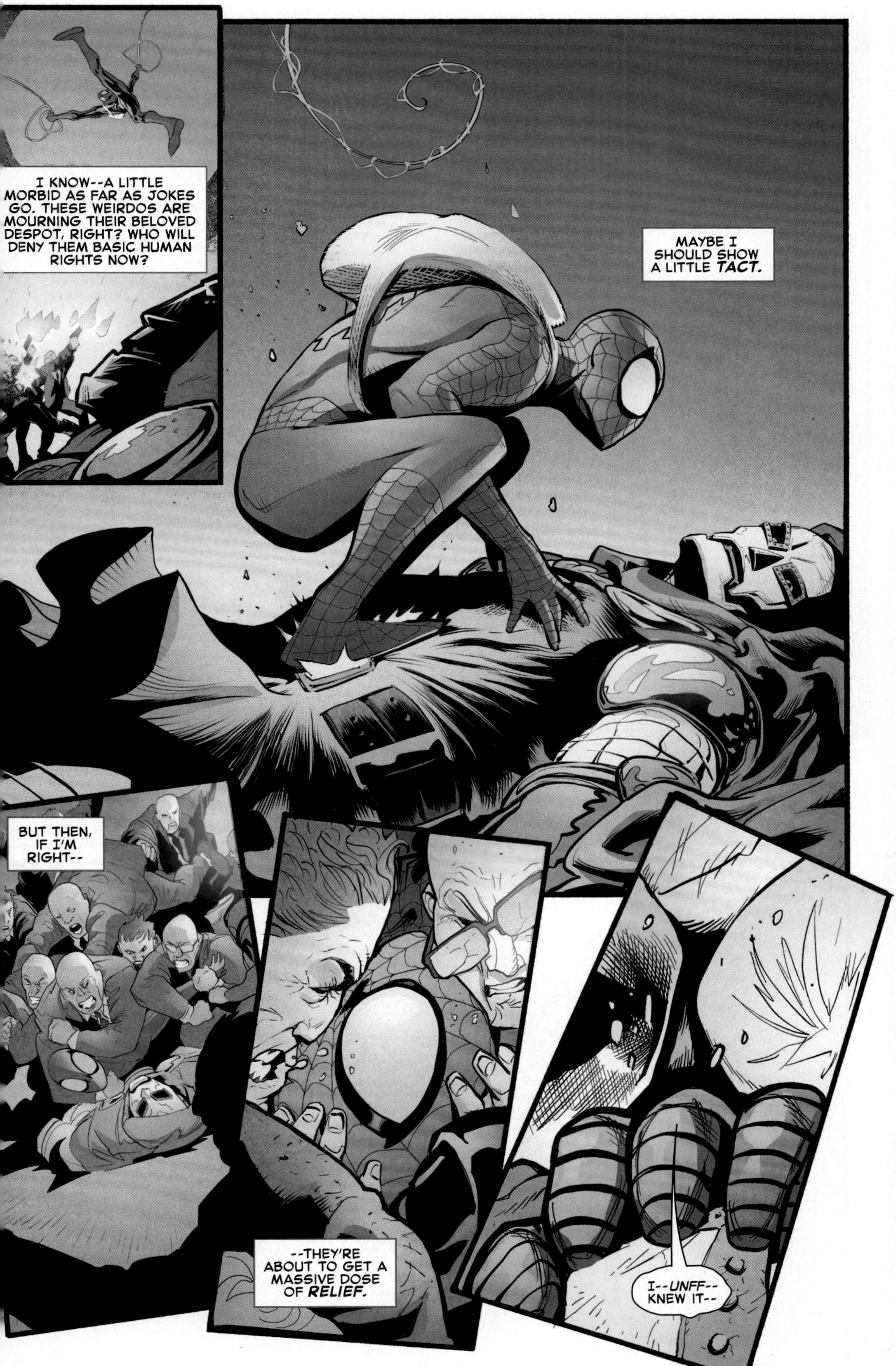
I KNOW--A LITTLE MORBID AS FAR AS JOKES GO. THESE WEIRDOS ARE MOURNING THEIR BELOVED DESPOT, RIGHT? WHO WILL DENY THEM BASIC HUMAN RIGHTS NOW?
MAYBE I SHOULD SHOW A LITTLE TACT.
BUT THEN, IF I'M RIGHT--
--THEY'RE ABOUT TO GET A MASSIVE DOSE OF RELIEF.
I--UNFF--KNEW IT--

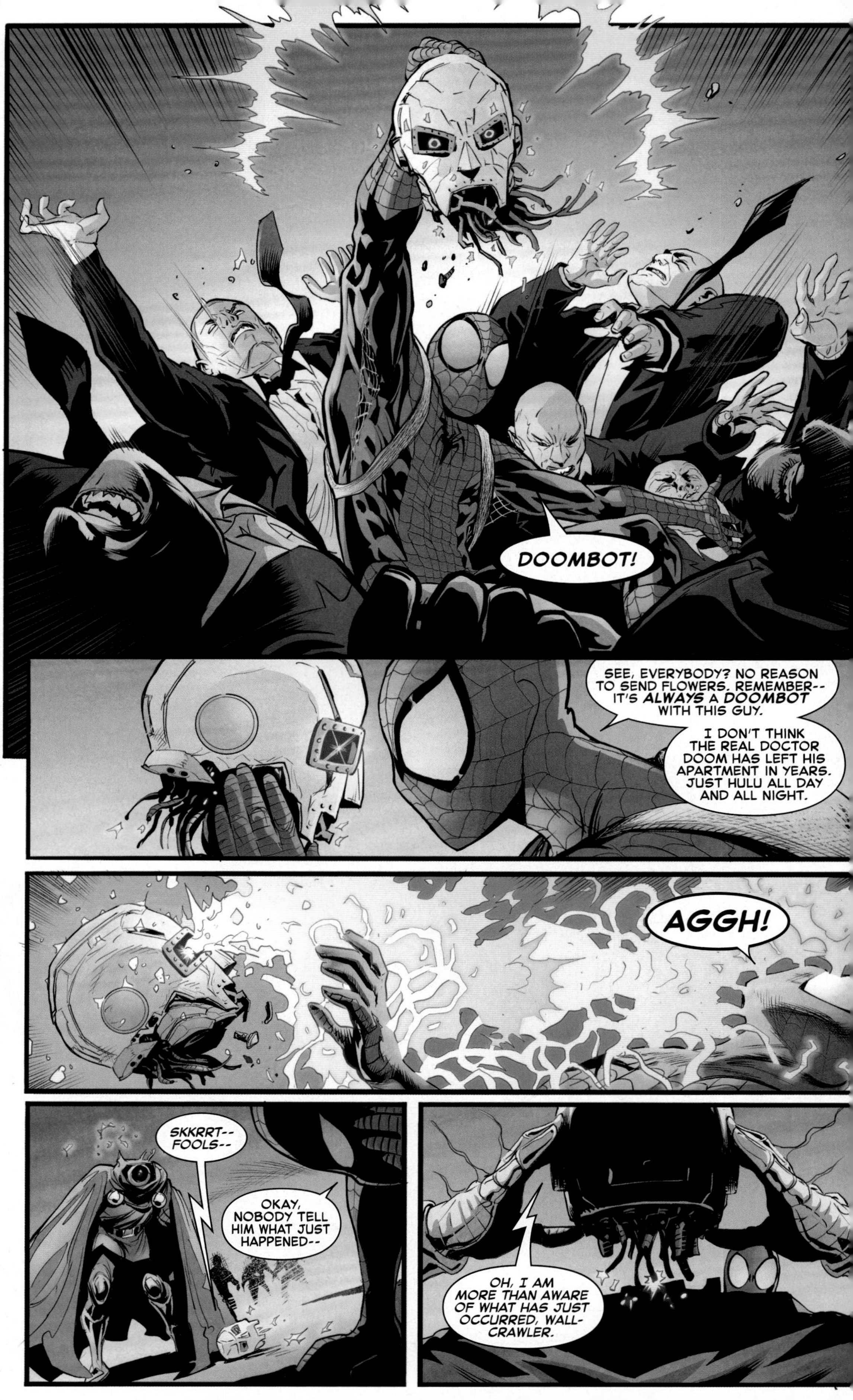
DOOMBOT!
SEE, EVERYBODY? NO REASON TO SEND FLOWERS. REMEMBER-- IT'S ALWAYS A DOOMBOT WITH THIS GUY.
I DON'T THINK THE REAL DOCTOR DOOM HAS LEFT HIS APARTMENT IN YEARS. JUST HULU ALL DAY AND ALL NIGHT.
AGGH!
SKKRRT-- FOOLS--
OKAY, NOBODY TELL HIM WHAT JUST HAPPENED--
OH, I AM MORE THAN AWARE OF WHAT HAS JUST OCCURRED, WALL-CRAWLER.

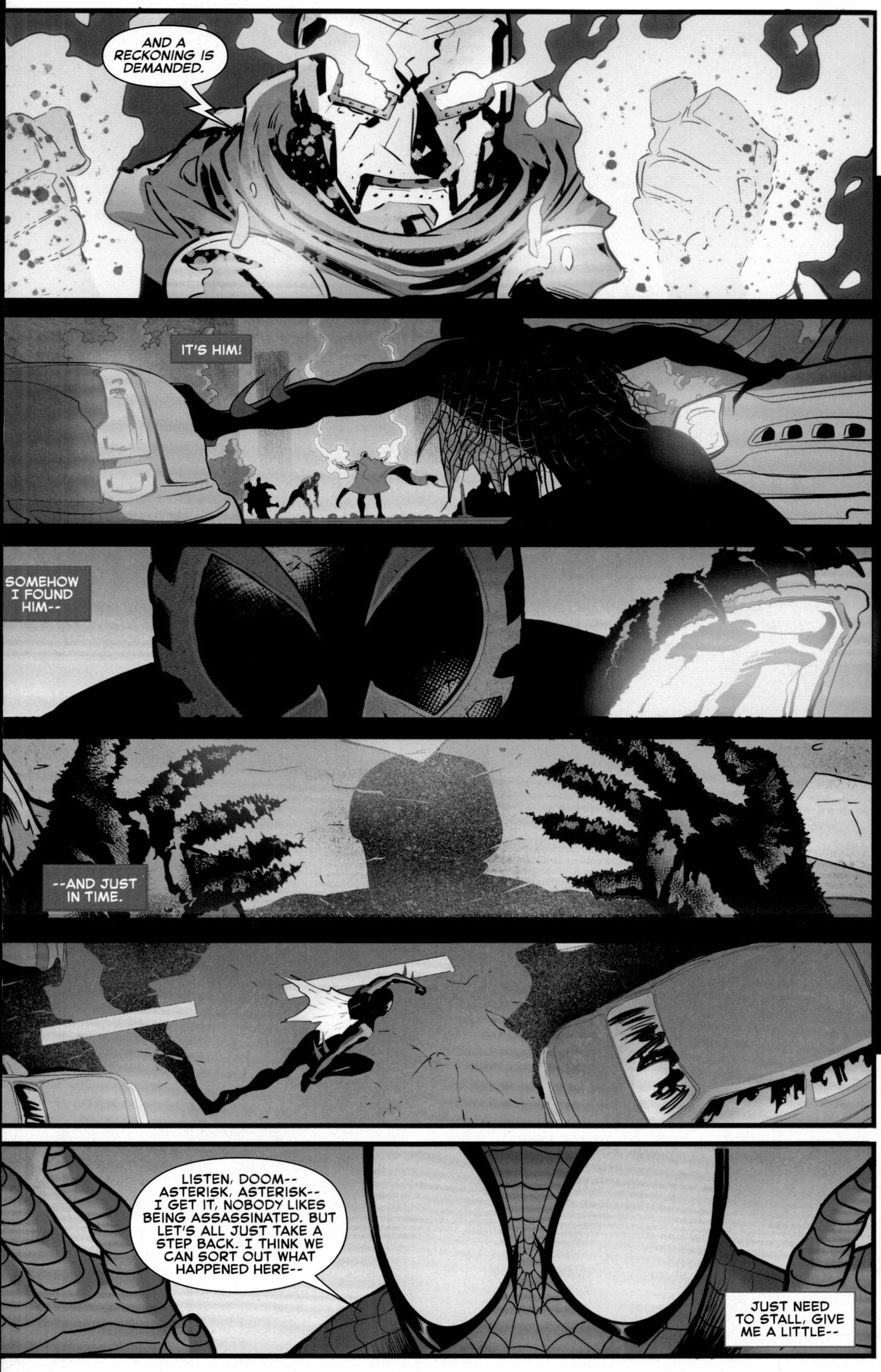
AND A RECKONING IS DEMANDED.
IT'S HIM!
SOMEHOW I FOUND HIM--
--AND JUST IN TIME.
LISTEN, DOOM-- ASTERISK, ASTERISK-- I GET IT, NOBODY LIKES BEING ASSASSINATED. BUT LET'S ALL JUST TAKE A STEP BACK. I THINK WE CAN SORT OUT WHAT HAPPENED HERE--
JUST NEED TO STALL, GIVE ME A LITTLE--

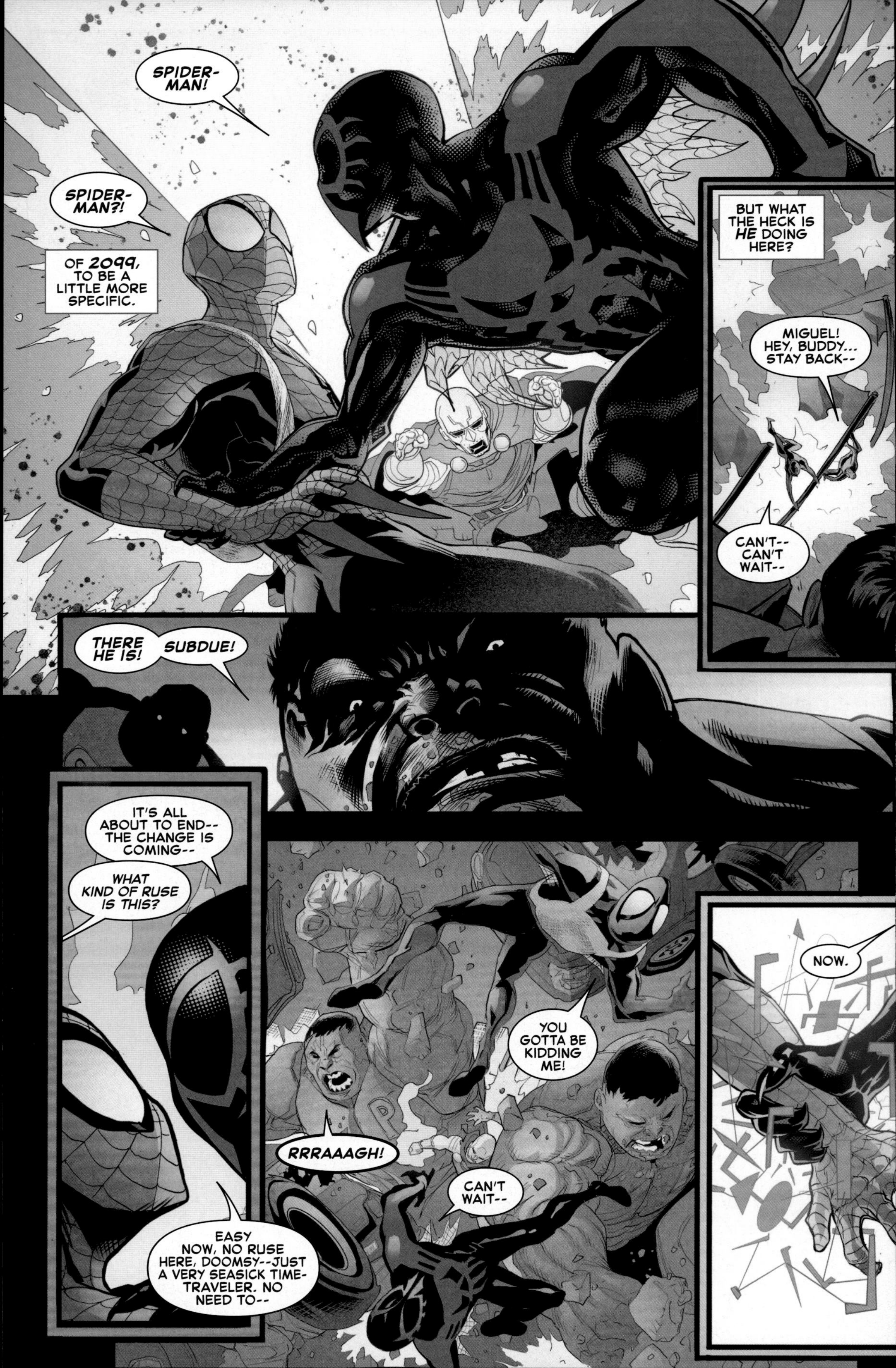
SPIDER-MAN!
SPIDER-MAN?!
OF 2099, TO BE A LITTLE MORE SPECIFIC.
BUT WHAT THE HECK IS HE DOING HERE?
MIGUEL! HEY, BUDDY... STAY BACK--
CAN'T-- CAN'T WAIT--
THERE HE IS!
SUBDUE!
IT'S ALL ABOUT TO END-- THE CHANGE IS COMING--
WHAT KIND OF RUSE IS THIS?
EASY NOW, NO RUSE HERE, DOOMSY--JUST A VERY SEASICK TIME-TRAVELER. NO NEED TO--
RRRAAAGH!
CAN'T WAIT--
YOU GOTTA BE KIDDING ME!
NOW.

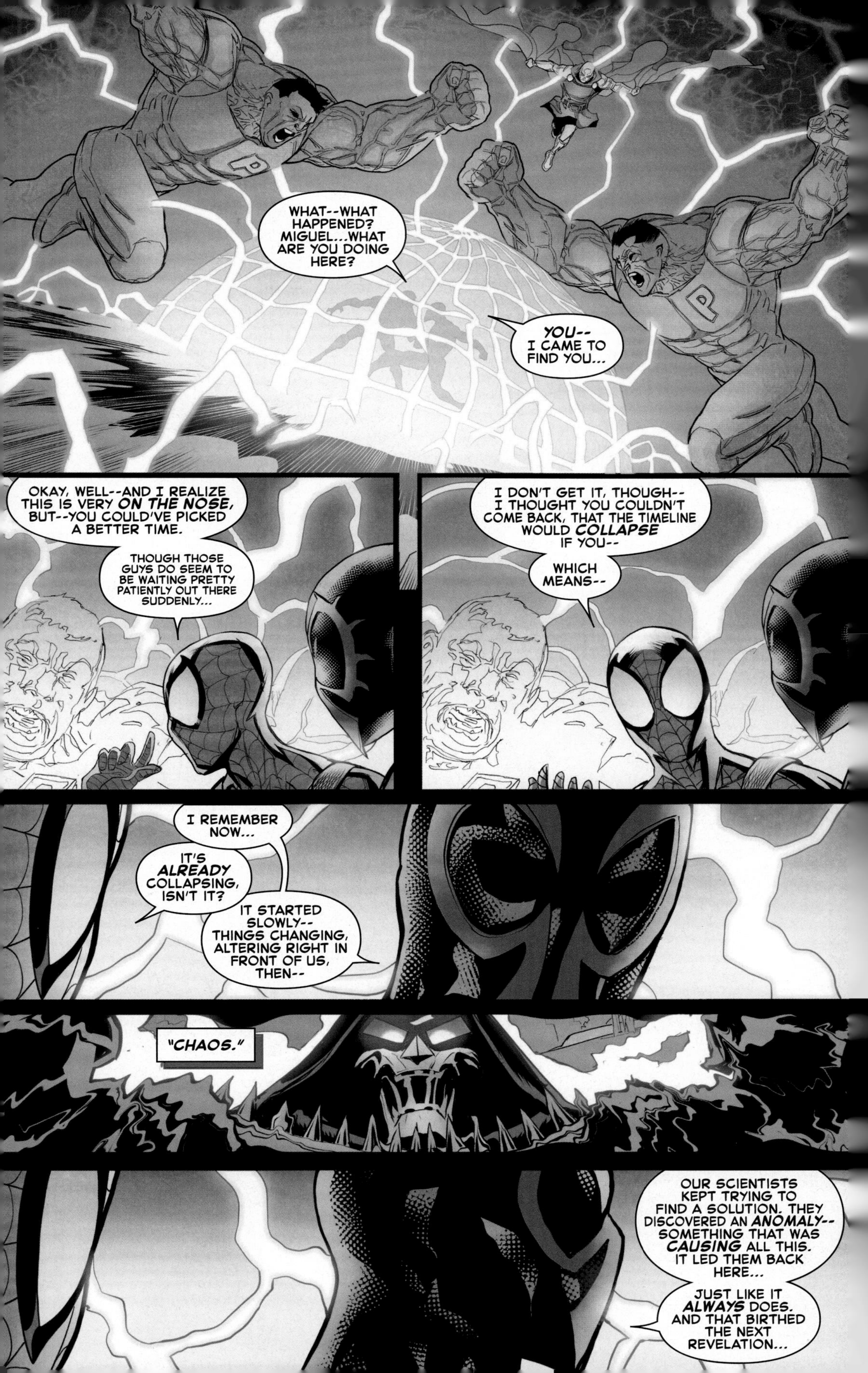
WHAT--WHAT HAPPENED? MIGUEL...WHAT ARE YOU DOING HERE?
YOU-- I CAME TO FIND YOU...
OKAY, WELL--AND I REALIZE THIS IS VERY ON THE NOSE, BUT--YOU COULD'VE PICKED A BETTER TIME.
THOUGH THOSE GUYS DO SEEM TO BE WAITING PRETTY PATIENTLY OUT THERE SUDDENLY...
I DON'T GET IT, THOUGH-- I THOUGHT YOU COULDN'T COME BACK, THAT THE TIMELINE WOULD COLLAPSE IF YOU--
WHICH MEANS--
I REMEMBER NOW...
IT'S ALREADY COLLAPSING, ISN'T IT?
IT STARTED SLOWLY-- THINGS CHANGING, ALTERING RIGHT IN FRONT OF US, THEN--
"CHAOS."
OUR SCIENTISTS KEPT TRYING TO FIND A SOLUTION. THEY DISCOVERED AN ANOMALY-- SOMETHING THAT WAS CAUSING ALL THIS. IT LED THEM BACK HERE...
JUST LIKE IT ALWAYS DOES. AND THAT BIRTHED THE NEXT REVELATION...

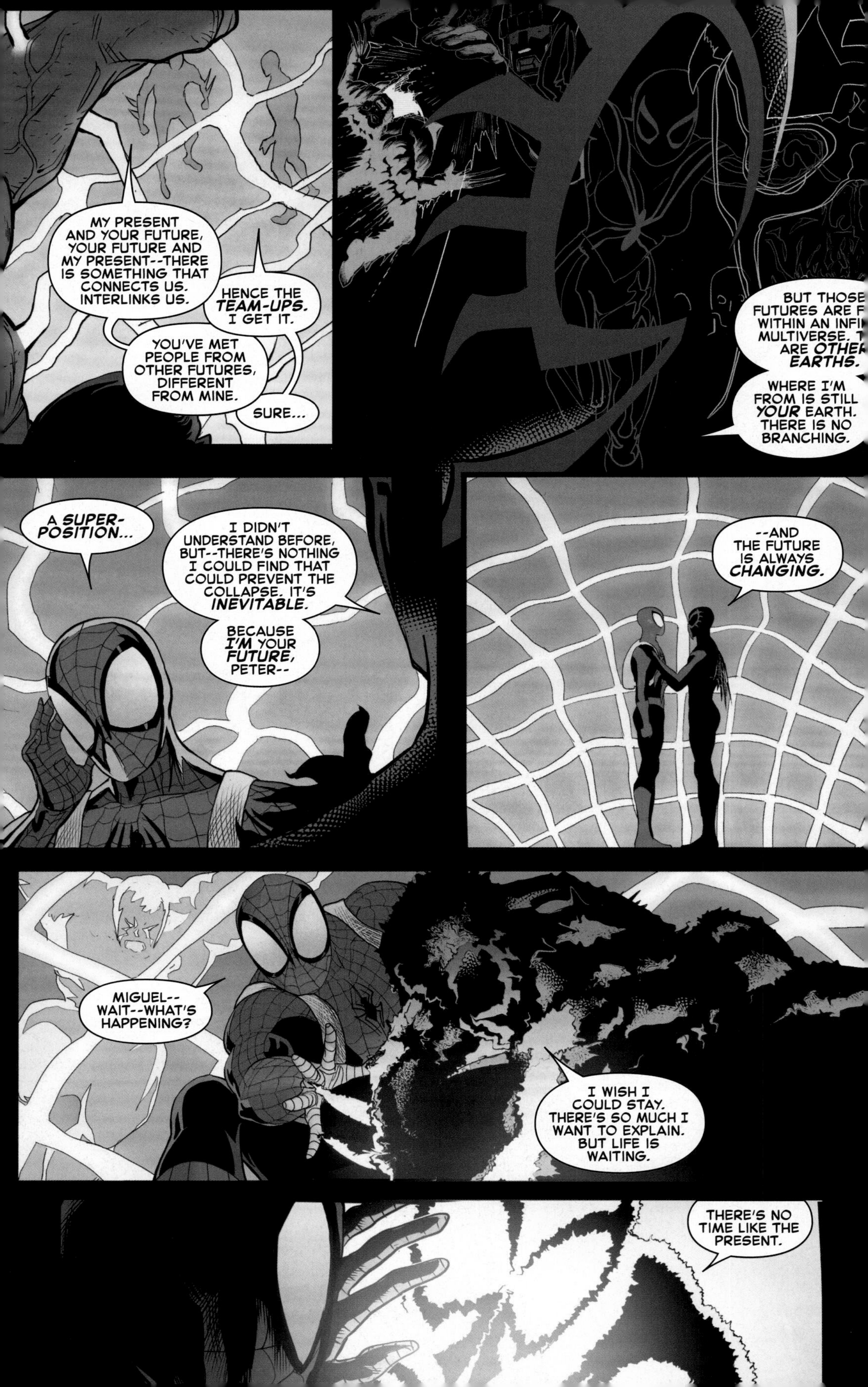
MY PRESENT AND YOUR FUTURE, YOUR FUTURE AND MY PRESENT--THERE IS SOMETHING THAT CONNECTS US. INTERLINKS US.
HENCE THE TEAM-UPS. I GET IT.
YOU'VE MET PEOPLE FROM OTHER FUTURES, DIFFERENT FROM MINE.
SURE...
BUT THOSE FUTURES ARE F WITHIN AN INFI MULTIVERSE. T ARE OTHER EARTHS.
WHERE I'M FROM IS STILL YOUR EARTH. THERE IS NO BRANCHING.
A SUPER-POSITION...
I DIDN'T UNDERSTAND BEFORE, BUT--THERE'S NOTHING I COULD FIND THAT COULD PREVENT THE COLLAPSE. IT'S INEVITABLE.
BECAUSE I'M YOUR FUTURE, PETER--
--AND THE FUTURE IS ALWAYS CHANGING.
MIGUEL--WAIT--WHAT'S HAPPENING?
I WISH I COULD STAY. THERE'S SO MUCH I WANT TO EXPLAIN. BUT LIFE IS WAITING.
THERE'S NO TIME LIKE THE PRESENT.

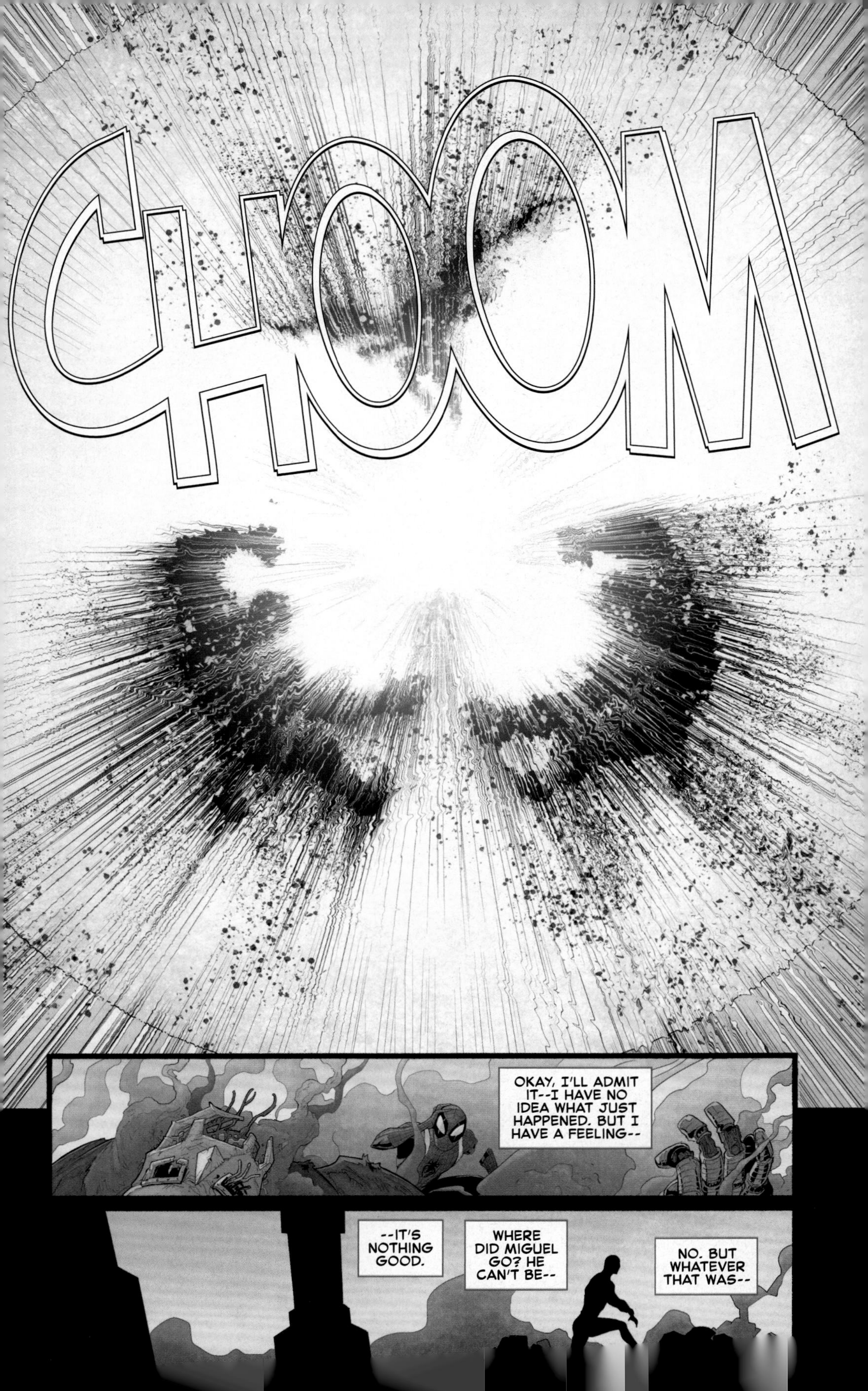
CHOOM
OKAY, I'LL ADMIT IT--I HAVE NO IDEA WHAT JUST HAPPENED. BUT I HAVE A FEELING--
--IT'S NOTHING GOOD.
WHERE DID MIGUEL GO? HE CAN'T BE--
NO. BUT WHATEVER THAT WAS--

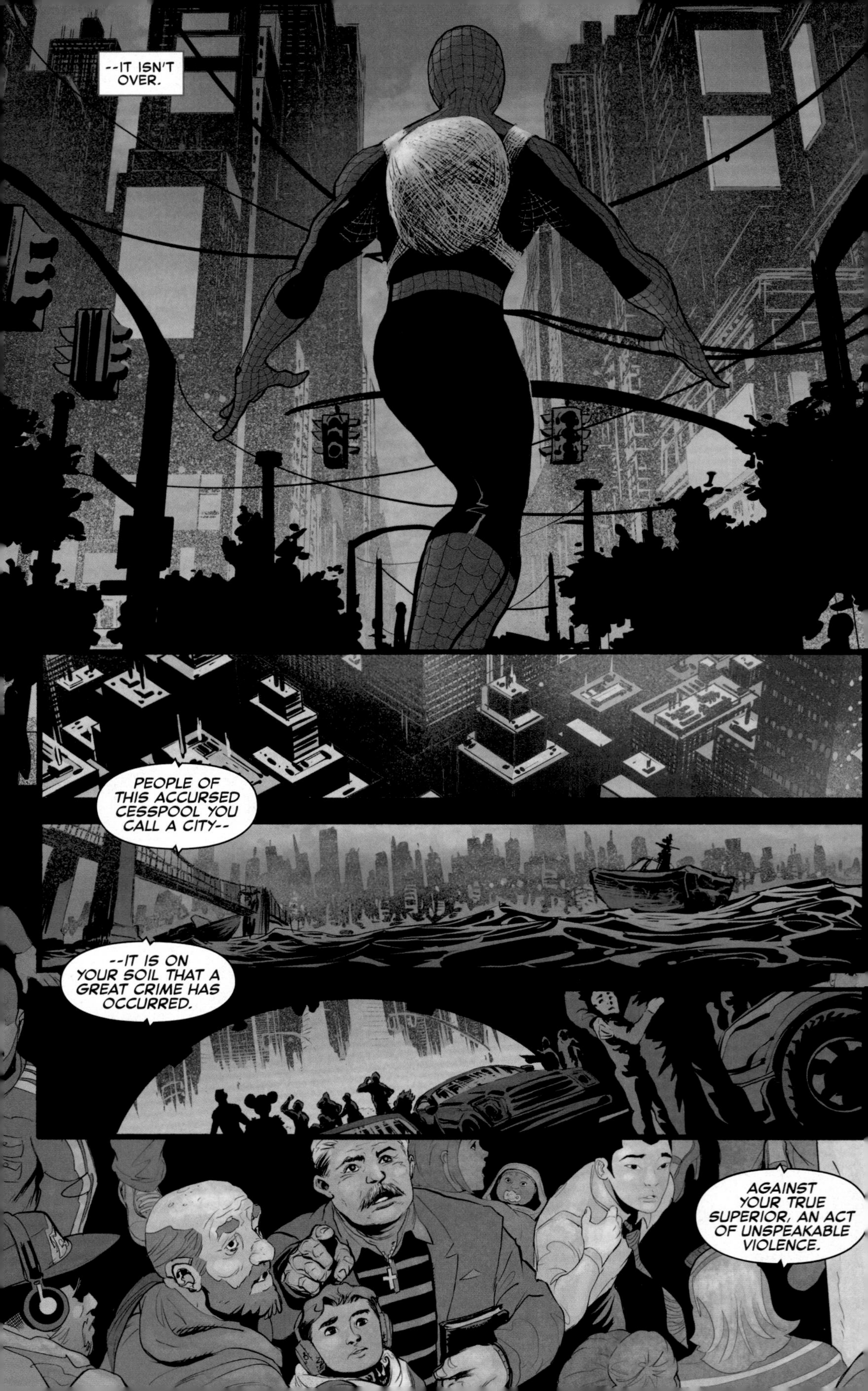
--IT ISN'T OVER.
PEOPLE OF THIS ACCURSED CESSPOOL YOU CALL A CITY--
--IT IS ON YOUR SOIL THAT A GREAT CRIME HAS OCCURRED.
AGAINST YOUR TRUE SUPERIOR, AN ACT OF UNSPEAKABLE VIOLENCE.

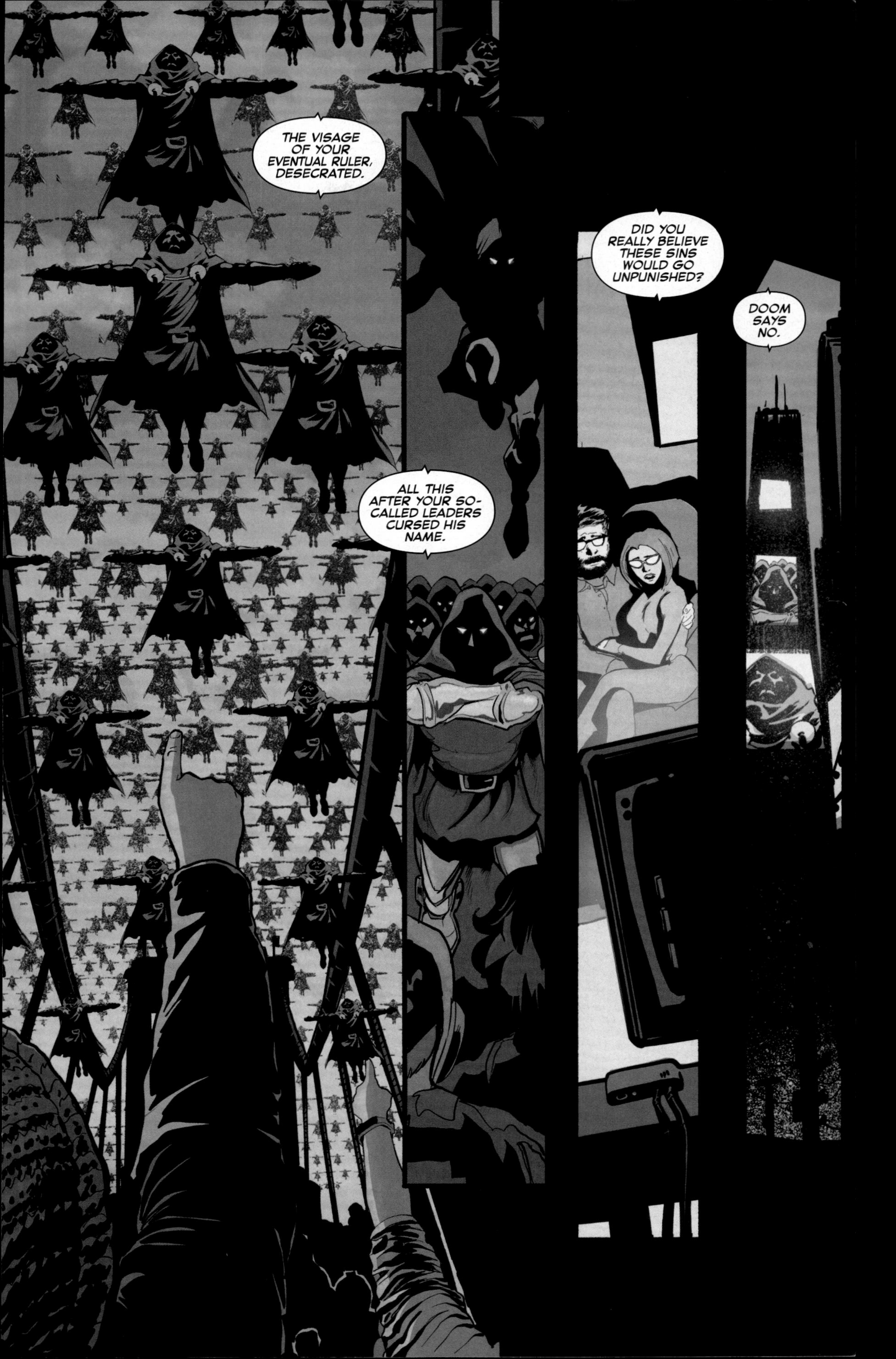
THE VISAGE OF YOUR EVENTUAL RULER, DESECRATED.
ALL THIS AFTER YOUR SO-CALLED LEADERS CURSED HIS NAME.
DID YOU REALLY BELIEVE THESE SINS WOULD GO UNPUNISHED?
DOOM SAYS NO.

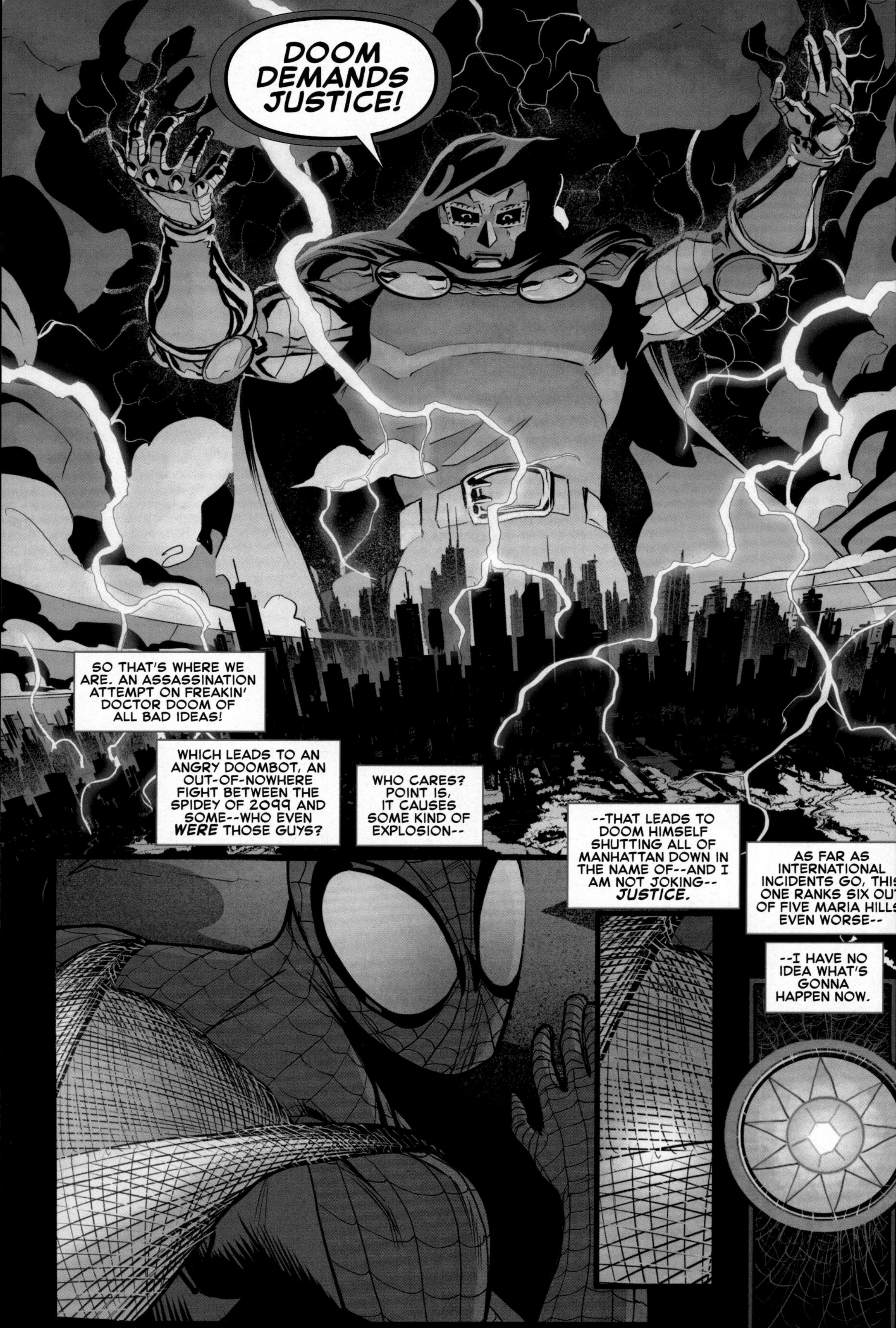
DOOM DEMANDS JUSTICE!
SO THAT'S WHERE WE ARE. AN ASSASSINATION ATTEMPT ON FREAKIN' DOCTOR DOOM OF ALL BAD IDEAS!
WHICH LEADS TO AN ANGRY DOOMBOT, AN OUT-OF-NOWHERE FIGHT BETWEEN THE SPIDEY OF 2099 AND SOME--WHO EVEN *WERE* THOSE GUYS?
WHO CARES? POINT IS, IT CAUSES SOME KIND OF EXPLOSION--
--THAT LEADS TO DOOM HIMSELF SHUTTING ALL OF MANHATTAN DOWN IN THE NAME OF--AND I AM NOT JOKING--*JUSTICE.*
AS FAR AS INTERNATIONAL INCIDENTS GO, THIS ONE RANKS SIX OUT OF FIVE MARIA HILLS EVEN WORSE--
--I HAVE NO IDEA WHAT'S GONNA HAPPEN NOW.

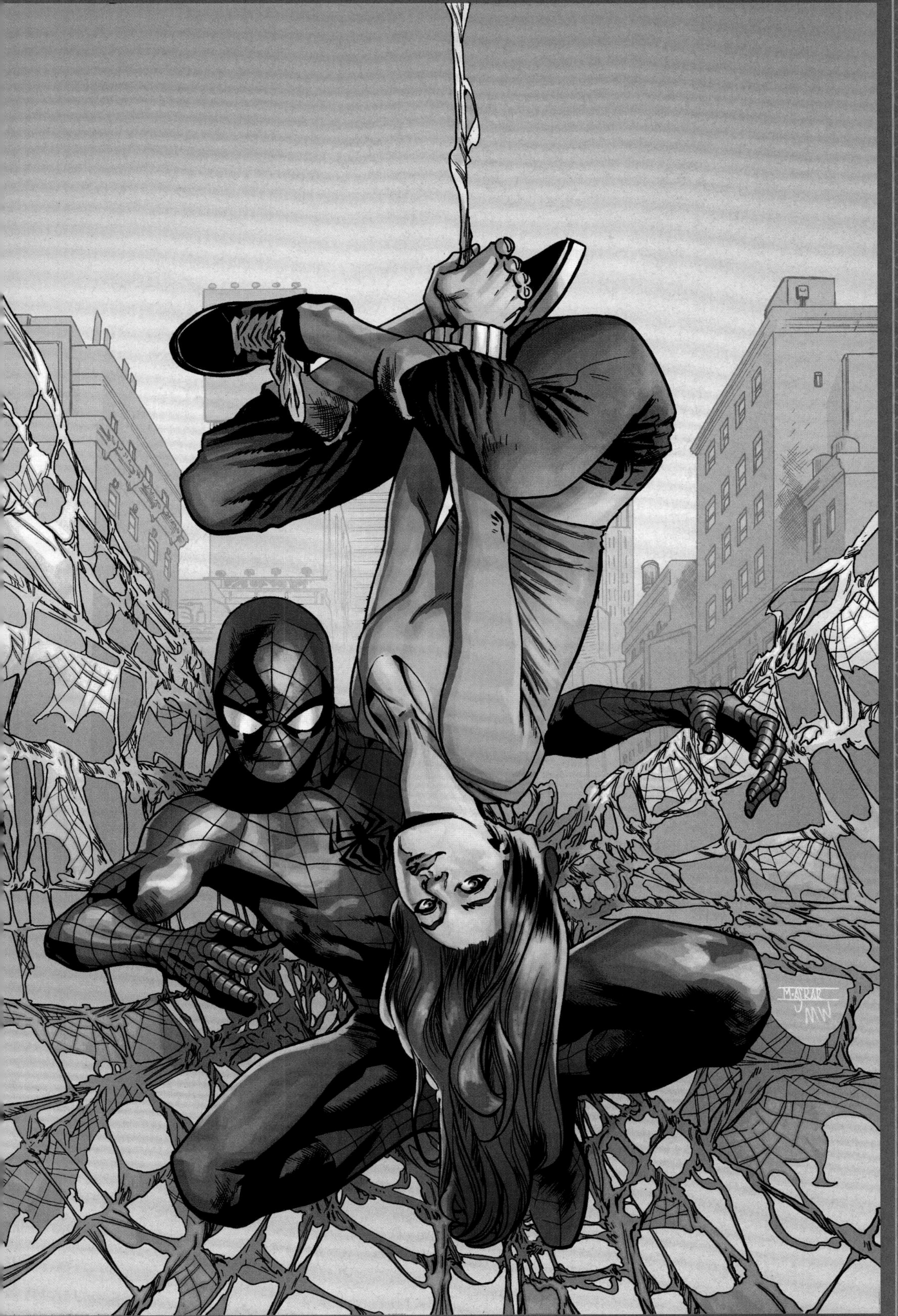
M.ASRAR
MW

#32 MARY JANE VARIANT BY MAHMUD ASRAR & MATTHEW WILSON

35

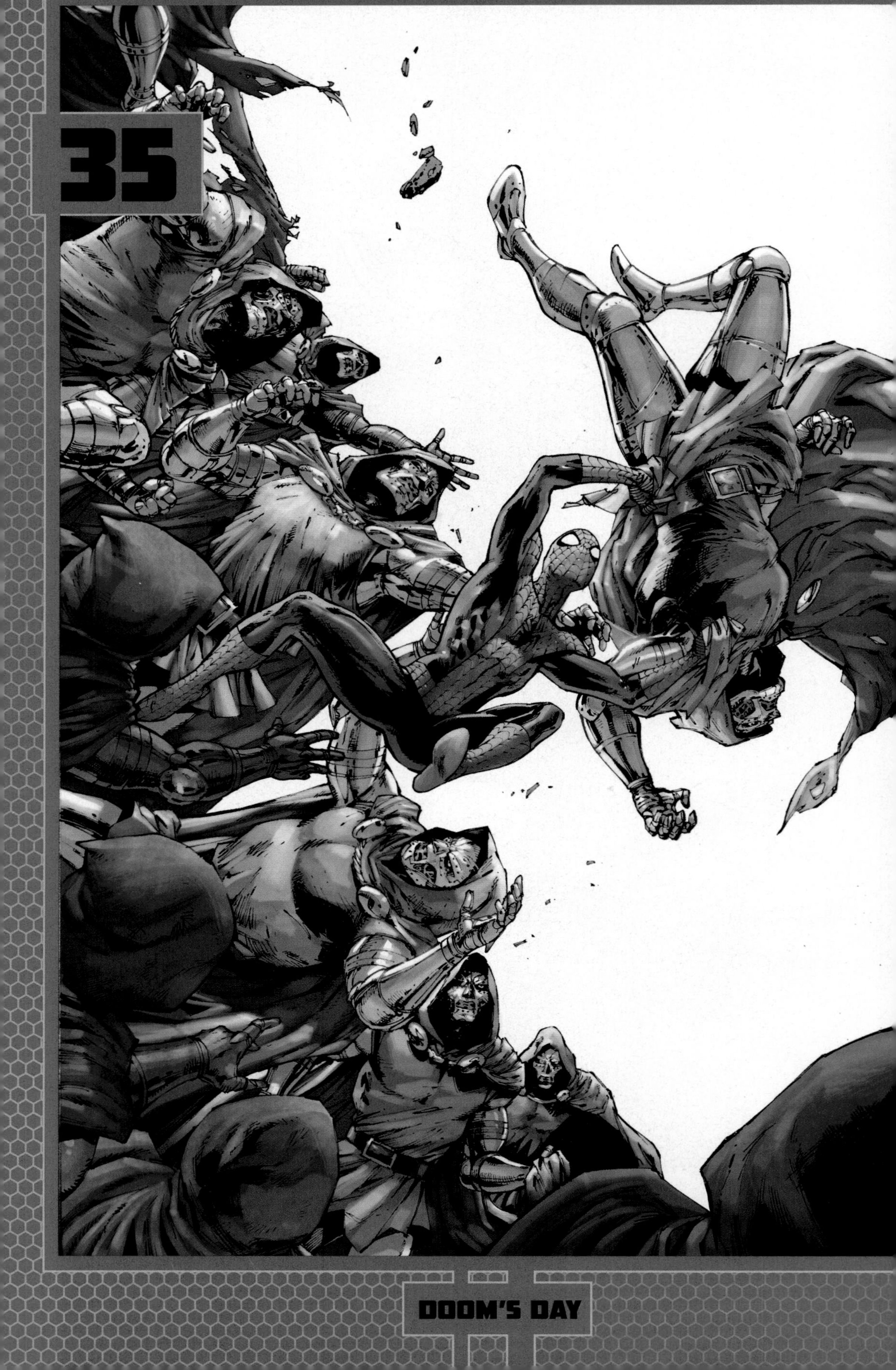

DOOM'S DAY

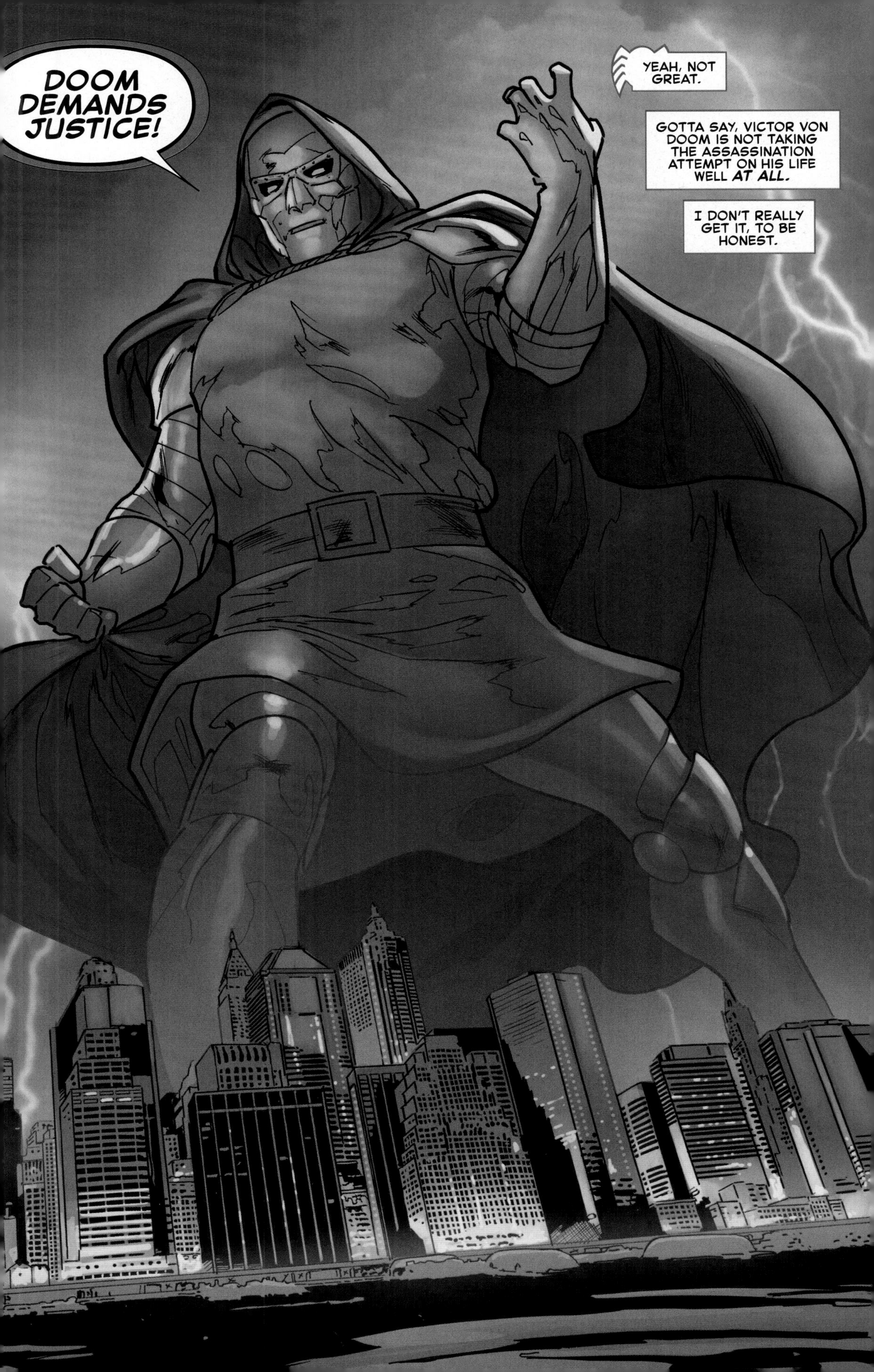
DOOM DEMANDS JUSTICE!
YEAH, NOT GREAT.
GOTTA SAY, VICTOR VON DOOM IS NOT TAKING THE ASSASSINATION ATTEMPT ON HIS LIFE WELL AT ALL.
I DON'T REALLY GET IT, TO BE HONEST.

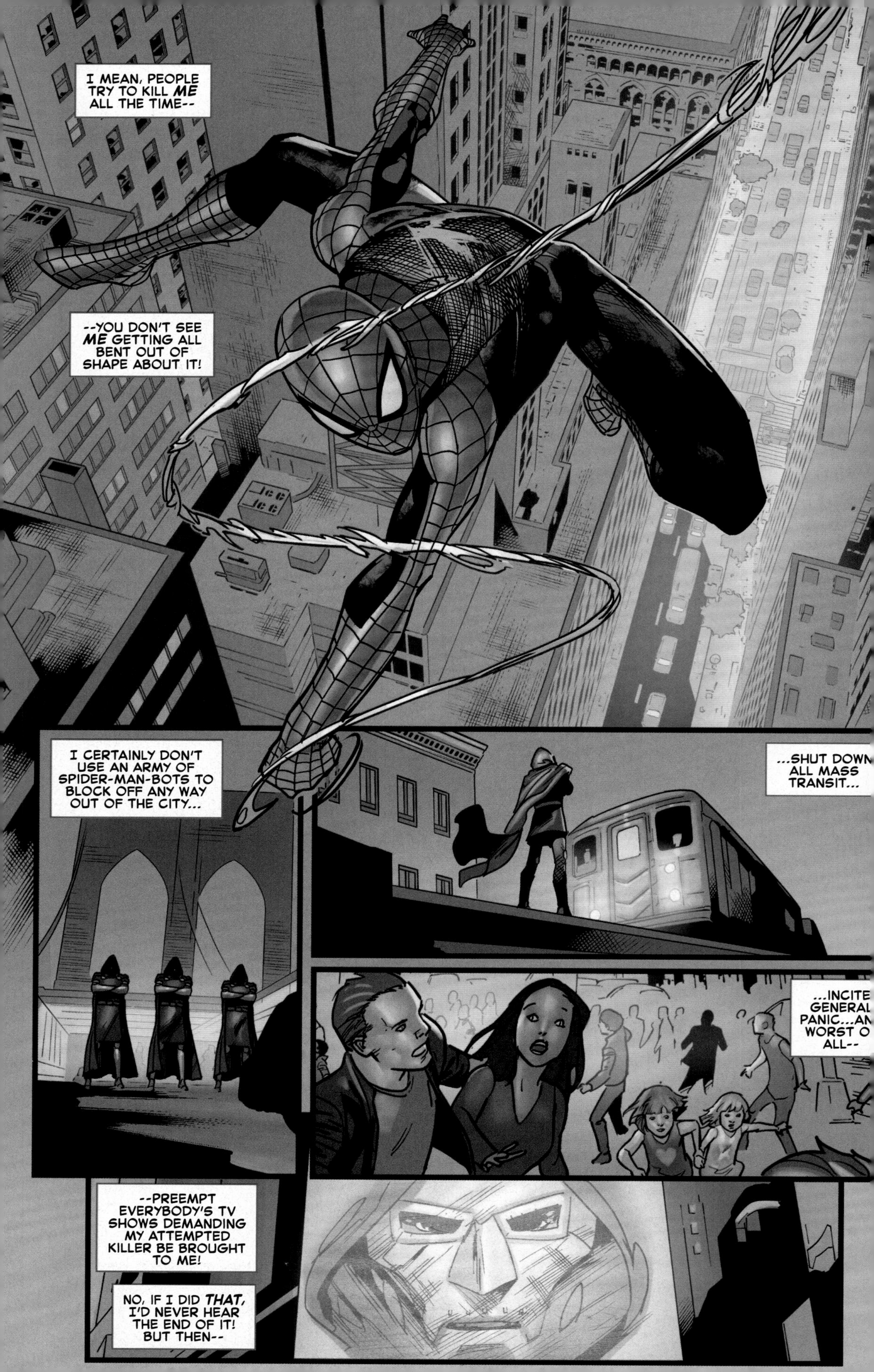

I MEAN, PEOPLE TRY TO KILL *ME* ALL THE TIME--
--YOU DON'T SEE *ME* GETTING ALL BENT OUT OF SHAPE ABOUT IT!
I CERTAINLY DON'T USE AN ARMY OF SPIDER-MAN-BOTS TO BLOCK OFF ANY WAY OUT OF THE CITY...
...SHUT DOWN ALL MASS TRANSIT...
...INCITE GENERAL PANIC...AN WORST O ALL--
--PREEMPT EVERYBODY'S TV SHOWS DEMANDING MY ATTEMPTED KILLER BE BROUGHT TO ME!
NO, IF I DID *THAT,* I'D NEVER HEAR THE END OF IT! BUT THEN--

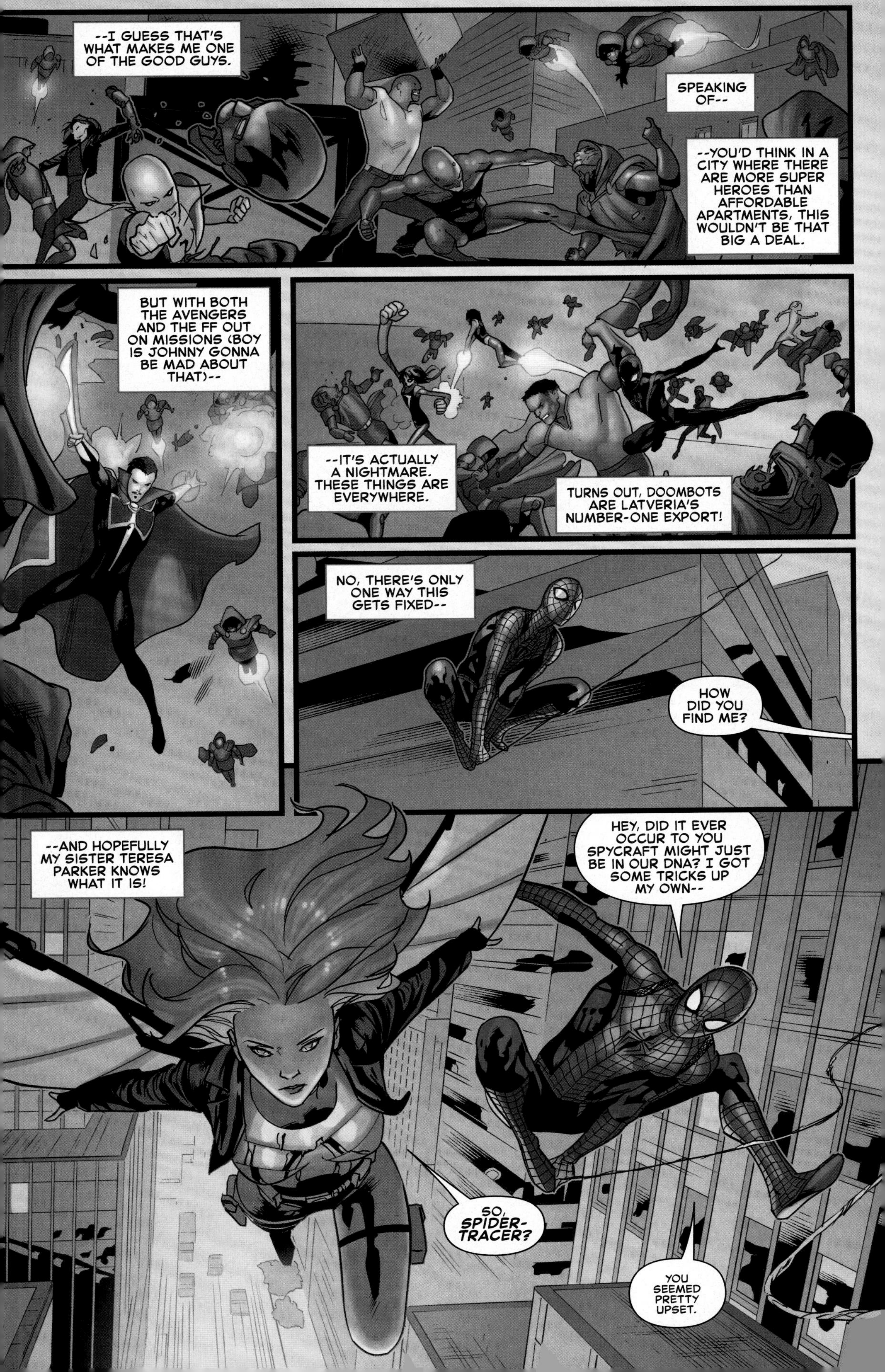
--I GUESS THAT'S WHAT MAKES ME ONE OF THE GOOD GUYS.
SPEAKING OF--
--YOU'D THINK IN A CITY WHERE THERE ARE MORE SUPER HEROES THAN AFFORDABLE APARTMENTS, THIS WOULDN'T BE THAT BIG A DEAL.
BUT WITH BOTH THE AVENGERS AND THE FF OUT ON MISSIONS (BOY IS JOHNNY GONNA BE MAD ABOUT THAT)--
--IT'S ACTUALLY A NIGHTMARE. THESE THINGS ARE EVERYWHERE.
TURNS OUT, DOOMBOTS ARE LATVERIA'S NUMBER-ONE EXPORT!
NO, THERE'S ONLY ONE WAY THIS GETS FIXED--
HOW DID YOU FIND ME?
--AND HOPEFULLY MY SISTER TERESA PARKER KNOWS WHAT IT IS!
HEY, DID IT EVER OCCUR TO YOU SPYCRAFT MIGHT JUST BE IN OUR DNA? I GOT SOME TRICKS UP MY OWN--
SO, SPIDER-TRACER?
YOU SEEMED PRETTY UPSET.

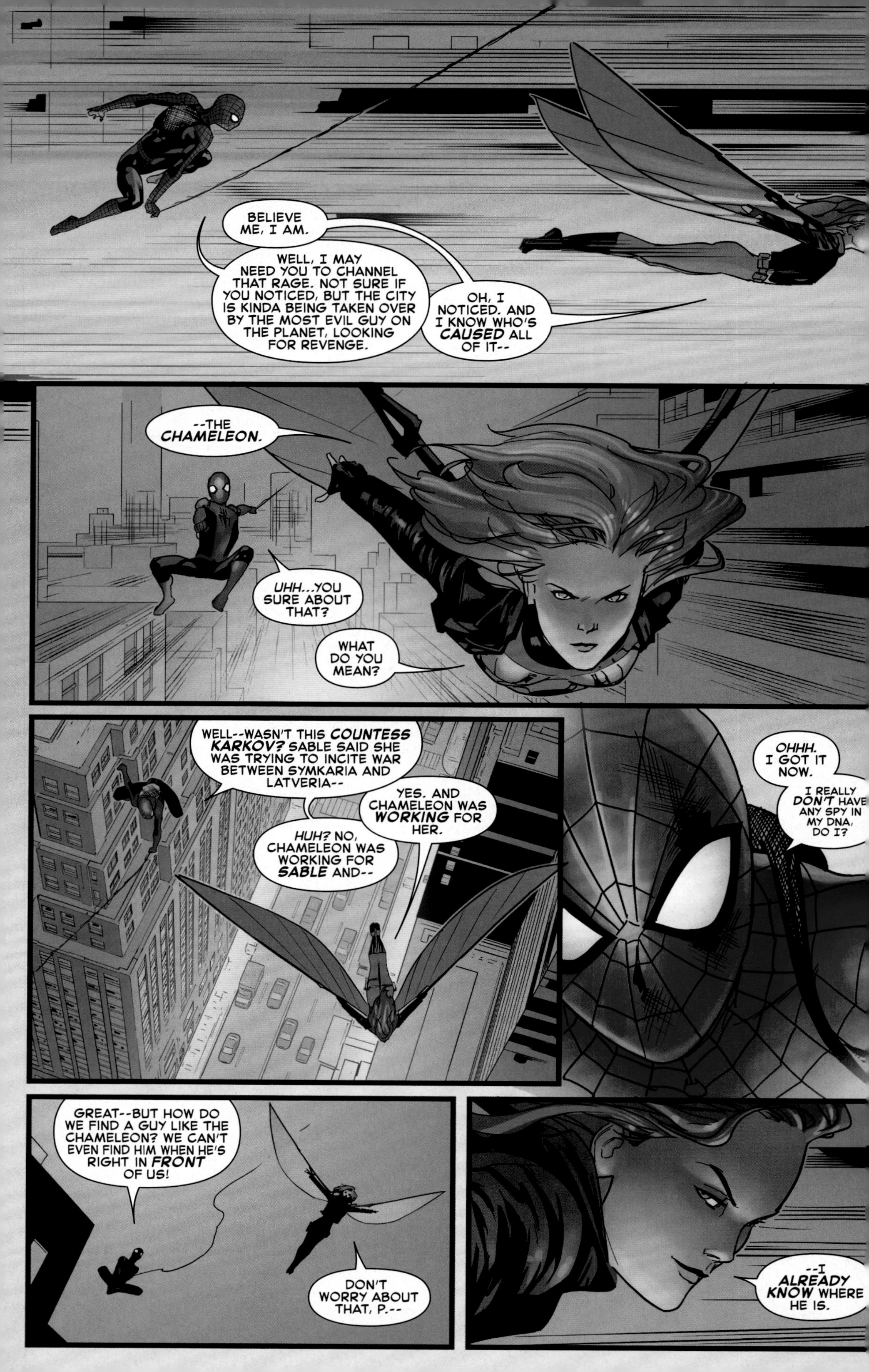
BELIEVE ME, I AM.
WELL, I MAY NEED YOU TO CHANNEL THAT RAGE. NOT SURE IF YOU NOTICED, BUT THE CITY IS KINDA BEING TAKEN OVER BY THE MOST EVIL GUY ON THE PLANET, LOOKING FOR REVENGE.
OH, I NOTICED. AND I KNOW WHO'S CAUSED ALL OF IT--
--THE CHAMELEON.
UHH...YOU SURE ABOUT THAT?
WHAT DO YOU MEAN?
WELL--WASN'T THIS COUNTESS KARKOV? SABLE SAID SHE WAS TRYING TO INCITE WAR BETWEEN SYMKARIA AND LATVERIA--
HUH? NO, CHAMELEON WAS WORKING FOR SABLE AND--
YES. AND CHAMELEON WAS WORKING FOR HER.
OHHH. I GOT IT NOW.
I REALLY DON'T HAVE ANY SPY IN MY DNA, DO I?
GREAT--BUT HOW DO WE FIND A GUY LIKE THE CHAMELEON? WE CAN'T EVEN FIND HIM WHEN HE'S RIGHT IN FRONT OF US!
DON'T WORRY ABOUT THAT, P.--
--I ALREADY KNOW WHERE HE IS.

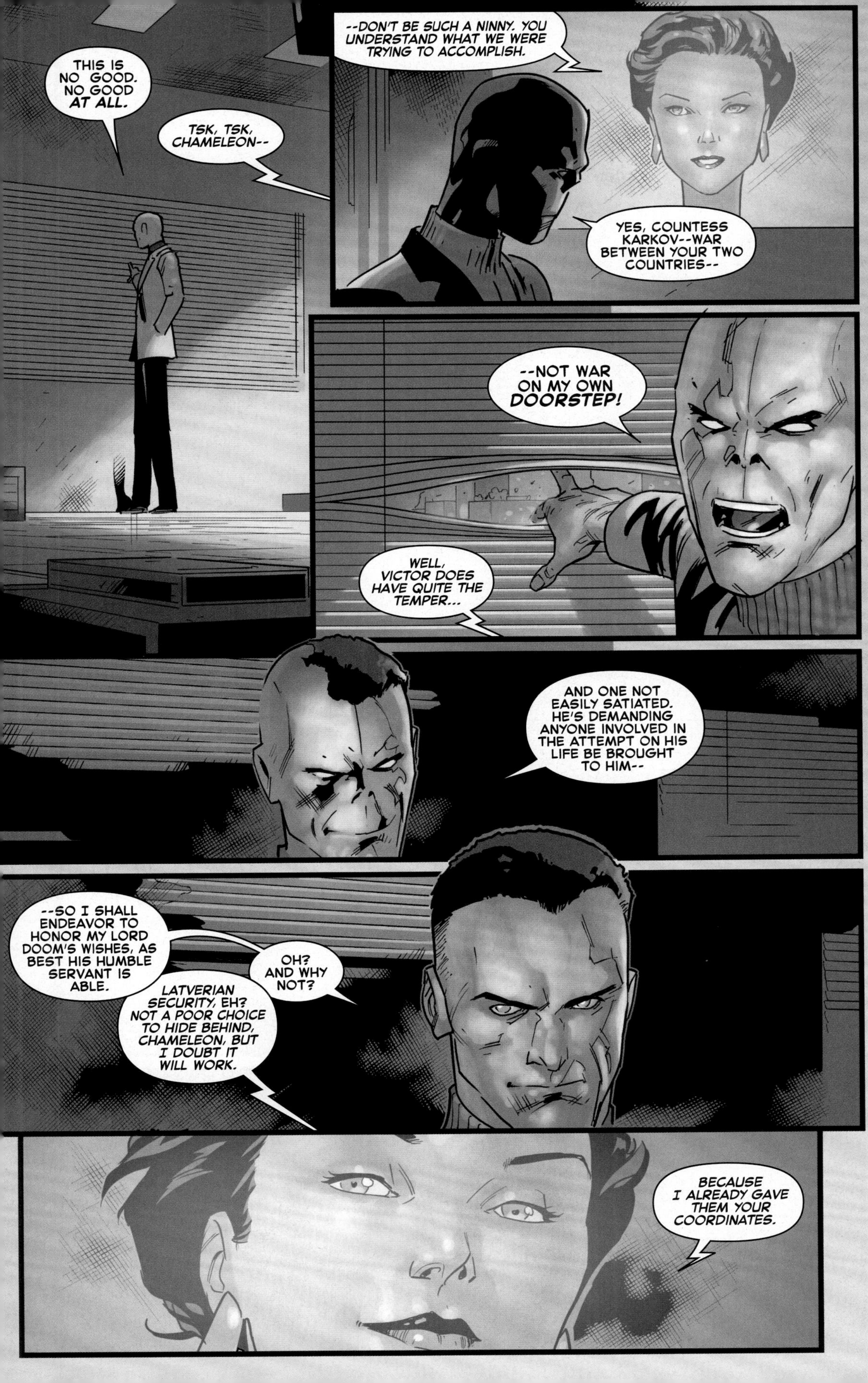
THIS IS NO GOOD. NO GOOD AT ALL.
TSK, TSK, CHAMELEON--
--DON'T BE SUCH A NINNY. YOU UNDERSTAND WHAT WE WERE TRYING TO ACCOMPLISH.
YES, COUNTESS KARKOV--WAR BETWEEN YOUR TWO COUNTRIES--
--NOT WAR ON MY OWN DOORSTEP!
WELL, VICTOR DOES HAVE QUITE THE TEMPER...
AND ONE NOT EASILY SATIATED. HE'S DEMANDING ANYONE INVOLVED IN THE ATTEMPT ON HIS LIFE BE BROUGHT TO HIM--
--SO I SHALL ENDEAVOR TO HONOR MY LORD DOOM'S WISHES, AS BEST HIS HUMBLE SERVANT IS ABLE.
LATVERIAN SECURITY, EH? NOT A POOR CHOICE TO HIDE BEHIND, CHAMELEON, BUT I DOUBT IT WILL WORK.
OH? AND WHY NOT?
BECAUSE I ALREADY GAVE THEM YOUR COORDINATES.

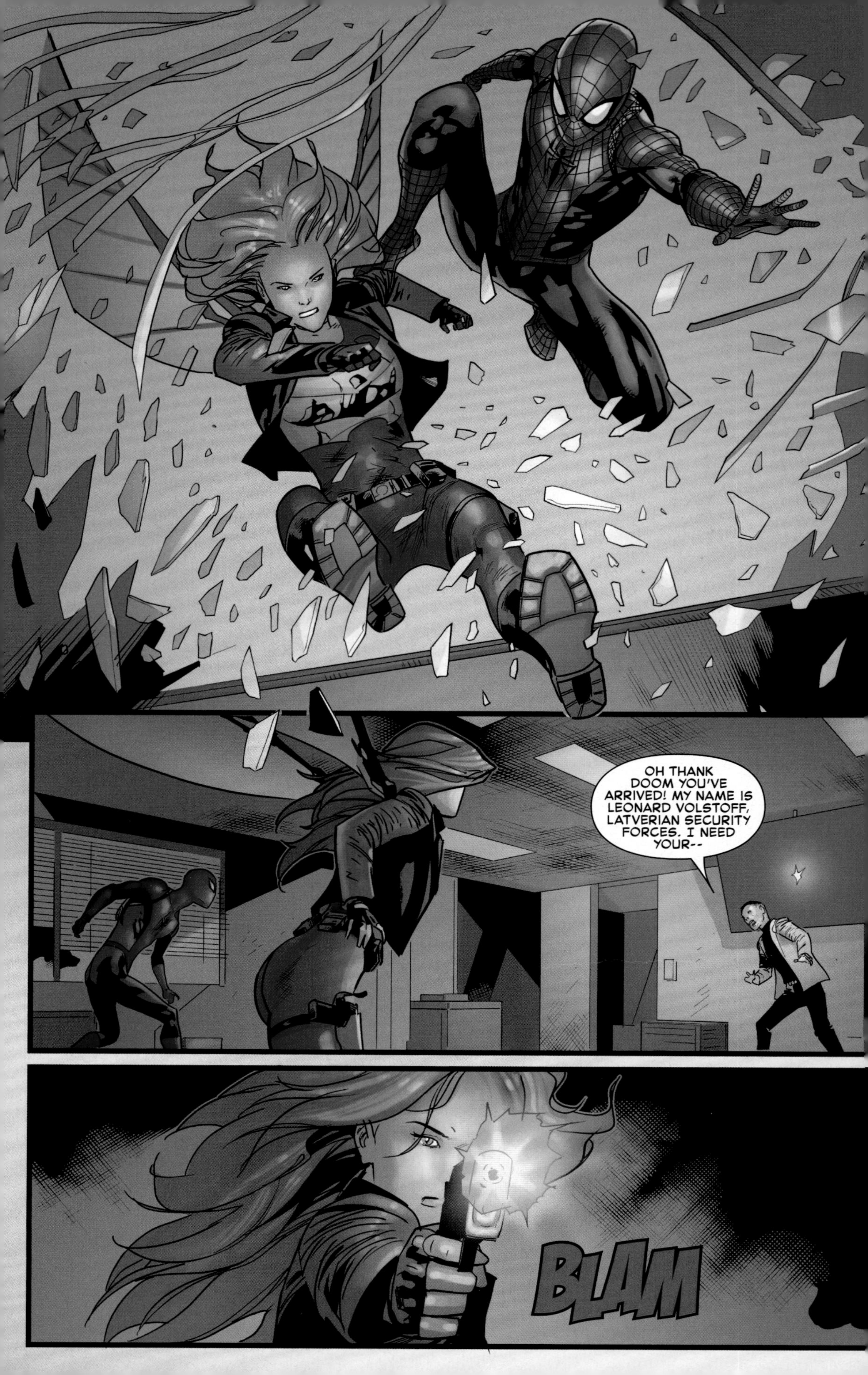
OH THANK DOOM YOU'VE ARRIVED! MY NAME IS LEONARD VOLSTOFF, LATVERIAN SECURITY FORCES. I NEED YOUR--
BLAM

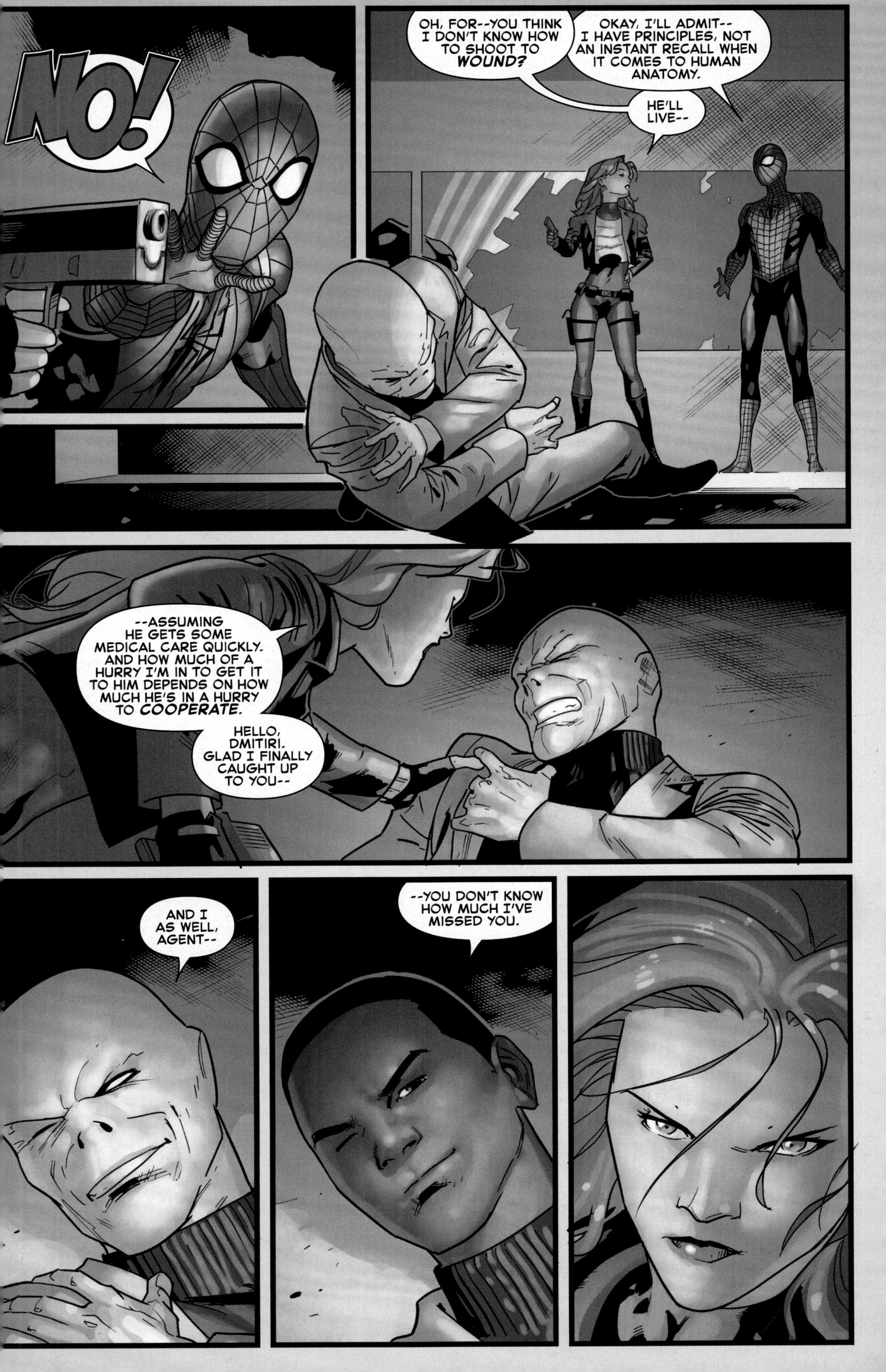
NO!
OH, FOR--YOU THINK I DON'T KNOW HOW TO SHOOT TO WOUND?
OKAY, I'LL ADMIT-- I HAVE PRINCIPLES, NOT AN INSTANT RECALL WHEN IT COMES TO HUMAN ANATOMY.
HE'LL LIVE--
--ASSUMING HE GETS SOME MEDICAL CARE QUICKLY. AND HOW MUCH OF A HURRY I'M IN TO GET IT TO HIM DEPENDS ON HOW MUCH HE'S IN A HURRY TO COOPERATE.
HELLO, DMITIRI. GLAD I FINALLY CAUGHT UP TO YOU--
AND I AS WELL, AGENT--
--YOU DON'T KNOW HOW MUCH I'VE MISSED YOU.

TERESA!

NOT BAD, GIRL. BUT NO ONE CAN HIT LIKE MY BROTHER.

TALK! YOU DID THIS, DIDN'T YOU?!

YOU MISUNDERSTAND-- I WASN'T THE *KILLER*, I ONLY PROVIDED THE *TRIGGER*--

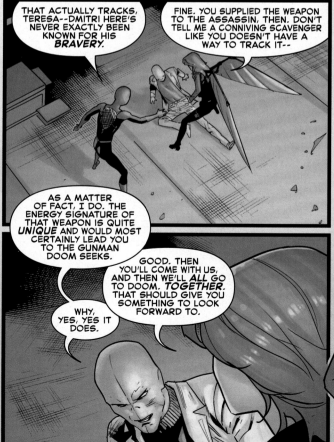

THAT ACTUALLY TRACKS, TERESA--DMITRI HERE'S NEVER EXACTLY BEEN KNOWN FOR HIS *BRAVERY*.

FINE. YOU SUPPLIED THE WEAPON TO THE ASSASSIN, THEN. DON'T TELL ME A CONNIVING SCAVENGER LIKE YOU DOESN'T HAVE A WAY TO TRACK IT--

AS A MATTER OF FACT, I DO. THE ENERGY SIGNATURE OF THAT WEAPON IS QUITE *UNIQUE* AND WOULD MOST CERTAINLY LEAD YOU TO THE GUNMAN DOOM SEEKS.

GOOD. THEN YOU'LL COME WITH US, AND THEN WE'LL *ALL* GO TO DOOM. *TOGETHER.* THAT SHOULD GIVE YOU SOMETHING TO LOOK FORWARD TO.

WHY, YES, YES IT DOES.

WOULDN'T MISS IT FOR THE WORLD.

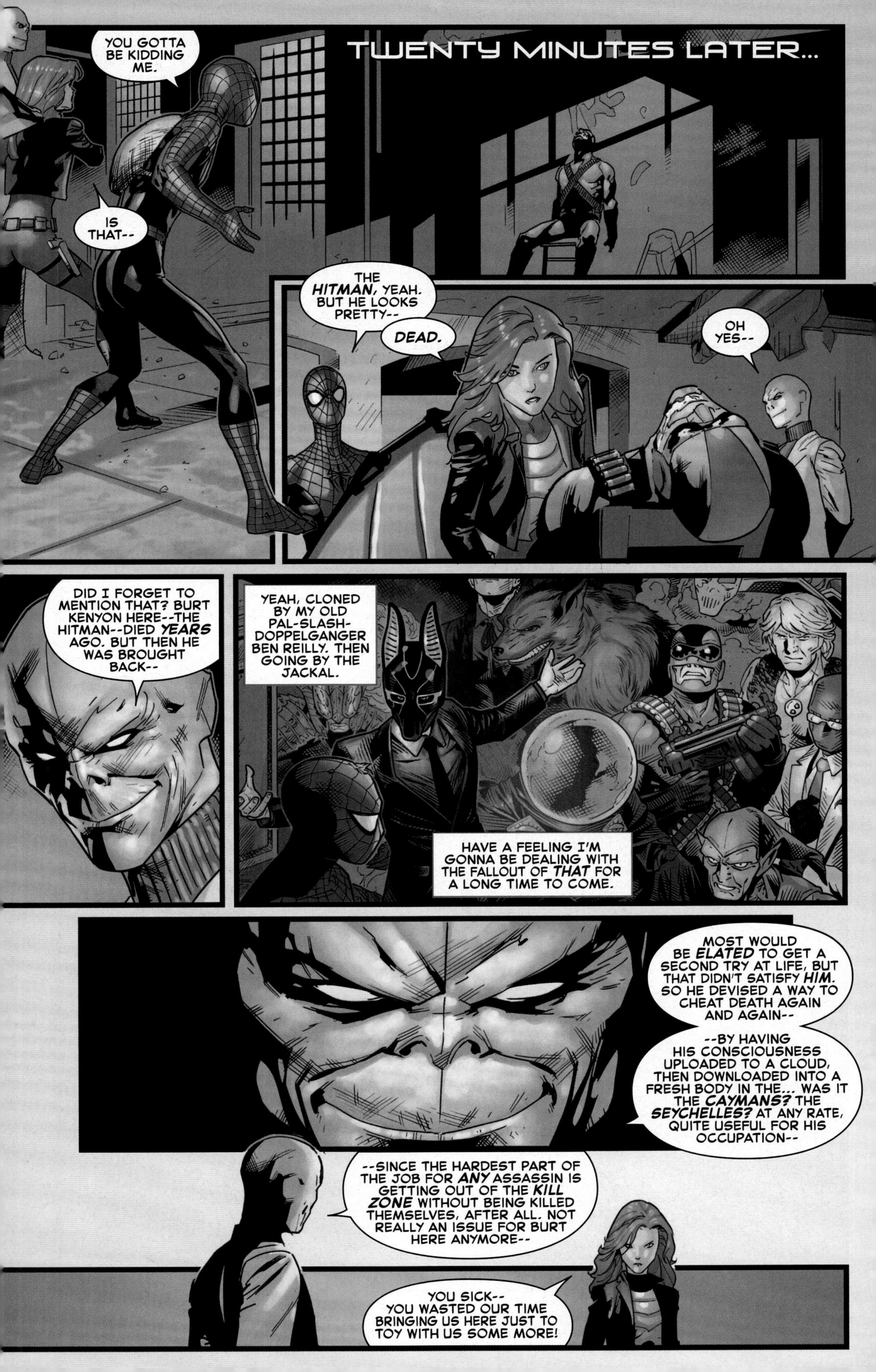
TWENTY MINUTES LATER...
YOU GOTTA BE KIDDING ME.
IS THAT--
THE HITMAN, YEAH. BUT HE LOOKS PRETTY--
DEAD.
OH YES--
DID I FORGET TO MENTION THAT? BURT KENYON HERE--THE HITMAN--DIED YEARS AGO. BUT THEN HE WAS BROUGHT BACK--
YEAH, CLONED BY MY OLD PAL-SLASH-DOPPELGANGER BEN REILLY. THEN GOING BY THE JACKAL.
HAVE A FEELING I'M GONNA BE DEALING WITH THE FALLOUT OF THAT FOR A LONG TIME TO COME.
MOST WOULD BE ELATED TO GET A SECOND TRY AT LIFE, BUT THAT DIDN'T SATISFY HIM. SO HE DEVISED A WAY TO CHEAT DEATH AGAIN AND AGAIN--
--BY HAVING HIS CONSCIOUSNESS UPLOADED TO A CLOUD, THEN DOWNLOADED INTO A FRESH BODY IN THE... WAS IT THE CAYMANS? THE SEYCHELLES? AT ANY RATE, QUITE USEFUL FOR HIS OCCUPATION--
--SINCE THE HARDEST PART OF THE JOB FOR ANY ASSASSIN IS GETTING OUT OF THE KILL ZONE WITHOUT BEING KILLED THEMSELVES, AFTER ALL. NOT REALLY AN ISSUE FOR BURT HERE ANYMORE--
YOU SICK-- YOU WASTED OUR TIME BRINGING US HERE JUST TO TOY WITH US SOME MORE!

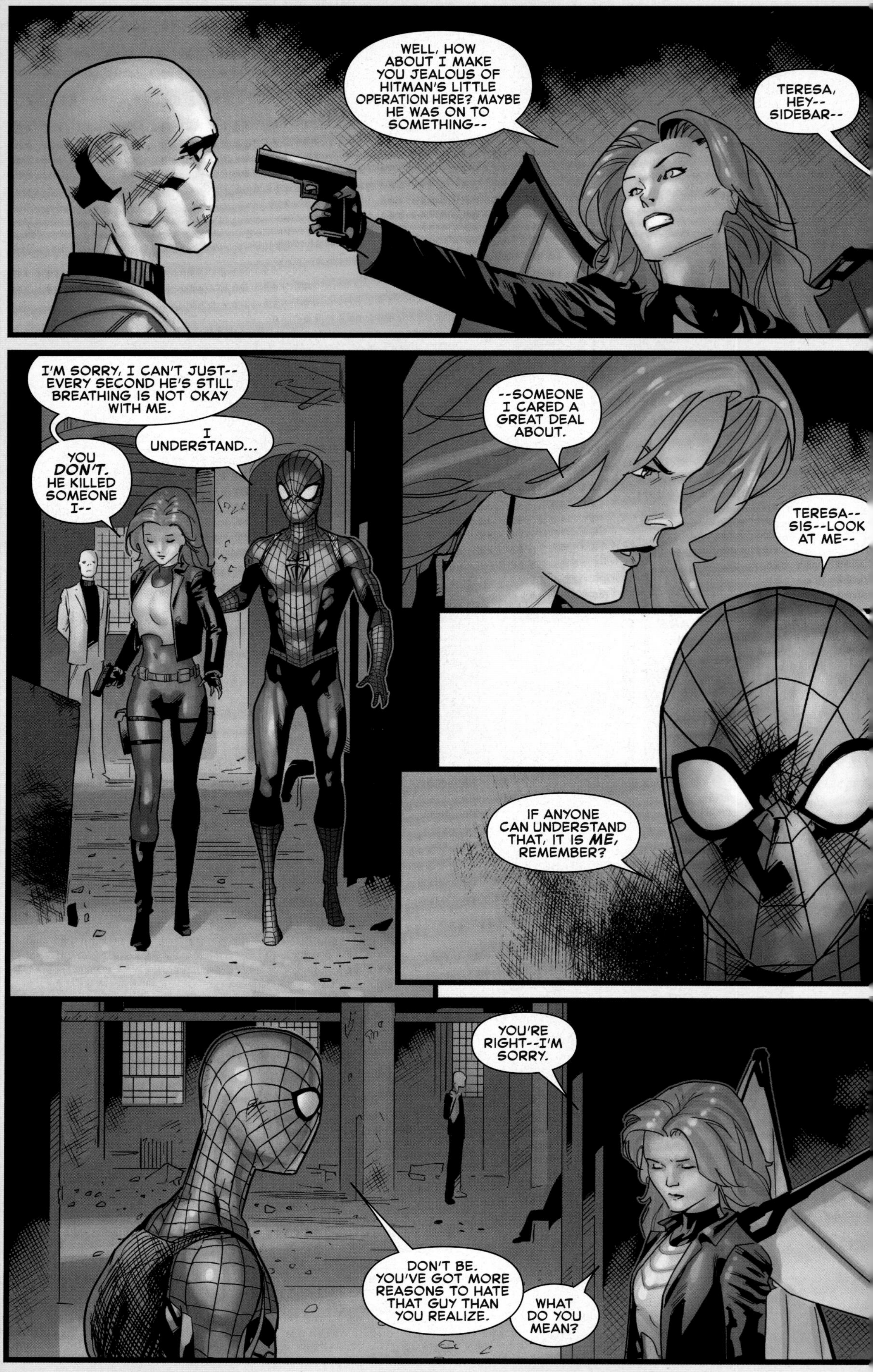
WELL, HOW ABOUT I MAKE YOU JEALOUS OF HITMAN'S LITTLE OPERATION HERE? MAYBE HE WAS ON TO SOMETHING--
TERESA, HEY-- SIDEBAR--
I'M SORRY, I CAN'T JUST-- EVERY SECOND HE'S STILL BREATHING IS NOT OKAY WITH ME.
I UNDERSTAND...
YOU *DON'T.* HE KILLED SOMEONE I--
--SOMEONE I CARED A GREAT DEAL ABOUT.
TERESA-- SIS--LOOK AT ME--
IF ANYONE CAN UNDERSTAND THAT, IT IS *ME,* REMEMBER?
YOU'RE RIGHT--I'M SORRY.
DON'T BE. YOU'VE GOT MORE REASONS TO HATE THAT GUY THAN YOU REALIZE.
WHAT DO YOU MEAN?

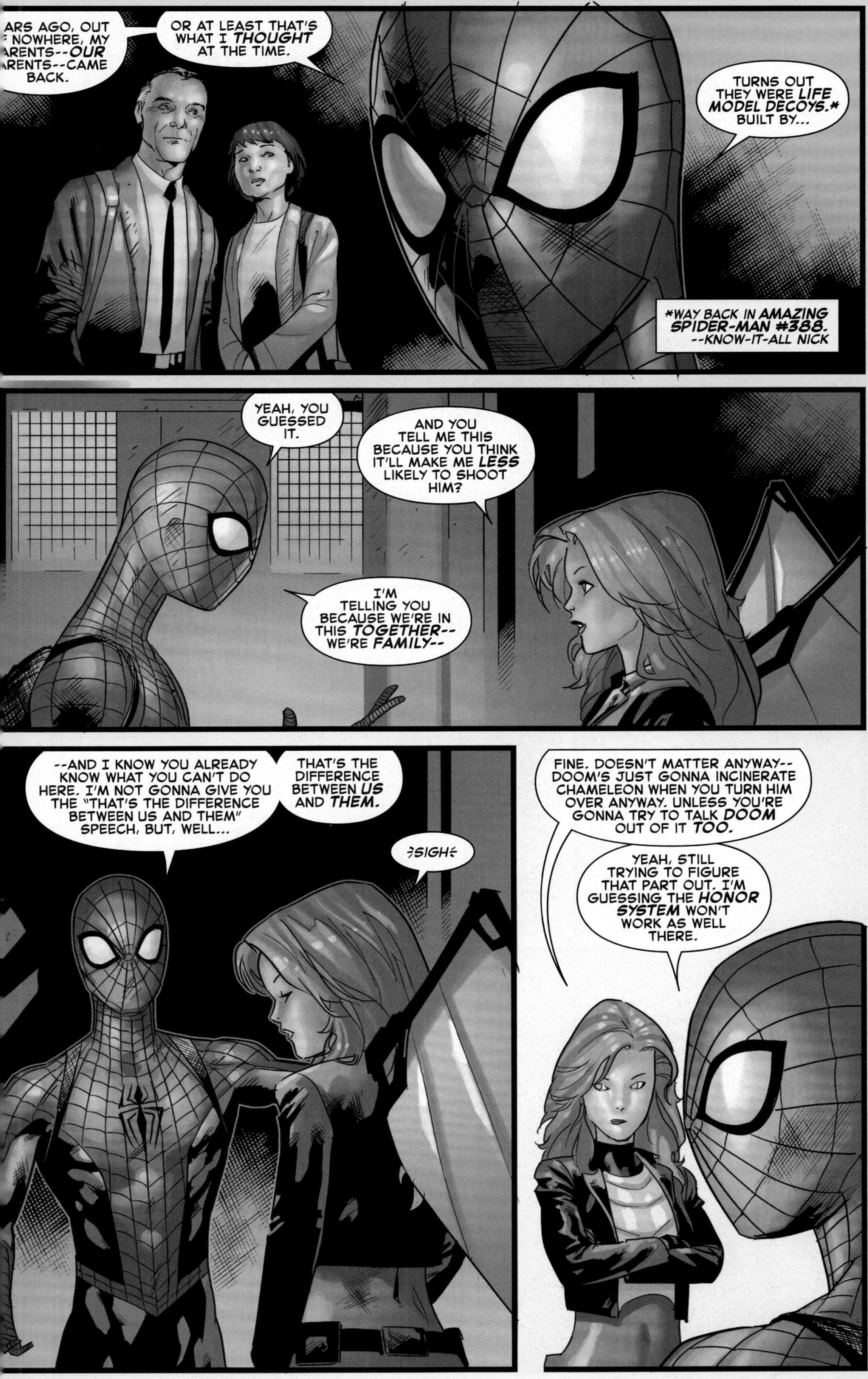
ARS AGO, OUT
F NOWHERE, MY
ARENTS--OUR
ARENTS--CAME
BACK.
OR AT LEAST THAT'S WHAT I THOUGHT AT THE TIME.
TURNS OUT THEY WERE LIFE MODEL DECOYS.* BUILT BY...
*WAY BACK IN AMAZING SPIDER-MAN #388. --KNOW-IT-ALL NICK
YEAH, YOU GUESSED IT.
AND YOU TELL ME THIS BECAUSE YOU THINK IT'LL MAKE ME LESS LIKELY TO SHOOT HIM?
I'M TELLING YOU BECAUSE WE'RE IN THIS TOGETHER-- WE'RE FAMILY--
--AND I KNOW YOU ALREADY KNOW WHAT YOU CAN'T DO HERE. I'M NOT GONNA GIVE YOU THE "THAT'S THE DIFFERENCE BETWEEN US AND THEM" SPEECH, BUT, WELL...
THAT'S THE DIFFERENCE BETWEEN US AND THEM.
SIGH
FINE. DOESN'T MATTER ANYWAY-- DOOM'S JUST GONNA INCINERATE CHAMELEON WHEN YOU TURN HIM OVER ANYWAY. UNLESS YOU'RE GONNA TRY TO TALK DOOM OUT OF IT TOO.
YEAH, STILL TRYING TO FIGURE THAT PART OUT. I'M GUESSING THE HONOR SYSTEM WON'T WORK AS WELL THERE.

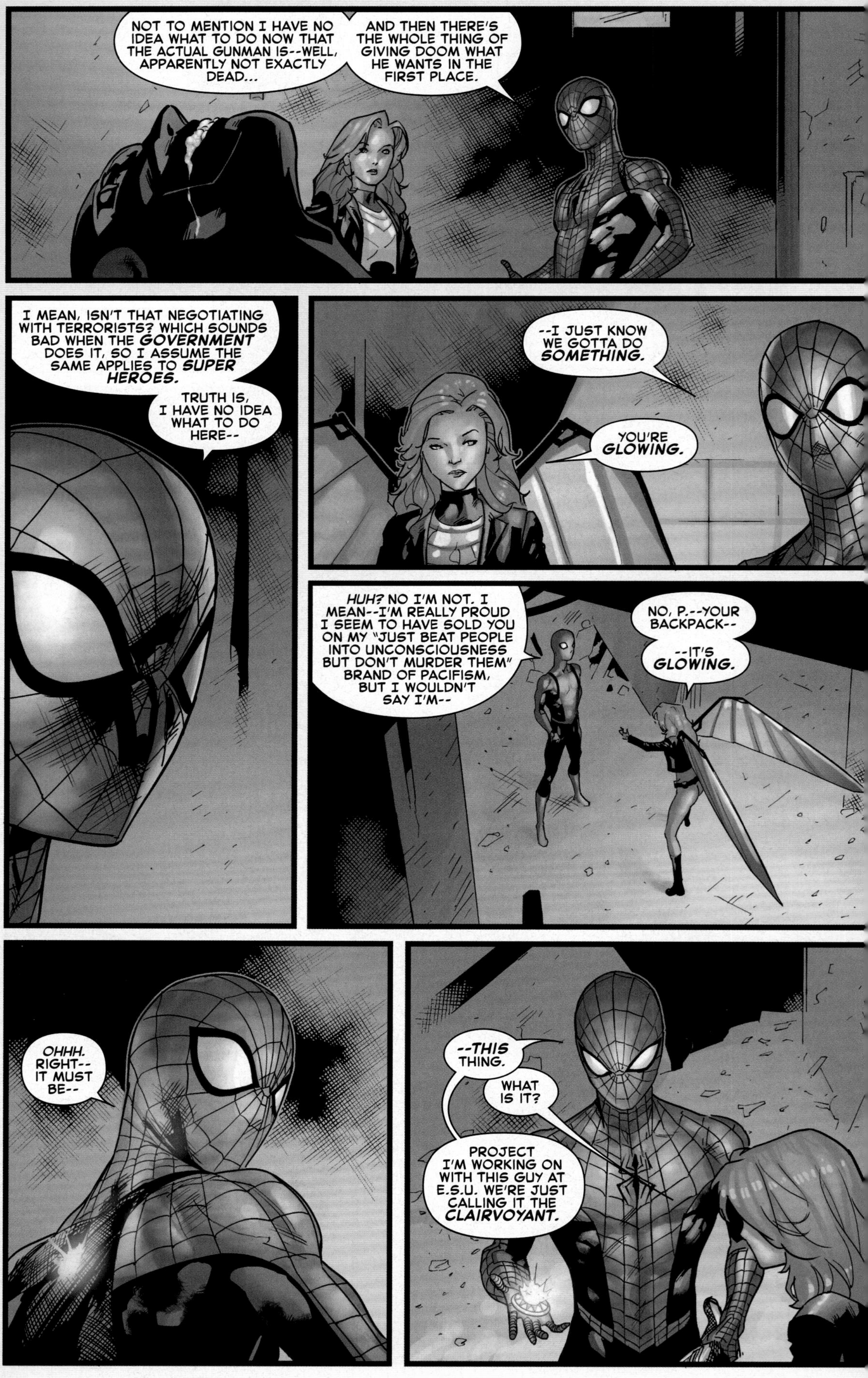
NOT TO MENTION I HAVE NO IDEA WHAT TO DO NOW THAT THE ACTUAL GUNMAN IS--WELL, APPARENTLY NOT EXACTLY DEAD...
AND THEN THERE'S THE WHOLE THING OF GIVING DOOM WHAT HE WANTS IN THE FIRST PLACE.
I MEAN, ISN'T THAT NEGOTIATING WITH TERRORISTS? WHICH SOUNDS BAD WHEN THE GOVERNMENT DOES IT, SO I ASSUME THE SAME APPLIES TO SUPER HEROES.
TRUTH IS, I HAVE NO IDEA WHAT TO DO HERE--
--I JUST KNOW WE GOTTA DO SOMETHING.
YOU'RE GLOWING.
HUH? NO I'M NOT. I MEAN--I'M REALLY PROUD I SEEM TO HAVE SOLD YOU ON MY "JUST BEAT PEOPLE INTO UNCONSCIOUSNESS BUT DON'T MURDER THEM" BRAND OF PACIFISM, BUT I WOULDN'T SAY I'M--
NO, P.--YOUR BACKPACK--
--IT'S GLOWING.
OHHH. RIGHT-- IT MUST BE--
--THIS THING.
WHAT IS IT?
PROJECT I'M WORKING ON WITH THIS GUY AT E.S.U. WE'RE JUST CALLING IT THE CLAIRVOYANT.

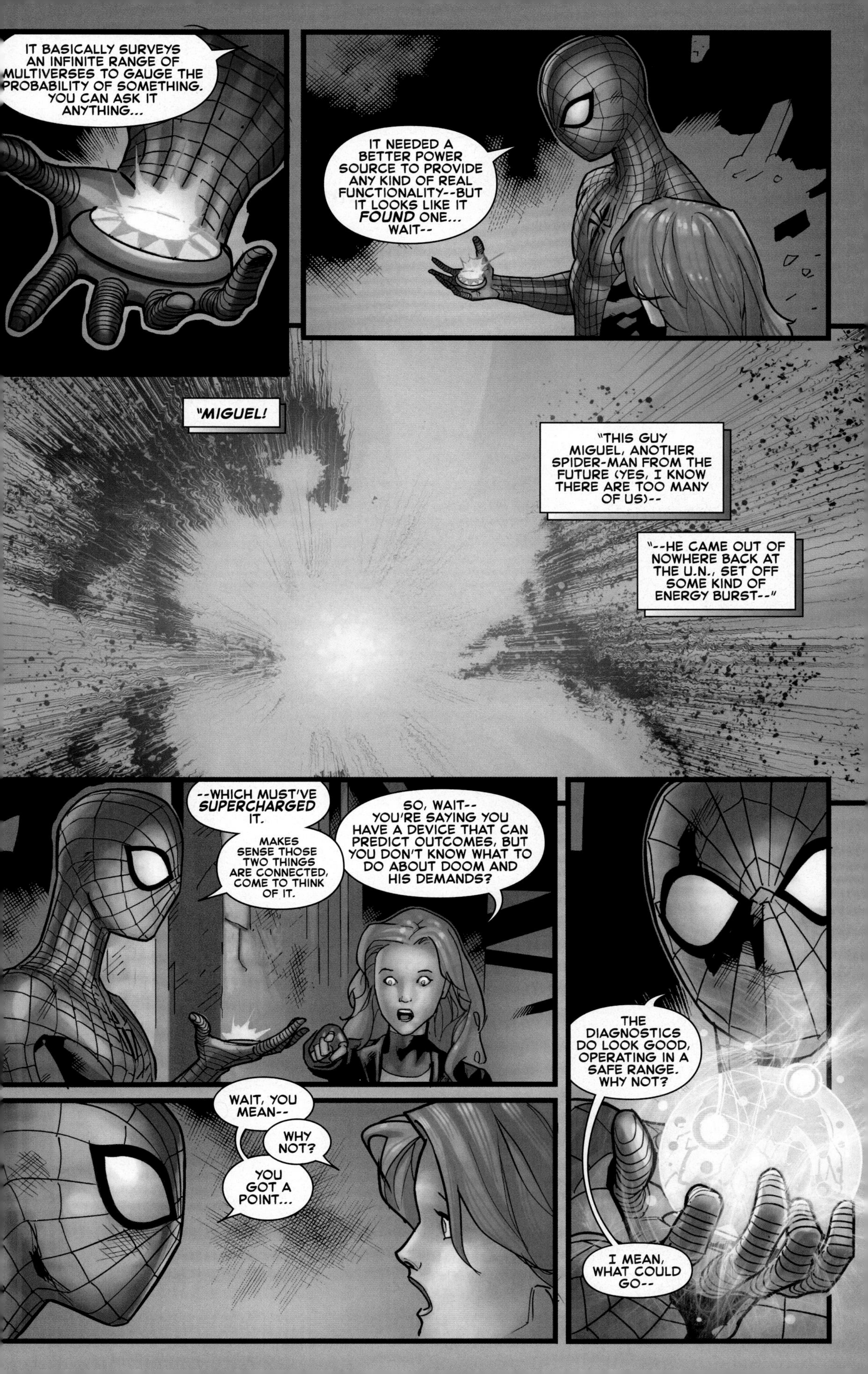
IT BASICALLY SURVEYS AN INFINITE RANGE OF MULTIVERSES TO GAUGE THE PROBABILITY OF SOMETHING. YOU CAN ASK IT ANYTHING...
IT NEEDED A BETTER POWER SOURCE TO PROVIDE ANY KIND OF REAL FUNCTIONALITY--BUT IT LOOKS LIKE IT FOUND ONE... WAIT--
"MIGUEL!
"THIS GUY MIGUEL, ANOTHER SPIDER-MAN FROM THE FUTURE (YES, I KNOW THERE ARE TOO MANY OF US)--
"--HE CAME OUT OF NOWHERE BACK AT THE U.N., SET OFF SOME KIND OF ENERGY BURST--"
--WHICH MUST'VE SUPERCHARGED IT.
MAKES SENSE THOSE TWO THINGS ARE CONNECTED, COME TO THINK OF IT.
SO, WAIT-- YOU'RE SAYING YOU HAVE A DEVICE THAT CAN PREDICT OUTCOMES, BUT YOU DON'T KNOW WHAT TO DO ABOUT DOOM AND HIS DEMANDS?
THE DIAGNOSTICS DO LOOK GOOD, OPERATING IN A SAFE RANGE. WHY NOT?
WAIT, YOU MEAN--
WHY NOT?
YOU GOT A POINT...
I MEAN, WHAT COULD GO--

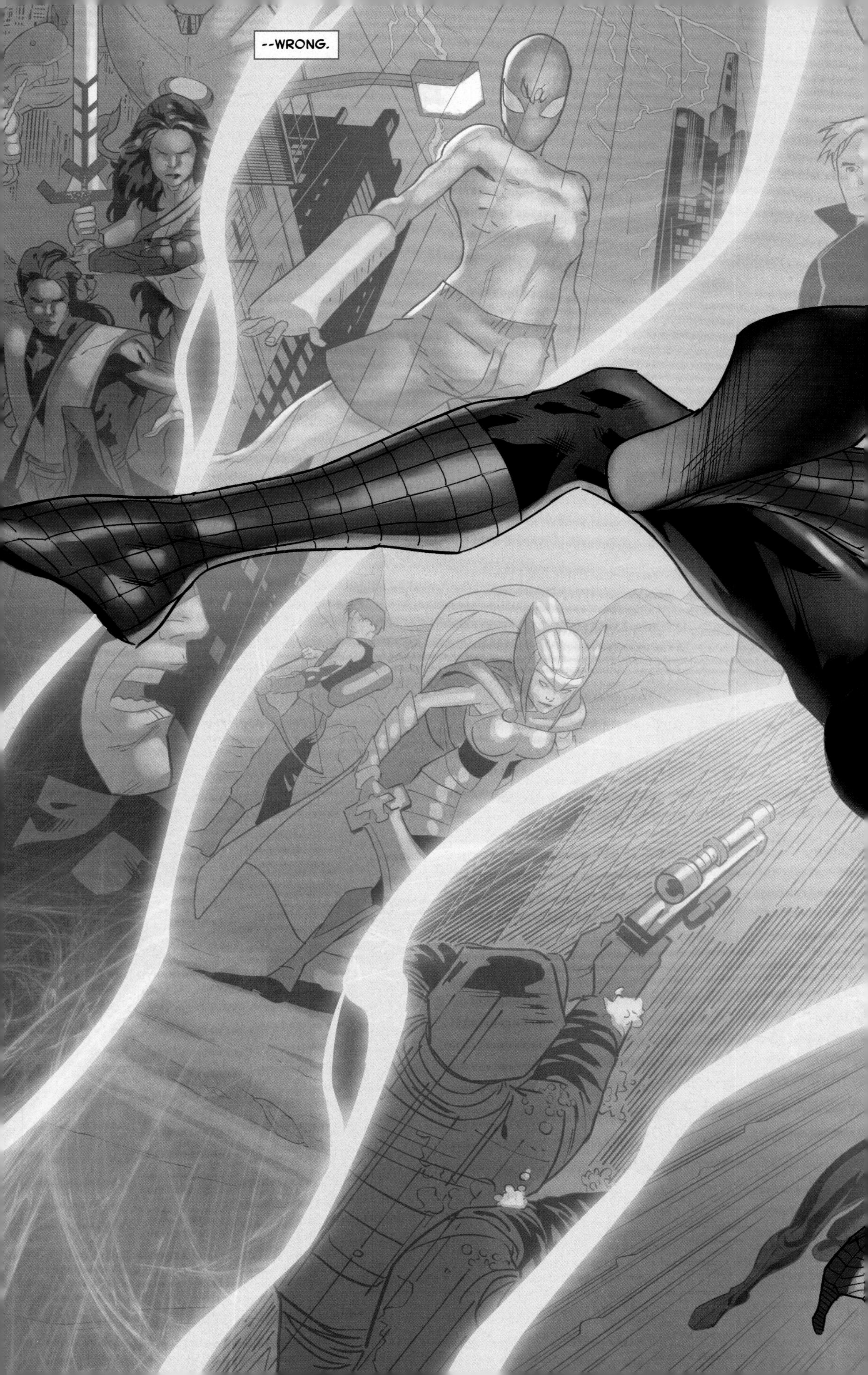
--WRONG.

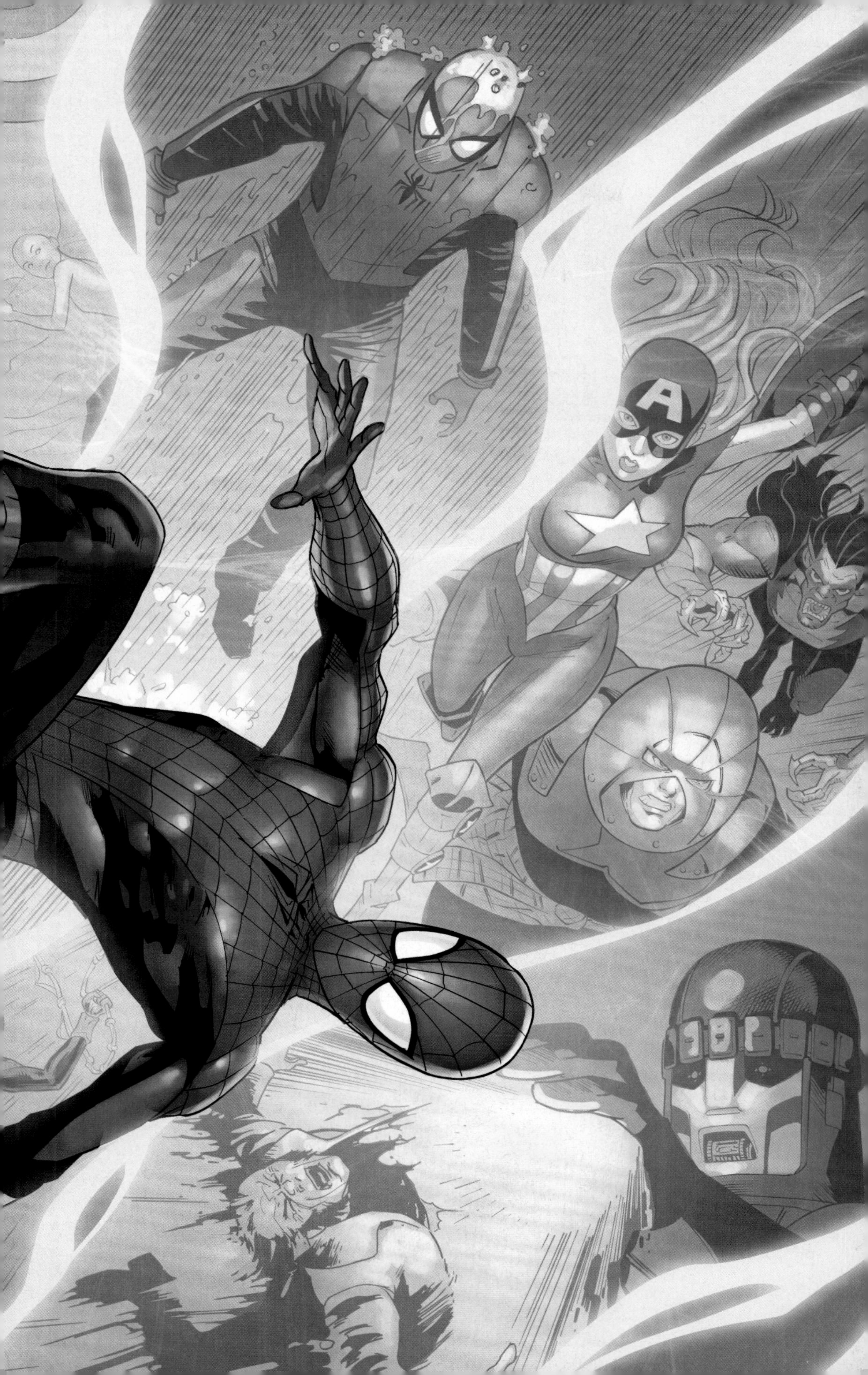

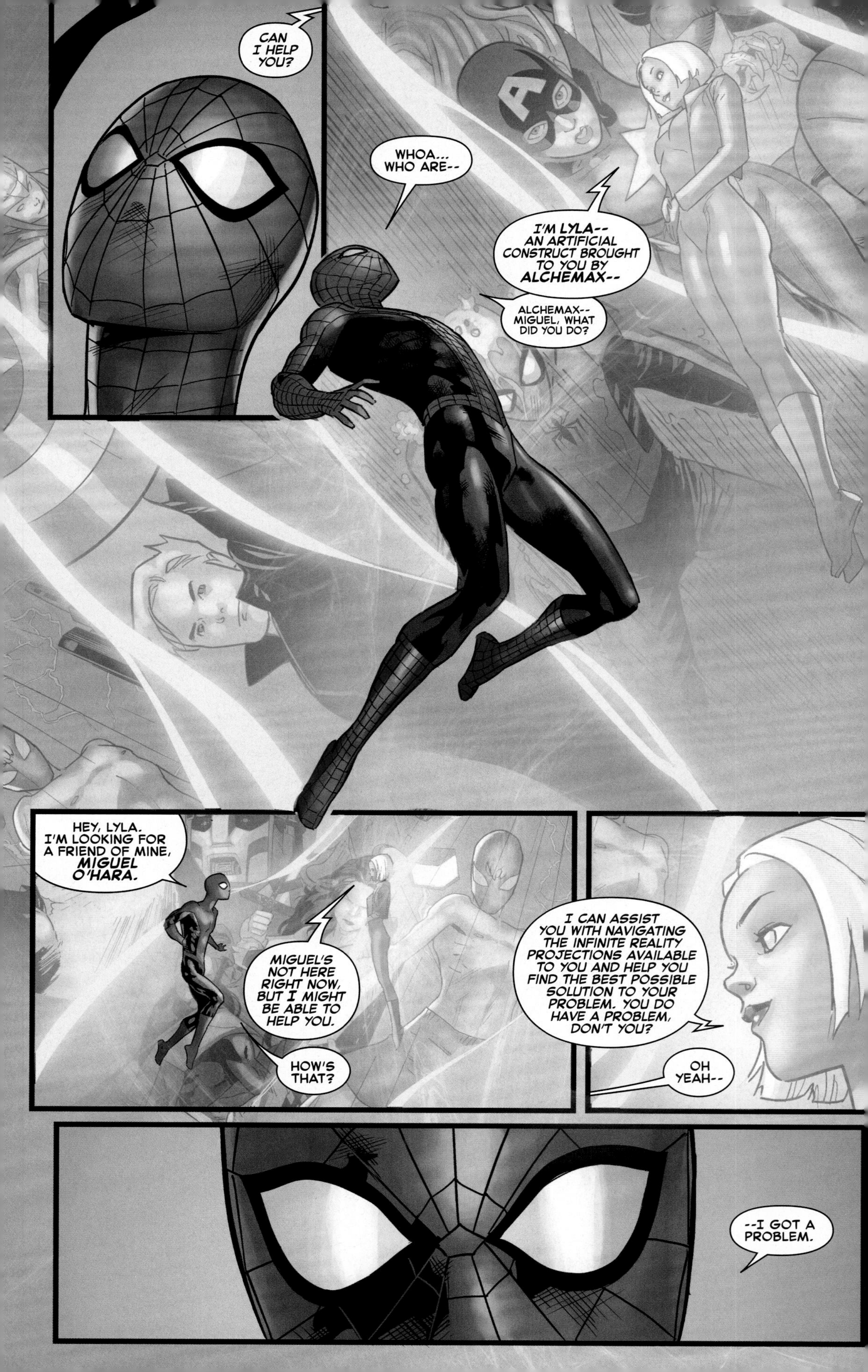
CAN I HELP YOU?
WHOA... WHO ARE--
I'M LYLA-- AN ARTIFICIAL CONSTRUCT BROUGHT TO YOU BY ALCHEMAX--
ALCHEMAX-- MIGUEL, WHAT DID YOU DO?
HEY, LYLA. I'M LOOKING FOR A FRIEND OF MINE, MIGUEL O'HARA.
MIGUEL'S NOT HERE RIGHT NOW, BUT I MIGHT BE ABLE TO HELP YOU.
HOW'S THAT?
I CAN ASSIST YOU WITH NAVIGATING THE INFINITE REALITY PROJECTIONS AVAILABLE TO YOU AND HELP YOU FIND THE BEST POSSIBLE SOLUTION TO YOUR PROBLEM. YOU DO HAVE A PROBLEM, DON'T YOU?
OH YEAH--
--I GOT A PROBLEM.

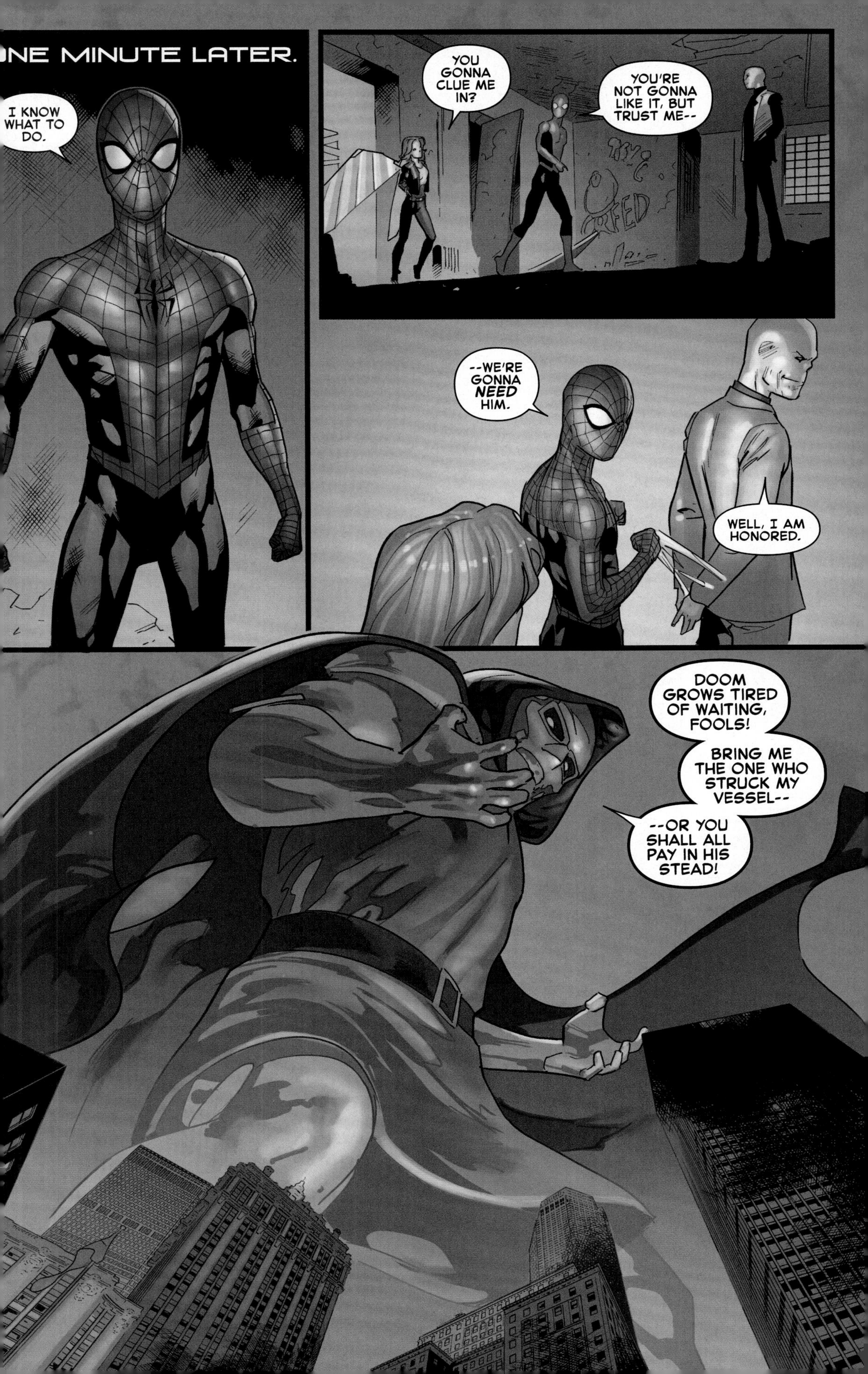
ONE MINUTE LATER.
I KNOW WHAT TO DO.
YOU GONNA CLUE ME IN?
YOU'RE NOT GONNA LIKE IT, BUT TRUST ME--
--WE'RE GONNA NEED HIM.
WELL, I AM HONORED.
DOOM GROWS TIRED OF WAITING, FOOLS!
BRING ME THE ONE WHO STRUCK MY VESSEL--
--OR YOU SHALL ALL PAY IN HIS STEAD!

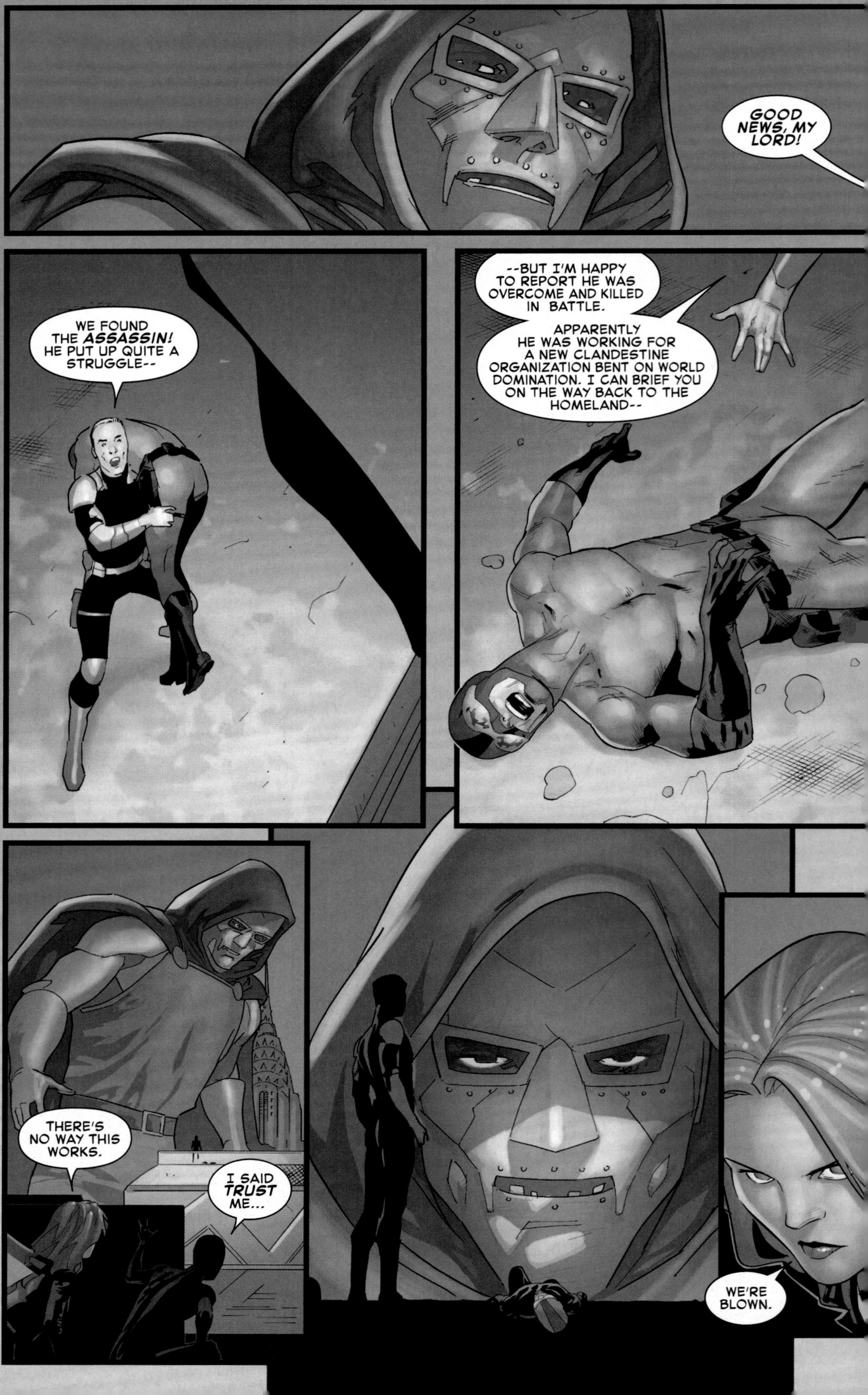
GOOD NEWS, MY LORD!
WE FOUND THE ASSASSIN! HE PUT UP QUITE A STRUGGLE--
--BUT I'M HAPPY TO REPORT HE WAS OVERCOME AND KILLED IN BATTLE.
APPARENTLY HE WAS WORKING FOR A NEW CLANDESTINE ORGANIZATION BENT ON WORLD DOMINATION. I CAN BRIEF YOU ON THE WAY BACK TO THE HOMELAND--
THERE'S NO WAY THIS WORKS.
I SAID TRUST ME...
WE'RE BLOWN.

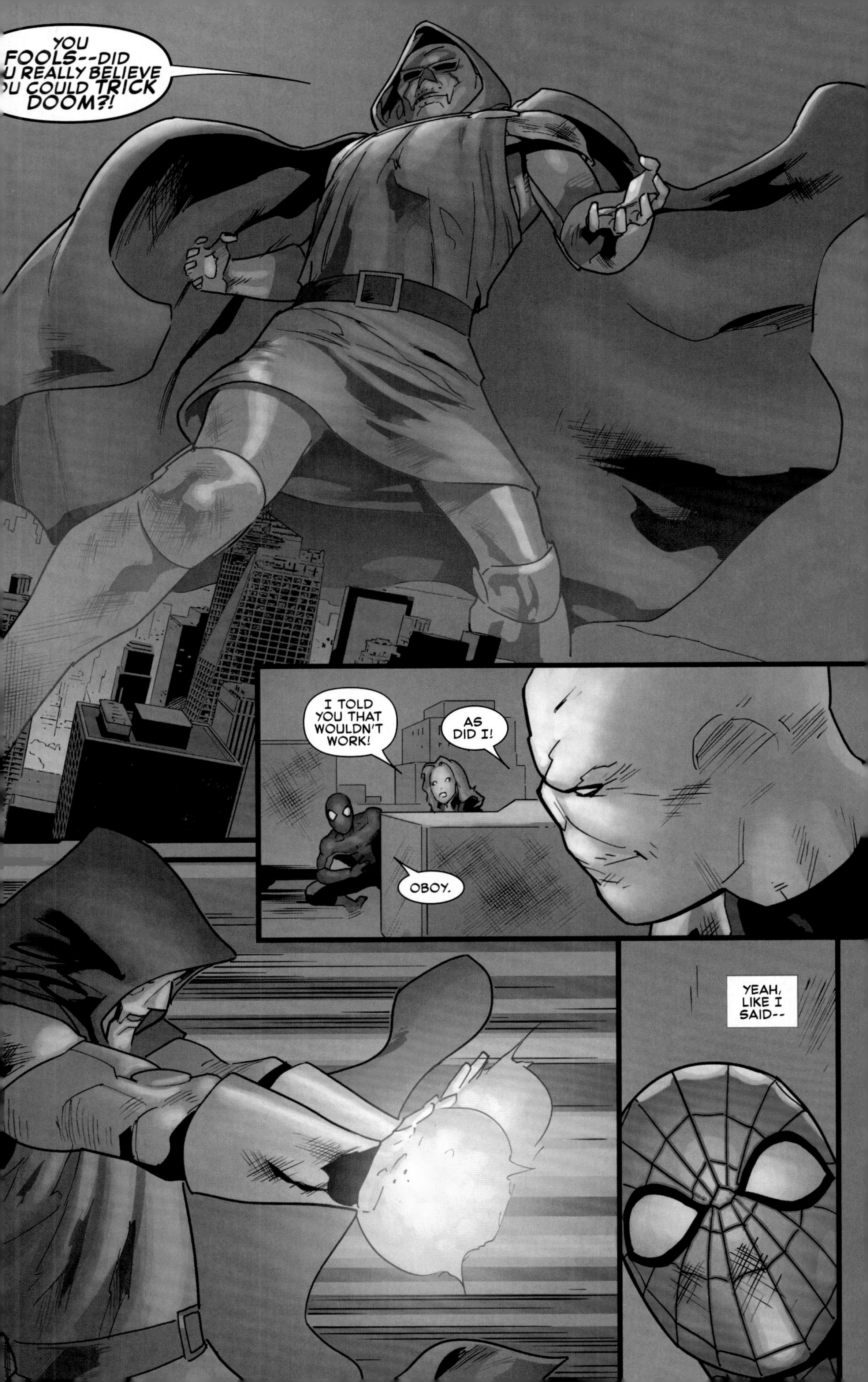
YOU FOOLS--DID U REALLY BELIEVE OU COULD TRICK DOOM?!
I TOLD YOU THAT WOULDN'T WORK!
AS DID I!
OBOY.
YEAH, LIKE I SAID--

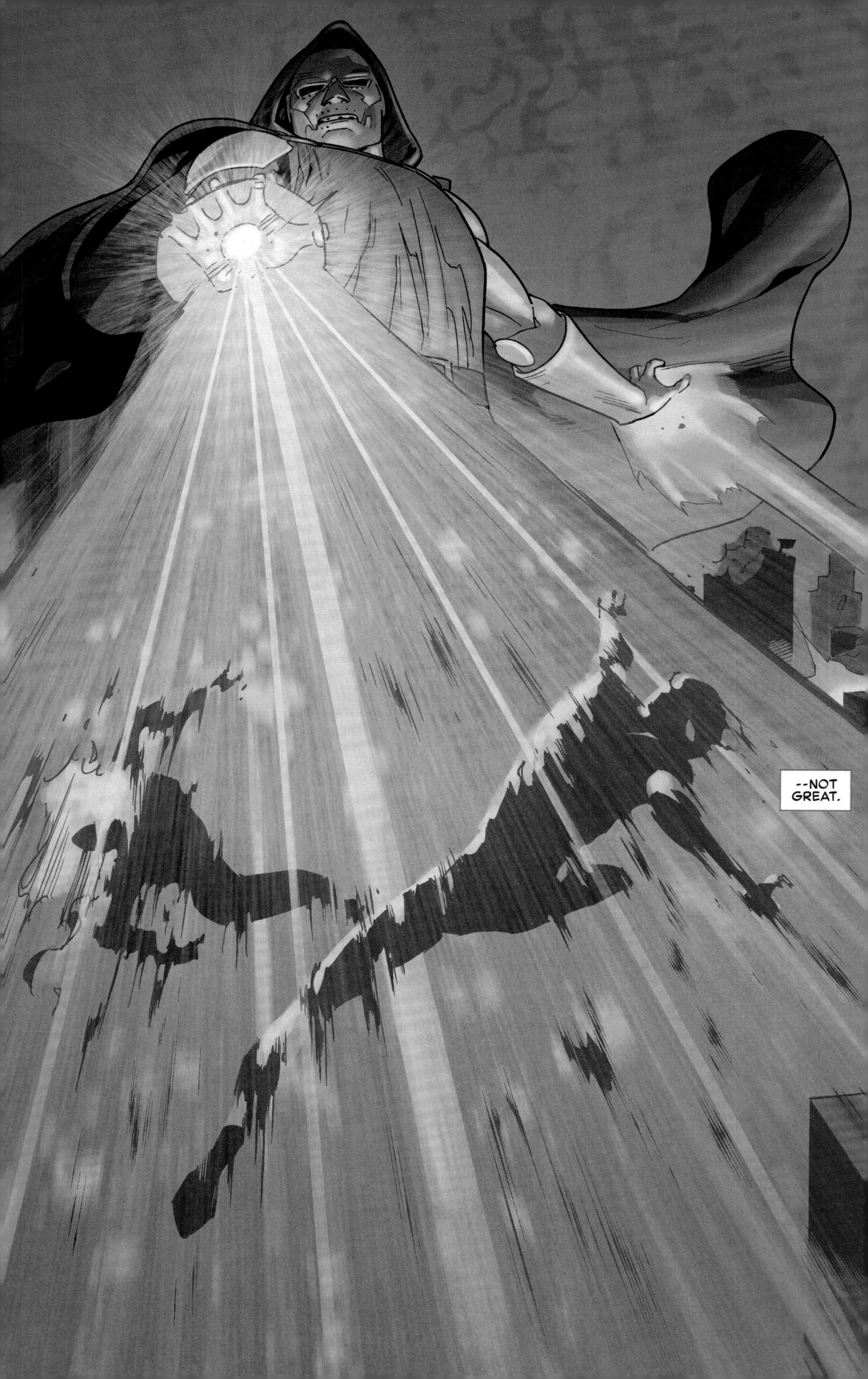
--NOT
GREAT.

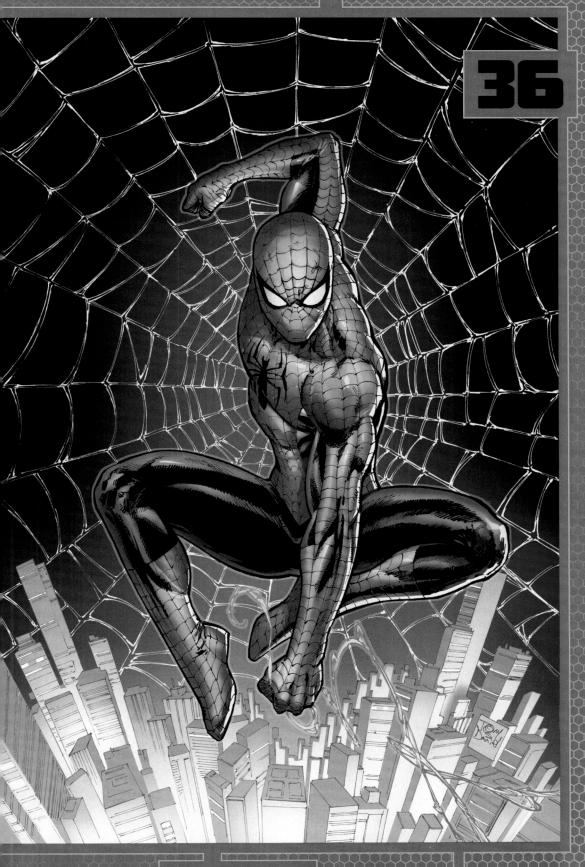

TIME AFTER TIME

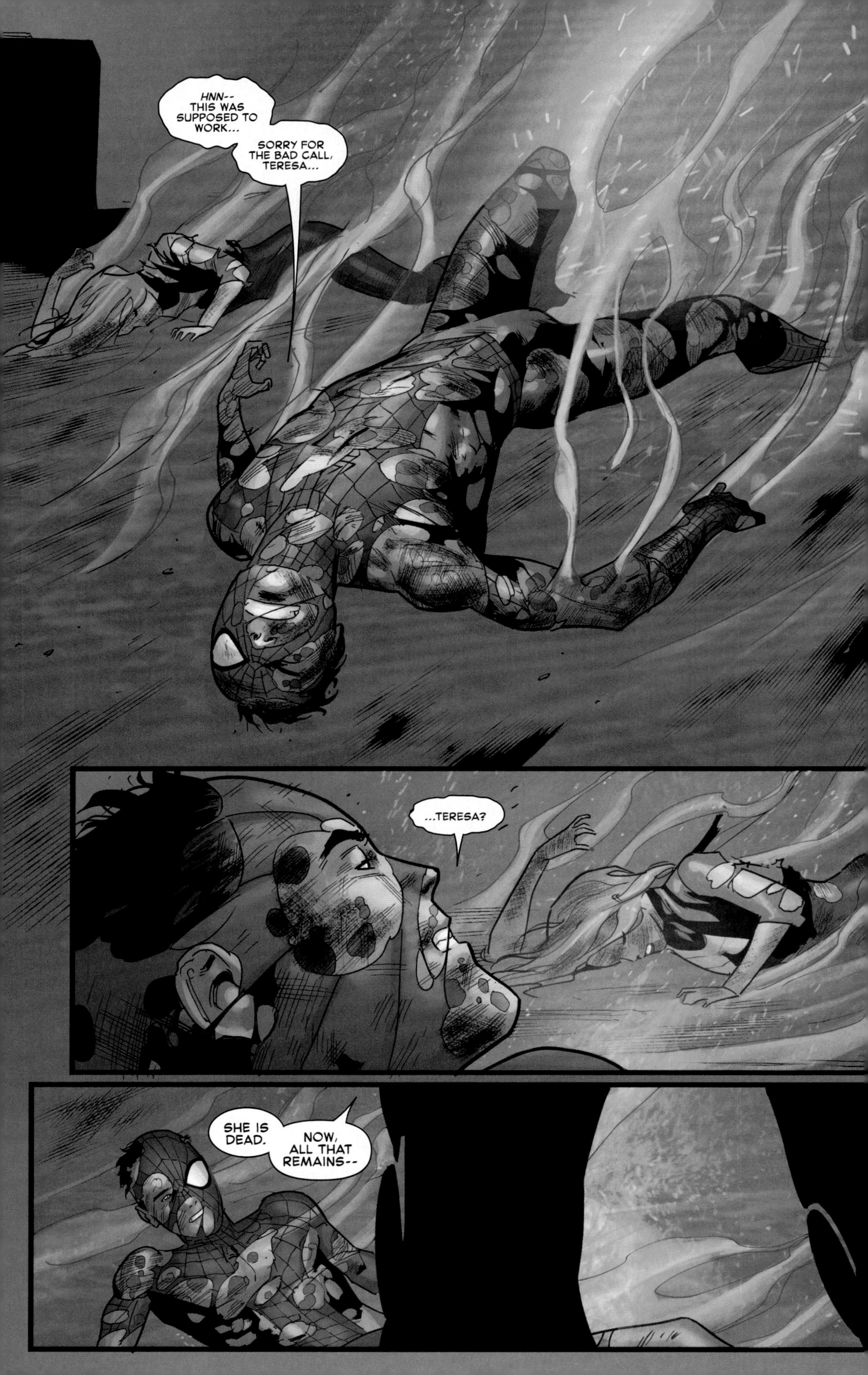
HNN-- THIS WAS SUPPOSED TO WORK...
SORRY FOR THE BAD CALL, TERESA...
...TERESA?
SHE IS DEAD.
NOW, ALL THAT REMAINS--

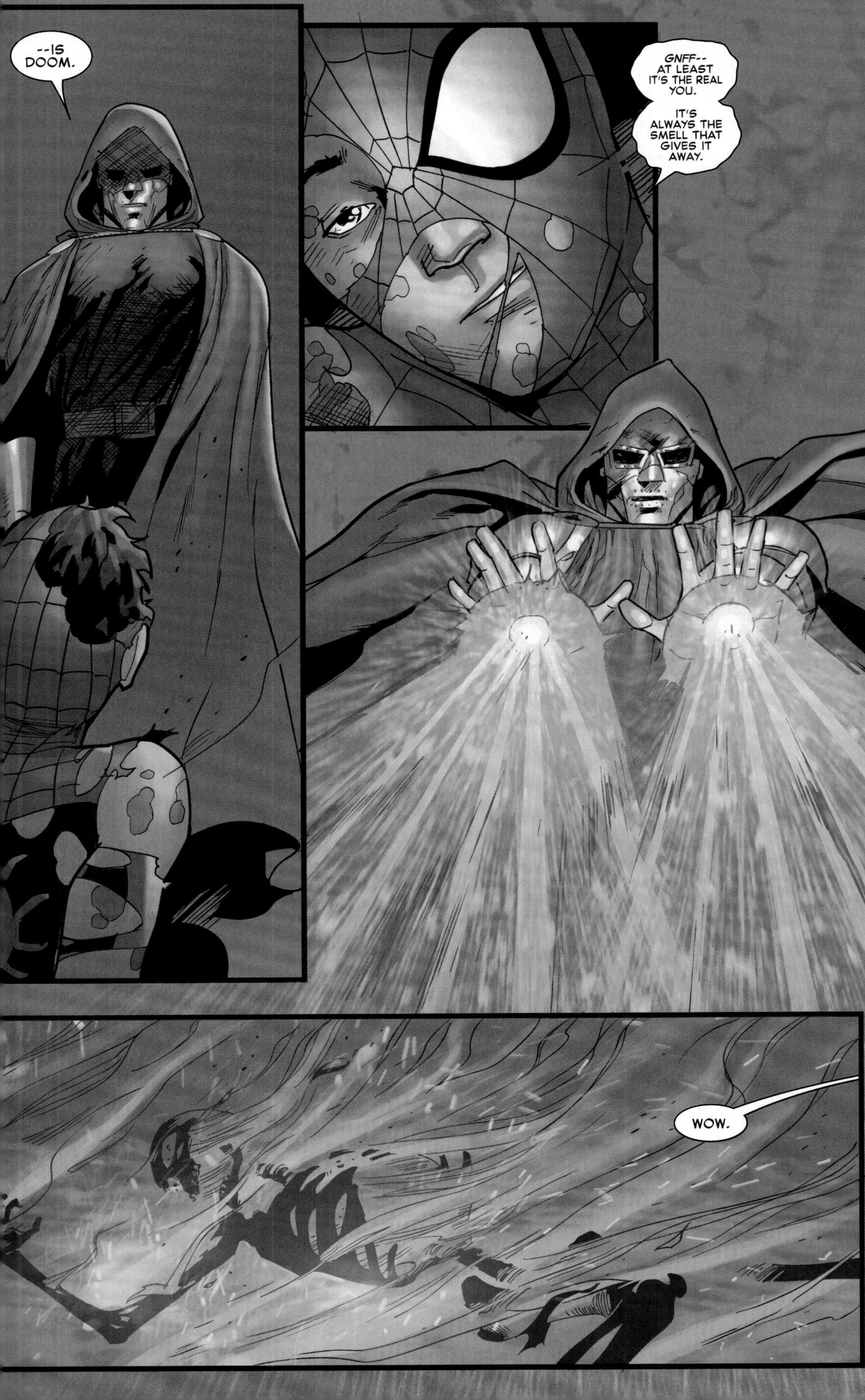
--IS DOOM.
GNFF-- AT LEAST IT'S THE REAL YOU.
IT'S ALWAYS THE SMELL THAT GIVES IT AWAY.
WOW.

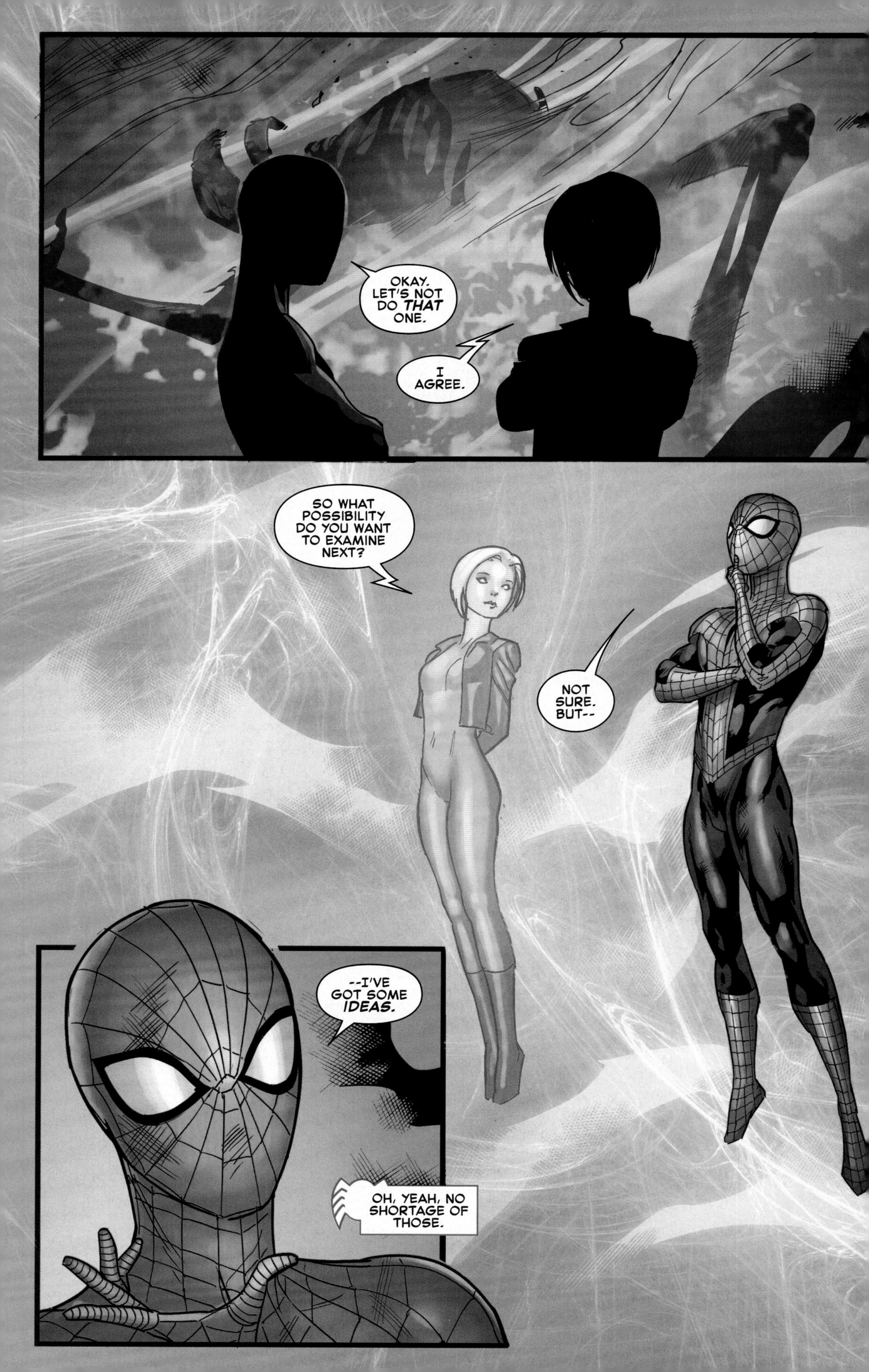
OKAY. LET'S NOT DO *THAT* ONE.
I AGREE.
SO WHAT POSSIBILITY DO YOU WANT TO EXAMINE NEXT?
NOT SURE. BUT--
--I'VE GOT SOME *IDEAS.*
OH, YEAH, NO SHORTAGE OF THOSE.

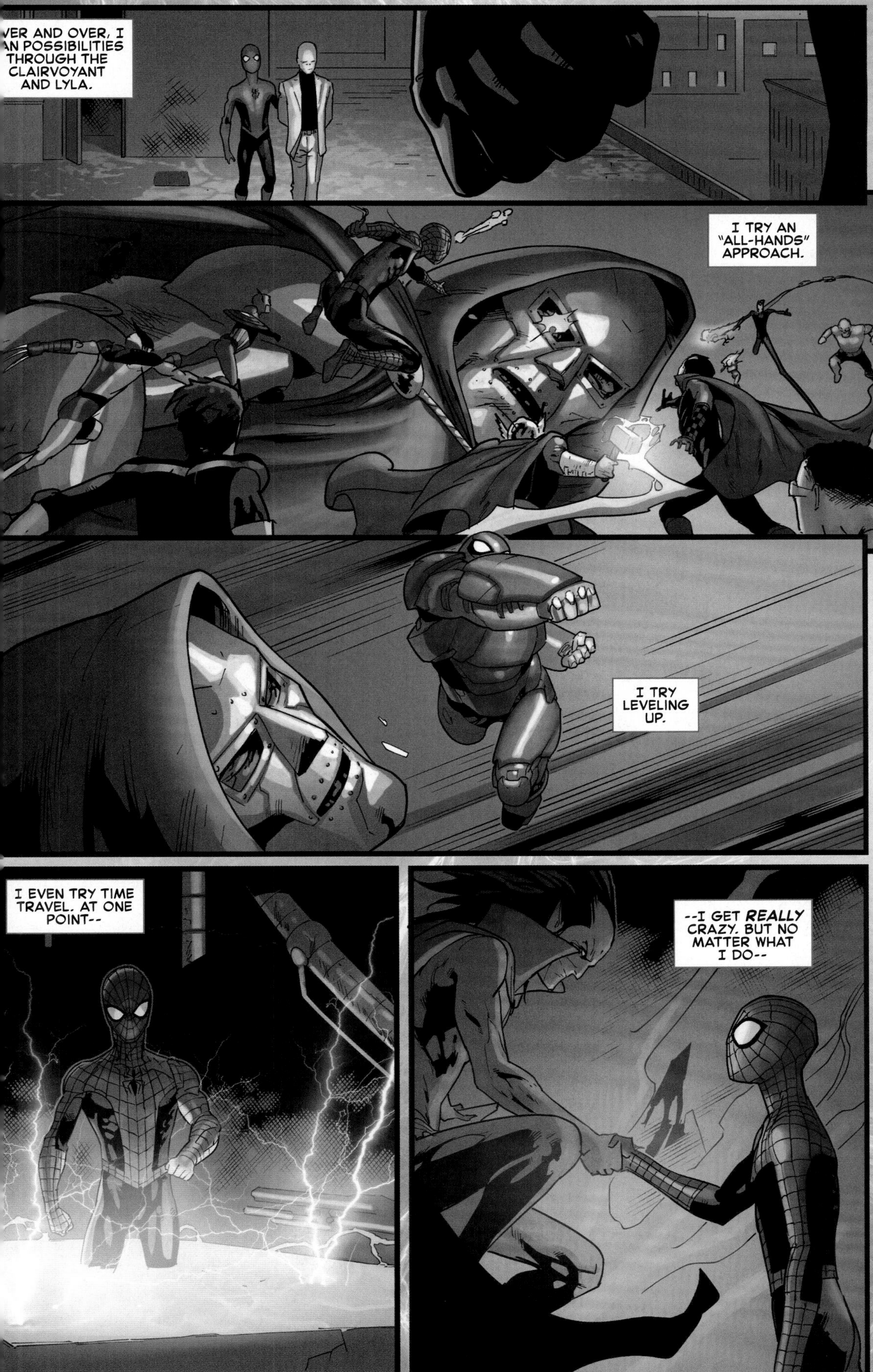
VER AND OVER, I
AN POSSIBILITIES THROUGH THE CLAIRVOYANT AND LYLA.
I TRY AN "ALL-HANDS" APPROACH.
I TRY LEVELING UP.
I EVEN TRY TIME TRAVEL. AT ONE POINT--
--I GET *REALLY* CRAZY. BUT NO MATTER WHAT I DO--

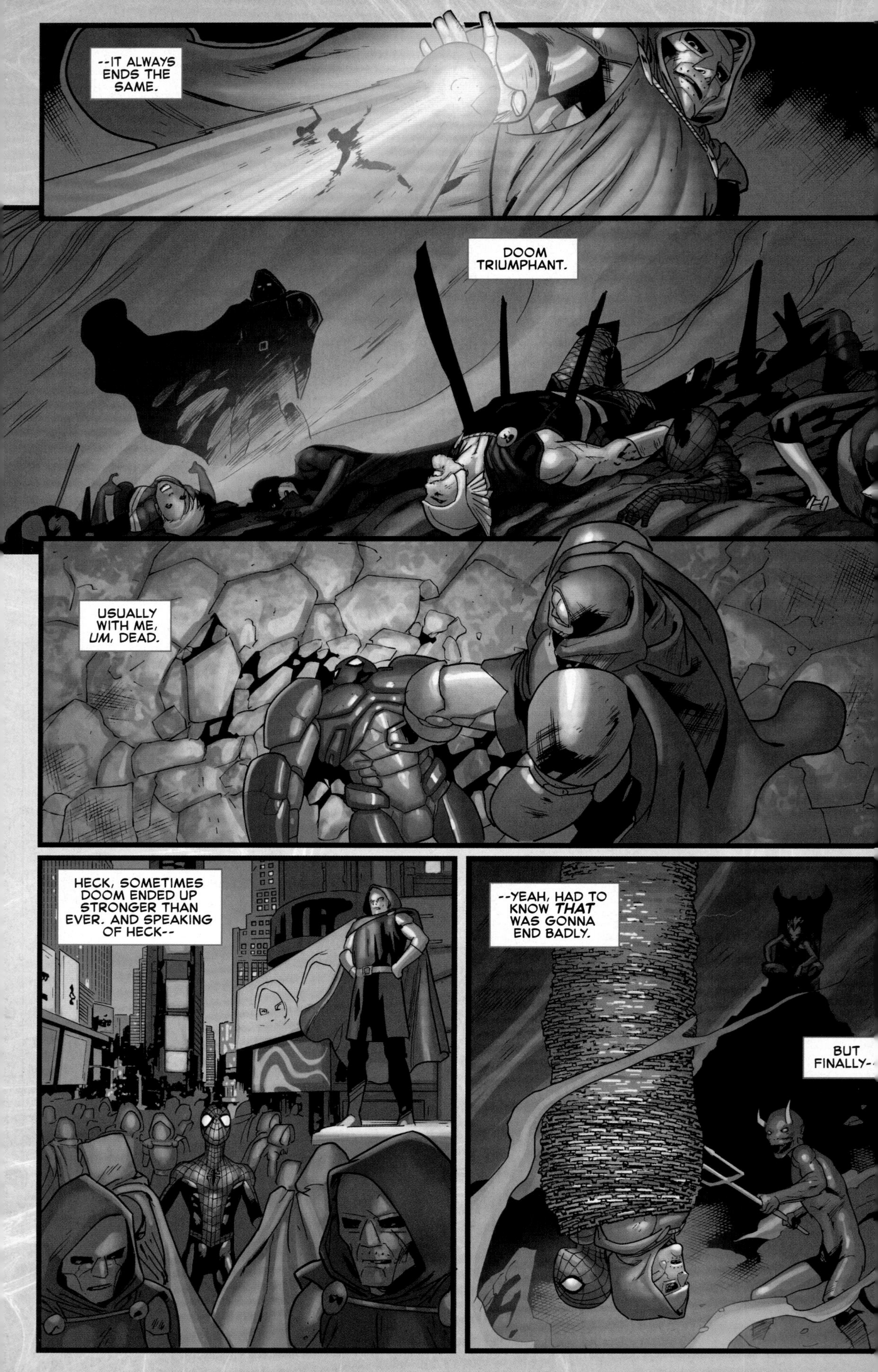
--IT ALWAYS ENDS THE SAME.
DOOM TRIUMPHANT.
USUALLY WITH ME, *UM*, DEAD.
HECK, SOMETIMES DOOM ENDED UP STRONGER THAN EVER. AND SPEAKING OF HECK--
--YEAH, HAD TO KNOW ***THAT*** WAS GONNA END BADLY.
BUT FINALLY--

A BREAKTHROUGH.

I KNOW WHAT TO DO.

OKAY, I'M IN POSITION.

GREAT. JUST KEEP EVERYONE CLEAR, OKAY? I'M SERIOUS.

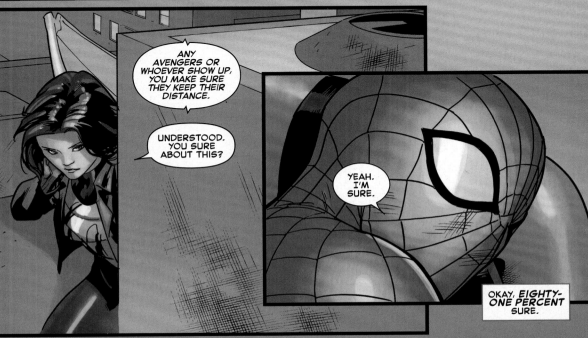

ANY AVENGERS OR WHOEVER SHOW UP, YOU MAKE SURE THEY KEEP THEIR DISTANCE.

UNDERSTOOD. YOU SURE ABOUT THIS?

YEAH. I'M SURE.

OKAY, EIGHTY-ONE PERCENT SURE.

BUT THAT'LL HAVE TO BE ENOUGH.

I MEAN, ISN'T THAT MY WHOLE THING?

YOU GET KNOCKED DOWN AND YOU GET BACK UP, OVER AND OVER. BELIEVING THAT EVENTUALLY--

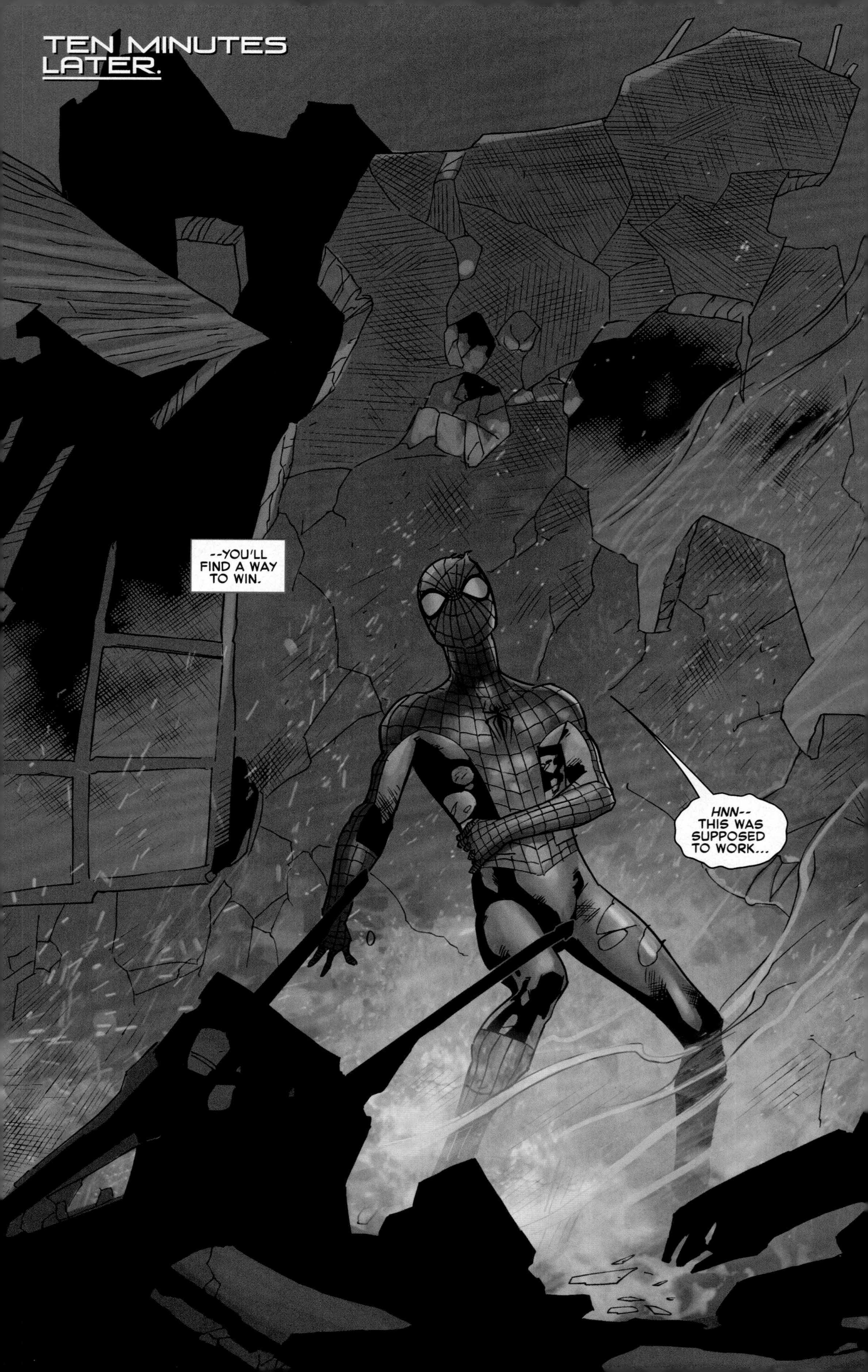
TEN MINUTES LATER.
--YOU'LL FIND A WAY TO WIN.
HNN-- THIS WAS SUPPOSED TO WORK...

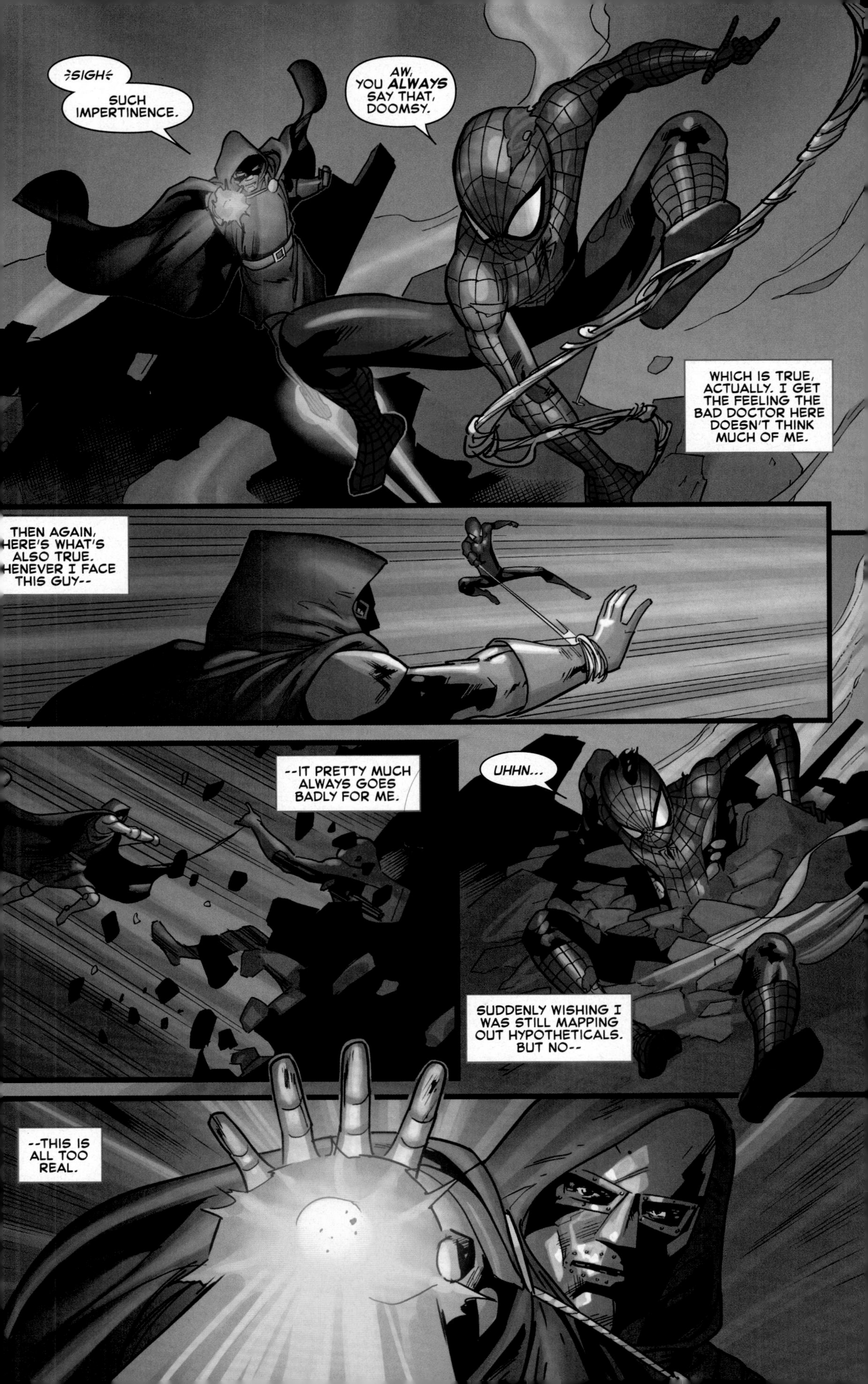

⁝SIGH⁝ SUCH IMPERTINENCE.
AW, YOU ALWAYS SAY THAT, DOOMSY.
WHICH IS TRUE, ACTUALLY. I GET THE FEELING THE BAD DOCTOR HERE DOESN'T THINK MUCH OF ME.
THEN AGAIN, HERE'S WHAT'S ALSO TRUE. HENEVER I FACE THIS GUY--
--IT PRETTY MUCH ALWAYS GOES BADLY FOR ME.
UHHN...
SUDDENLY WISHING I WAS STILL MAPPING OUT HYPOTHETICALS. BUT NO--
--THIS IS ALL TOO REAL.

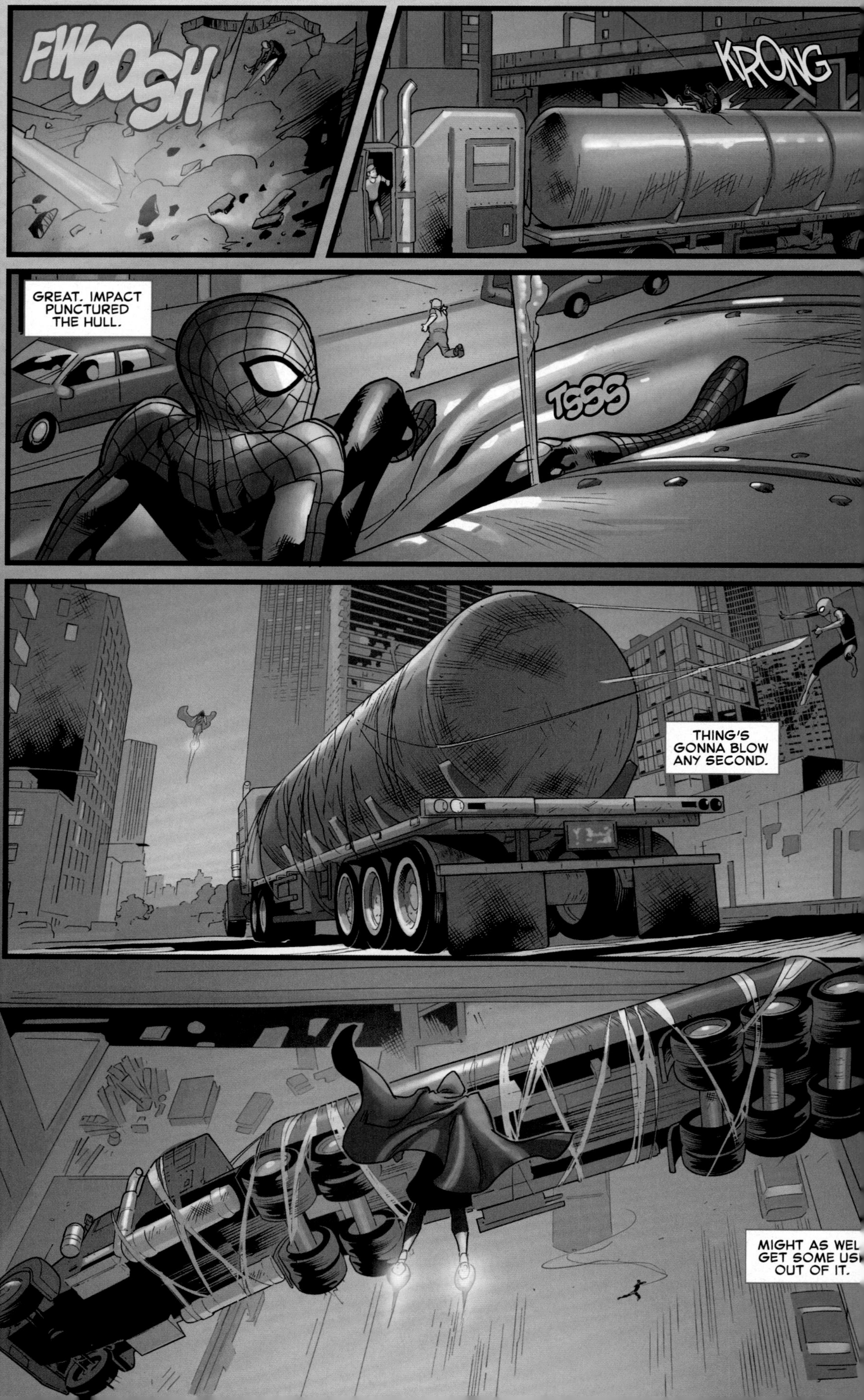
FWOOSH
KRONG
GREAT. IMPACT PUNCTURED THE HULL.
TSSS
THING'S GONNA BLOW ANY SECOND.
MIGHT AS WEL GET SOME US OUT OF IT.

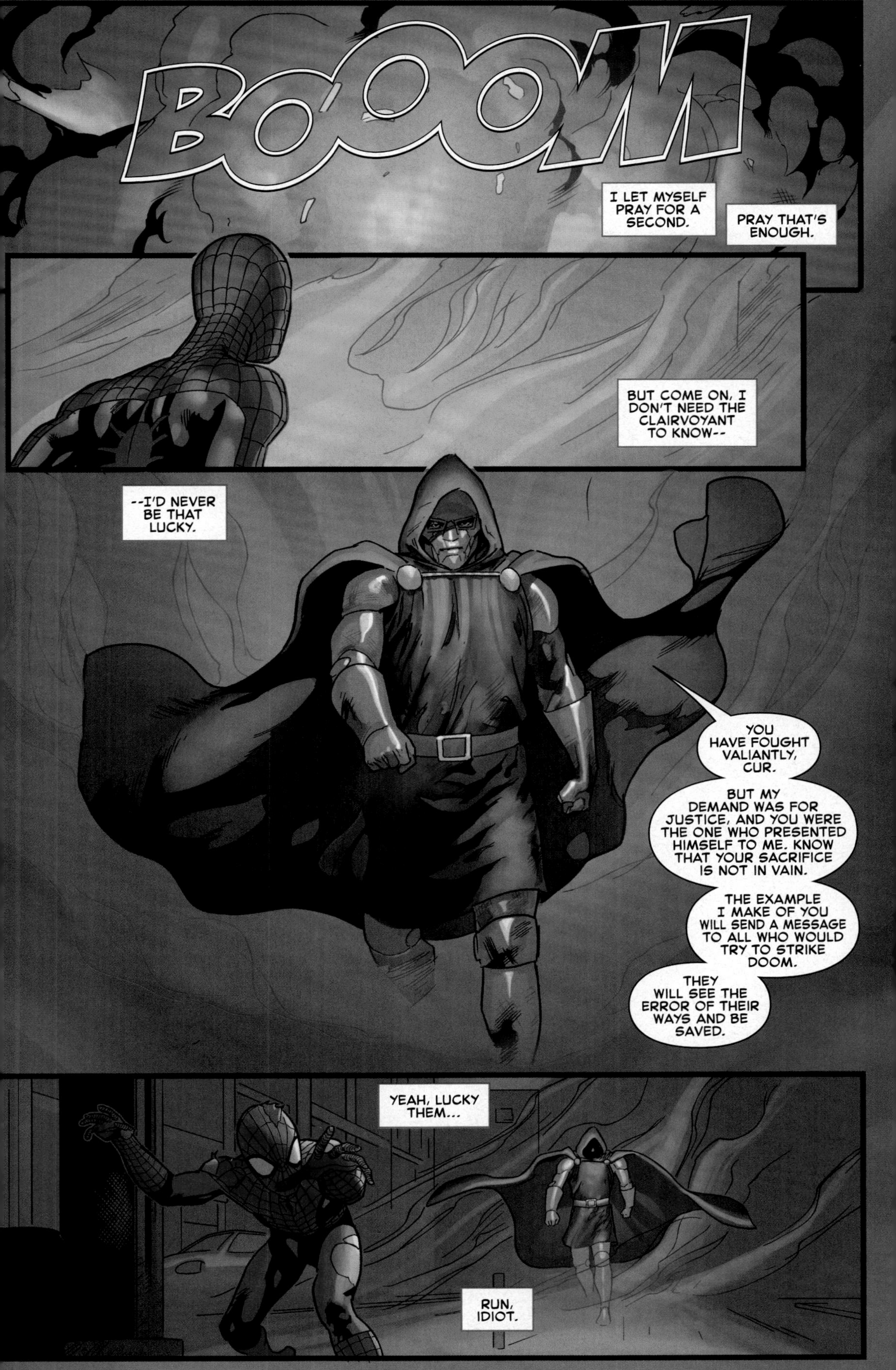
BOOOM
I LET MYSELF PRAY FOR A SECOND.
PRAY THAT'S ENOUGH.
BUT COME ON, I DON'T NEED THE CLAIRVOYANT TO KNOW--
--I'D NEVER BE THAT LUCKY.
YOU HAVE FOUGHT VALIANTLY, CUR.
BUT MY DEMAND WAS FOR JUSTICE, AND YOU WERE THE ONE WHO PRESENTED HIMSELF TO ME. KNOW THAT YOUR SACRIFICE IS NOT IN VAIN.
THE EXAMPLE I MAKE OF YOU WILL SEND A MESSAGE TO ALL WHO WOULD TRY TO STRIKE DOOM.
THEY WILL SEE THE ERROR OF THEIR WAYS AND BE SAVED.
YEAH, LUCKY THEM...
RUN, IDIOT.

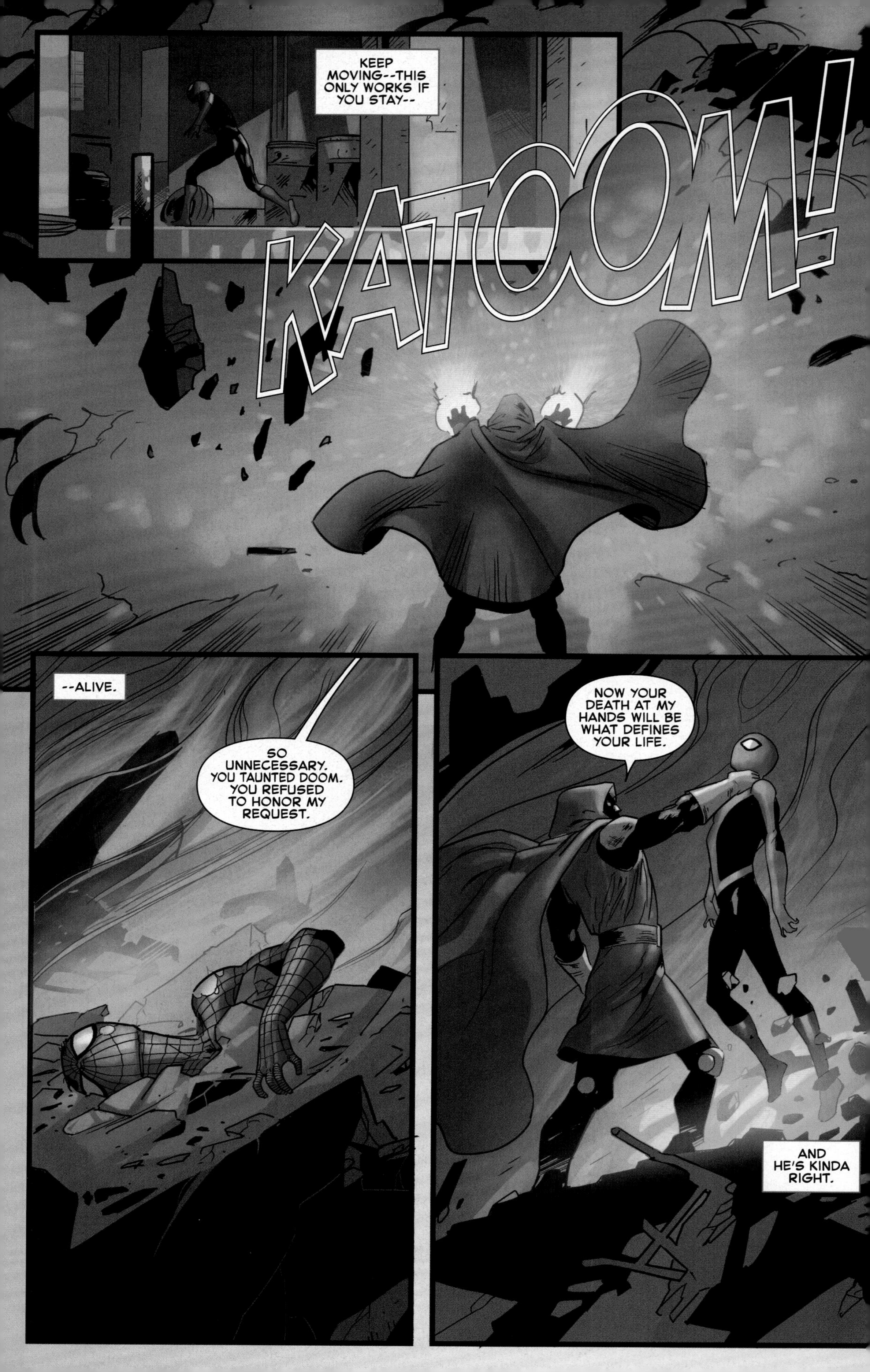
KEEP MOVING--THIS ONLY WORKS IF YOU STAY--
KATOOM!
--ALIVE.
SO UNNECESSARY. YOU TAUNTED DOOM. YOU REFUSED TO HONOR MY REQUEST.
NOW YOUR DEATH AT MY HANDS WILL BE WHAT DEFINES YOUR LIFE.
AND HE'S KINDA RIGHT.

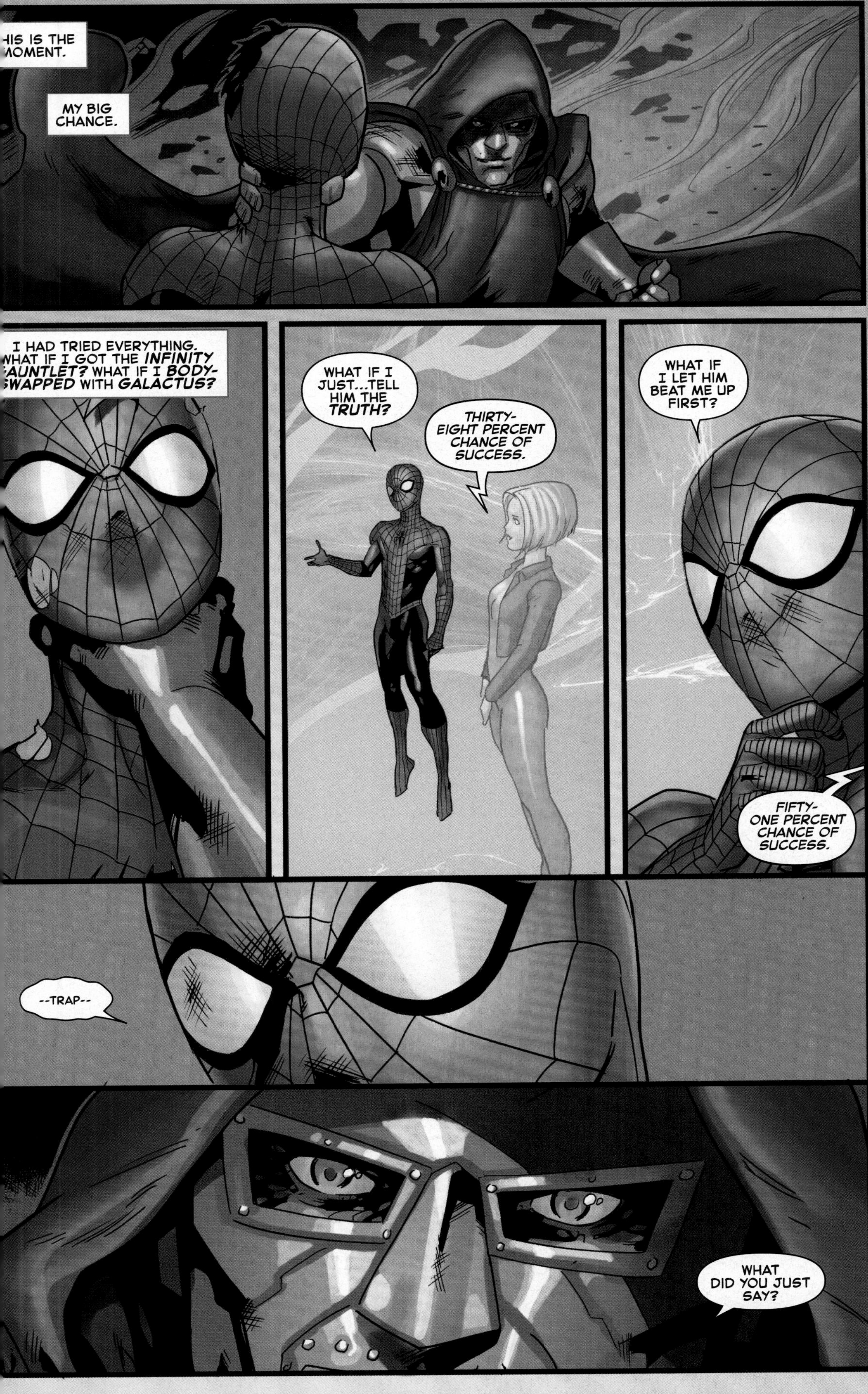
HIS IS THE
MOMENT.
MY BIG
CHANCE.
I HAD TRIED EVERYTHING.
WHAT IF I GOT THE *INFINITY*
GAUNTLET? WHAT IF I *BODY-*
SWAPPED WITH *GALACTUS?*
WHAT IF I JUST...TELL HIM THE *TRUTH?*
THIRTY-EIGHT PERCENT CHANCE OF SUCCESS.
WHAT IF I LET HIM BEAT ME UP FIRST?
FIFTY-ONE PERCENT CHANCE OF SUCCESS.
--TRAP--
WHAT DID YOU JUST SAY?

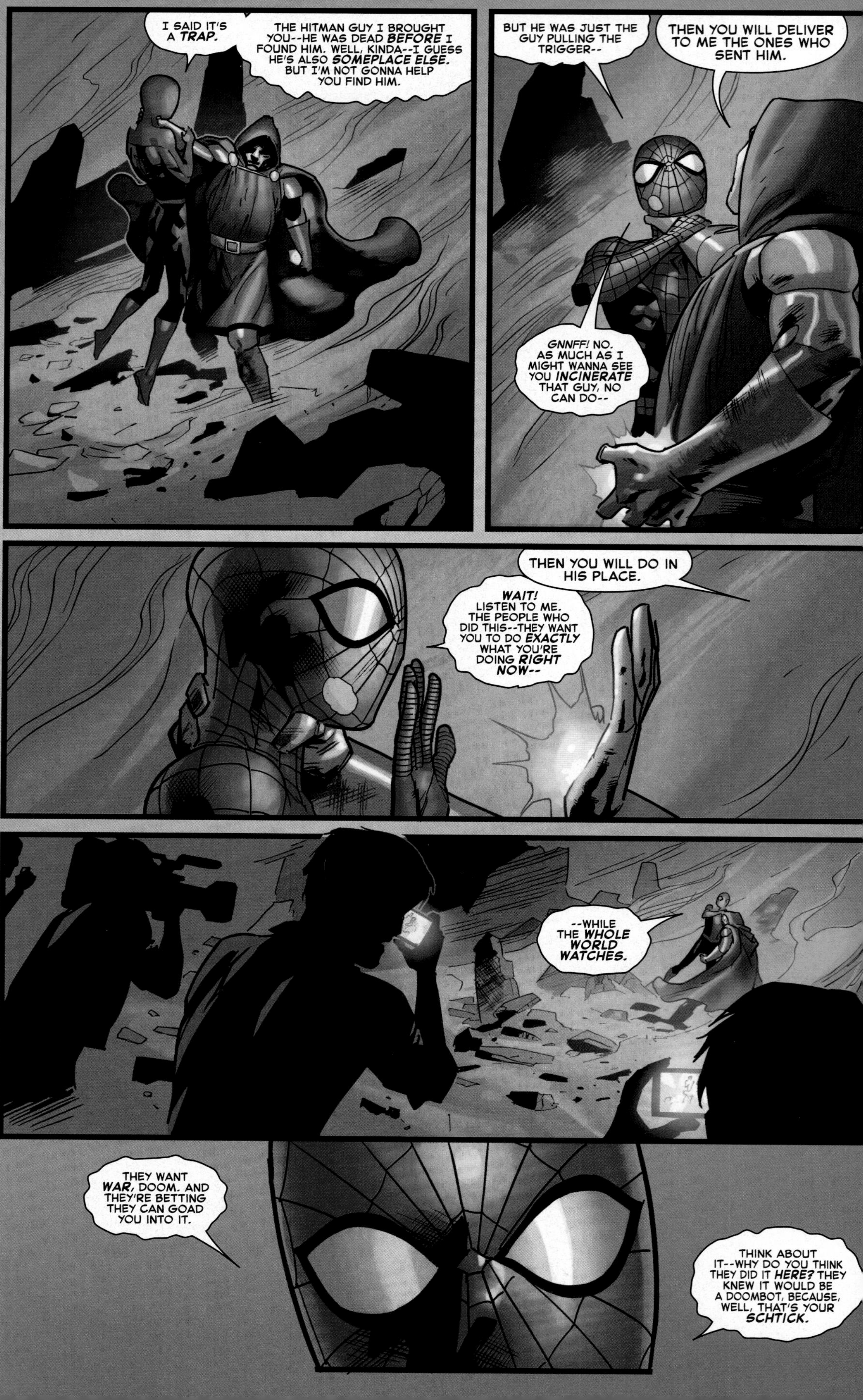
I SAID IT'S A TRAP.
THE HITMAN GUY I BROUGHT YOU--HE WAS DEAD BEFORE I FOUND HIM. WELL, KINDA--I GUESS HE'S ALSO SOMEPLACE ELSE. BUT I'M NOT GONNA HELP YOU FIND HIM.
BUT HE WAS JUST THE GUY PULLING THE TRIGGER--
THEN YOU WILL DELIVER TO ME THE ONES WHO SENT HIM.
GNNFF! NO. AS MUCH AS I MIGHT WANNA SEE YOU INCINERATE THAT GUY, NO CAN DO--
THEN YOU WILL DO IN HIS PLACE.
WAIT! LISTEN TO ME. THE PEOPLE WHO DID THIS--THEY WANT YOU TO DO EXACTLY WHAT YOU'RE DOING RIGHT NOW--
--WHILE THE WHOLE WORLD WATCHES.
THEY WANT WAR, DOOM. AND THEY'RE BETTING THEY CAN GOAD YOU INTO IT.
THINK ABOUT IT--WHY DO YOU THINK THEY DID IT HERE? THEY KNEW IT WOULD BE A DOOMBOT, BECAUSE, WELL, THAT'S YOUR SCHTICK.

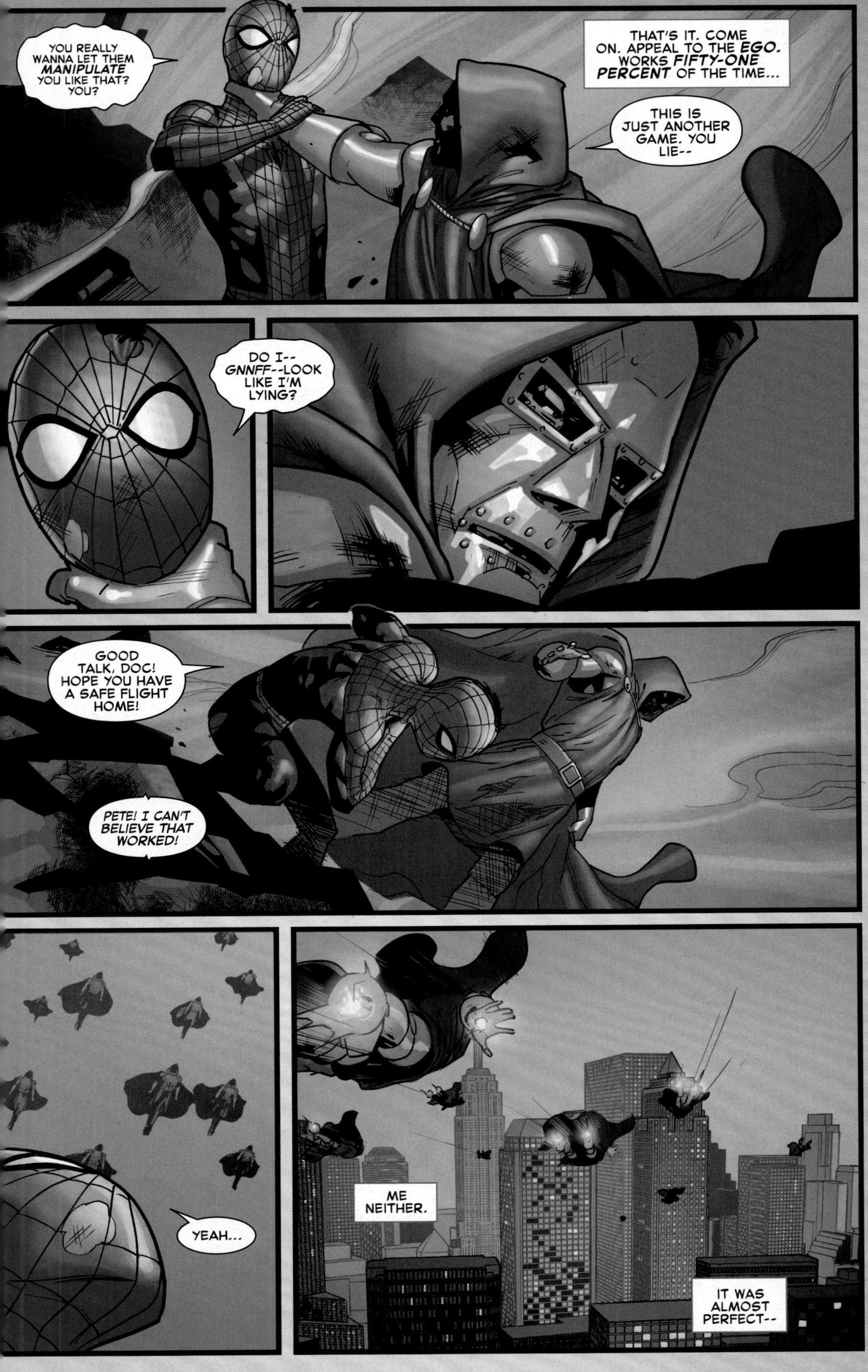
YOU REALLY WANNA LET THEM MANIPULATE YOU LIKE THAT? YOU?
THAT'S IT. COME ON. APPEAL TO THE EGO. WORKS FIFTY-ONE PERCENT OF THE TIME...
THIS IS JUST ANOTHER GAME. YOU LIE--
DO I-- GNNFF--LOOK LIKE I'M LYING?
GOOD TALK, DOC! HOPE YOU HAVE A SAFE FLIGHT HOME!
PETE! I CAN'T BELIEVE THAT WORKED!
YEAH...
ME NEITHER.
IT WAS ALMOST PERFECT--

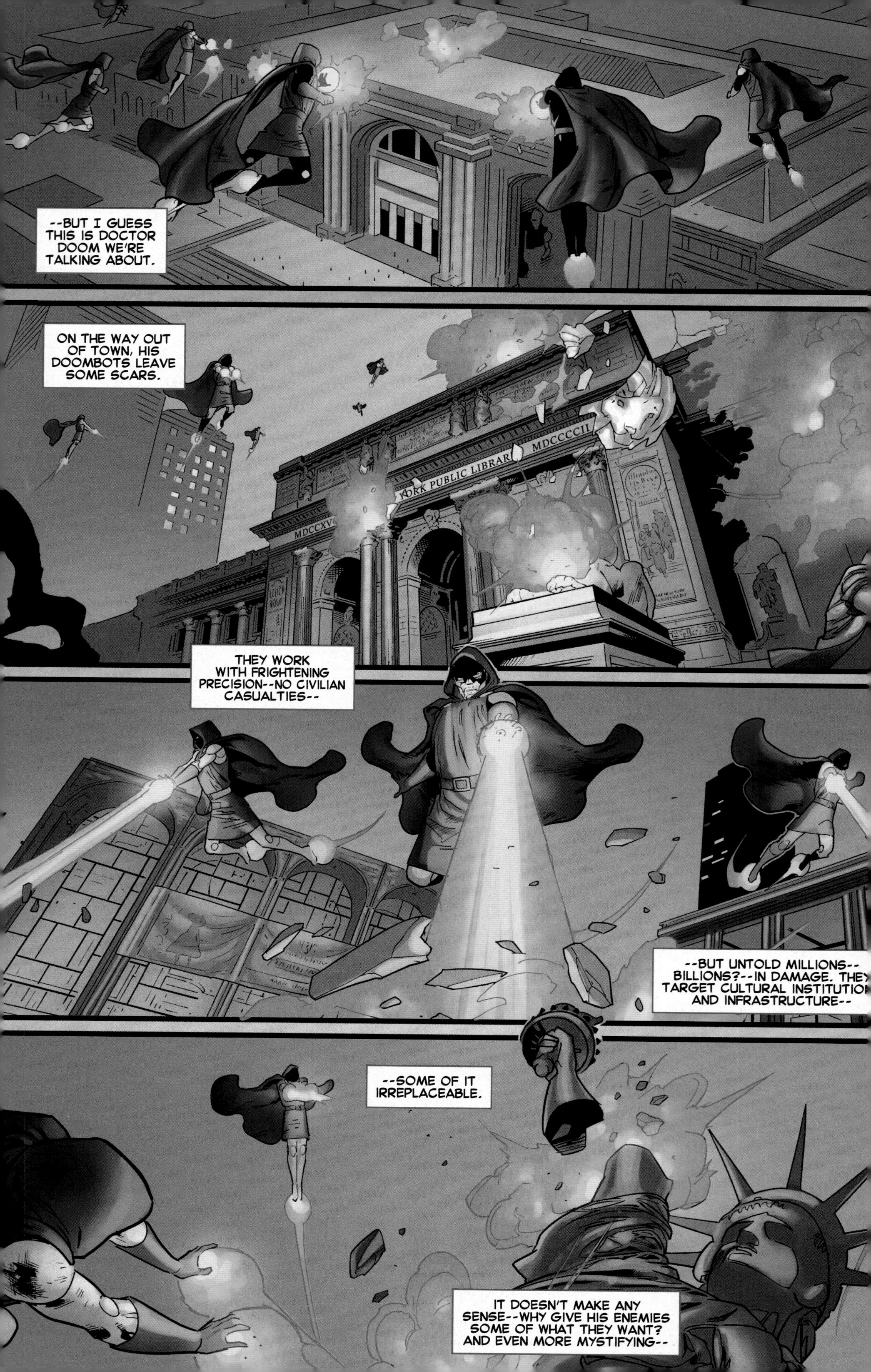
--BUT I GUESS THIS IS DOCTOR DOOM WE'RE TALKING ABOUT.
ON THE WAY OUT OF TOWN, HIS DOOMBOTS LEAVE SOME SCARS.
YORK PUBLIC LIBRARY MDCCCCII
MDCCXV
THEY WORK WITH FRIGHTENING PRECISION--NO CIVILIAN CASUALTIES--
--BUT UNTOLD MILLIONS--BILLIONS?--IN DAMAGE. THEY TARGET CULTURAL INSTITUTION AND INFRASTRUCTURE--
--SOME OF IT IRREPLACEABLE.
IT DOESN'T MAKE ANY SENSE--WHY GIVE HIS ENEMIES SOME OF WHAT THEY WANT? AND EVEN MORE MYSTIFYING--

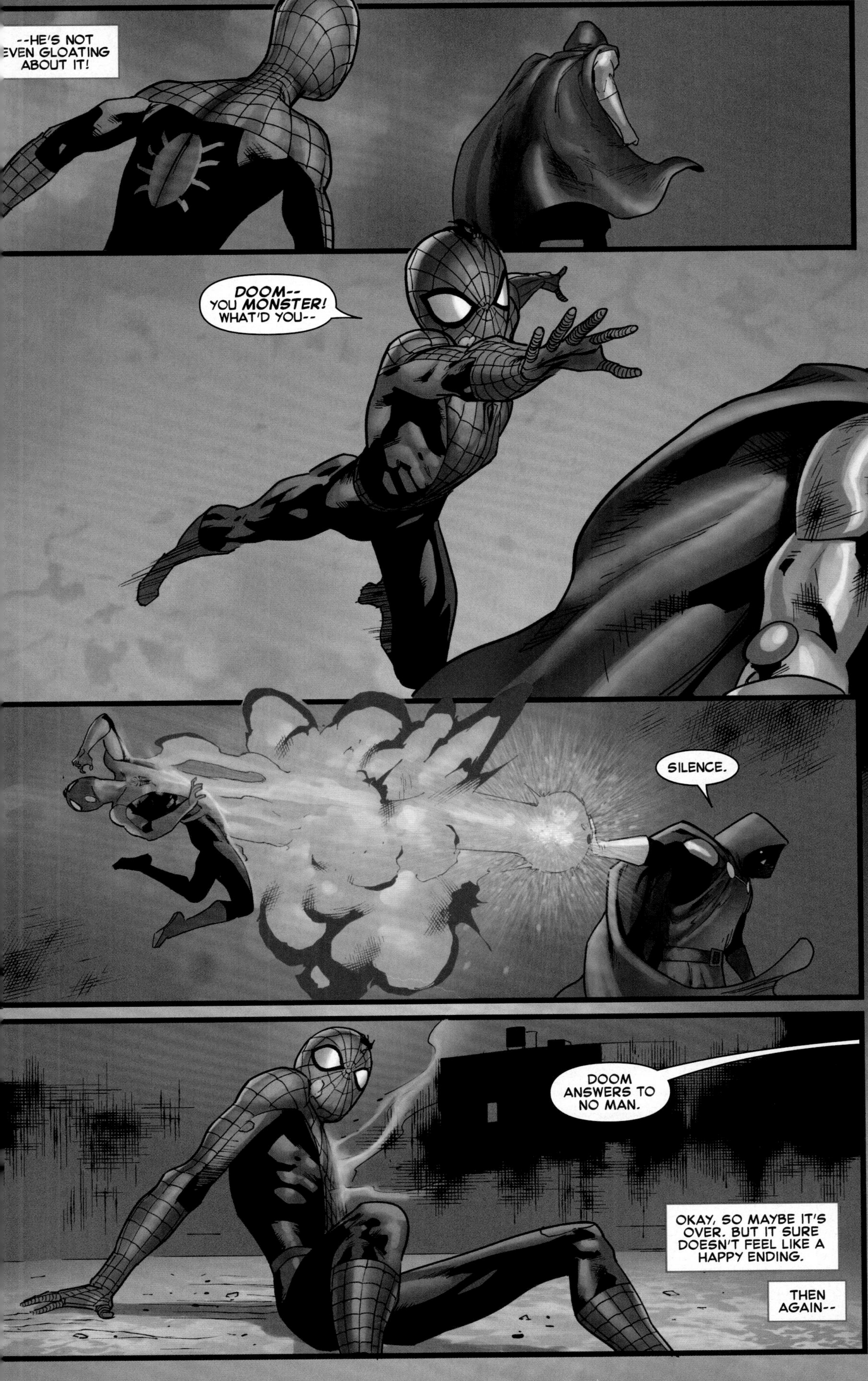
--HE'S NOT EVEN GLOATING ABOUT IT!
DOOM-- YOU MONSTER! WHAT'D YOU--
SILENCE.
DOOM ANSWERS TO NO MAN.
OKAY, SO MAYBE IT'S OVER. BUT IT SURE DOESN'T FEEL LIKE A HAPPY ENDING.
THEN AGAIN--

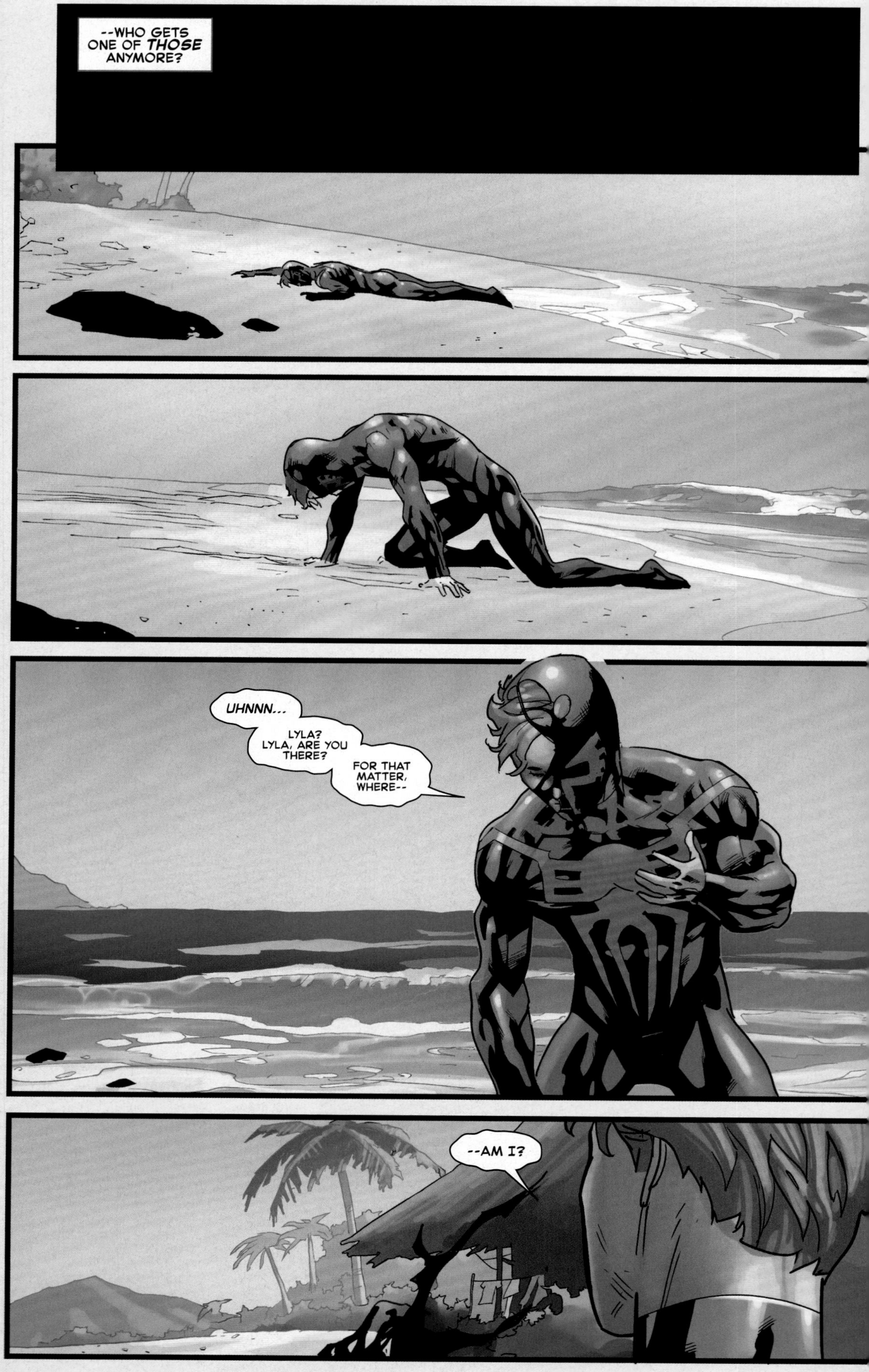
--WHO GETS ONE OF *THOSE* ANYMORE?
UHNNN...
LYLA? LYLA, ARE YOU THERE?
FOR THAT MATTER, WHERE--
--AM I?

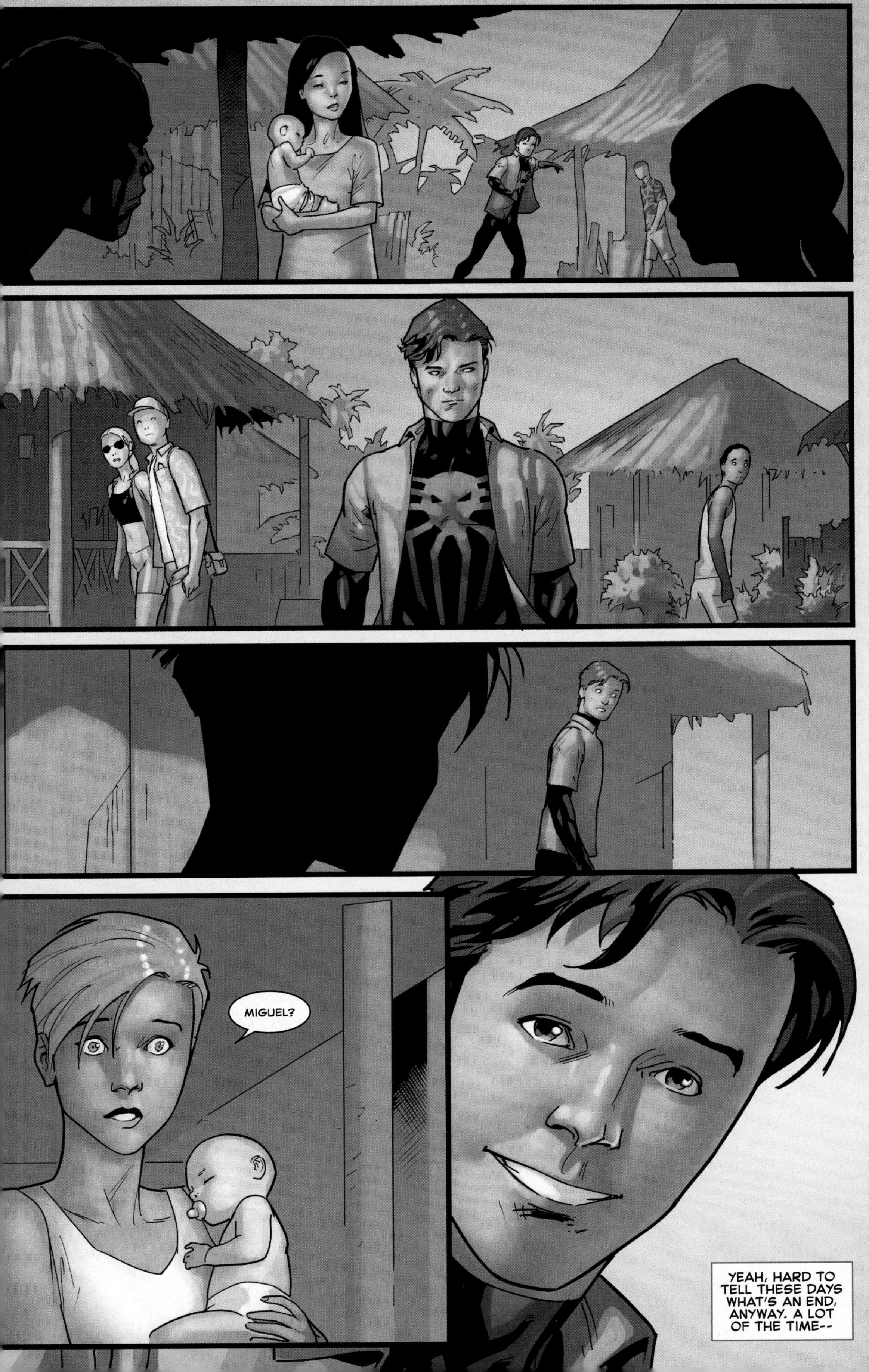
MIGUEL?
YEAH, HARD TO TELL THESE DAYS WHAT'S AN END, ANYWAY. A LOT OF THE TIME--

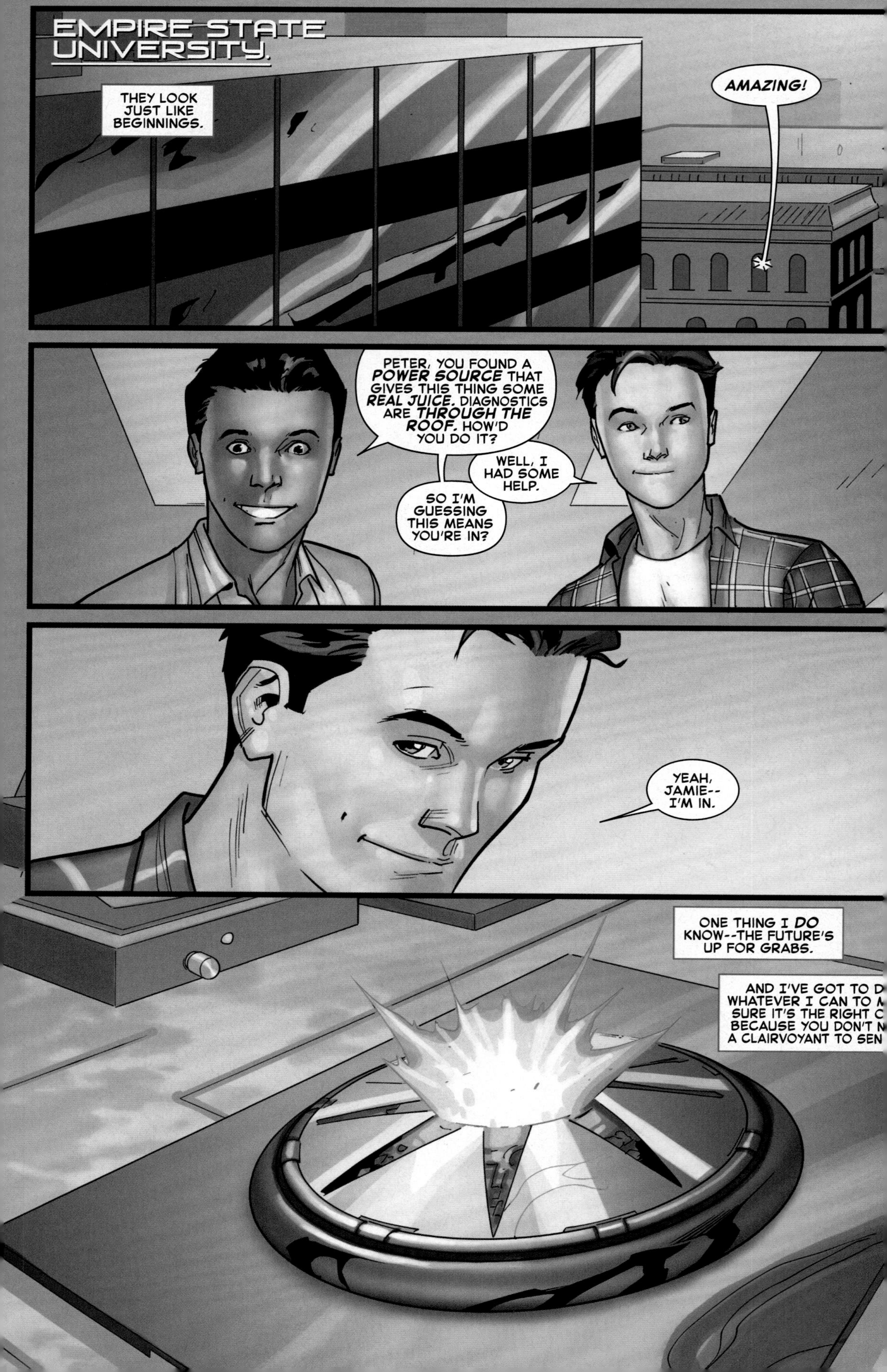

EMPIRE STATE UNIVERSITY.
THEY LOOK JUST LIKE BEGINNINGS.
AMAZING!
PETER, YOU FOUND A POWER SOURCE THAT GIVES THIS THING SOME REAL JUICE. DIAGNOSTICS ARE THROUGH THE ROOF. HOW'D YOU DO IT?
WELL, I HAD SOME HELP.
SO I'M GUESSING THIS MEANS YOU'RE IN?
YEAH, JAMIE-- I'M IN.
ONE THING I DO KNOW--THE FUTURE'S UP FOR GRABS.

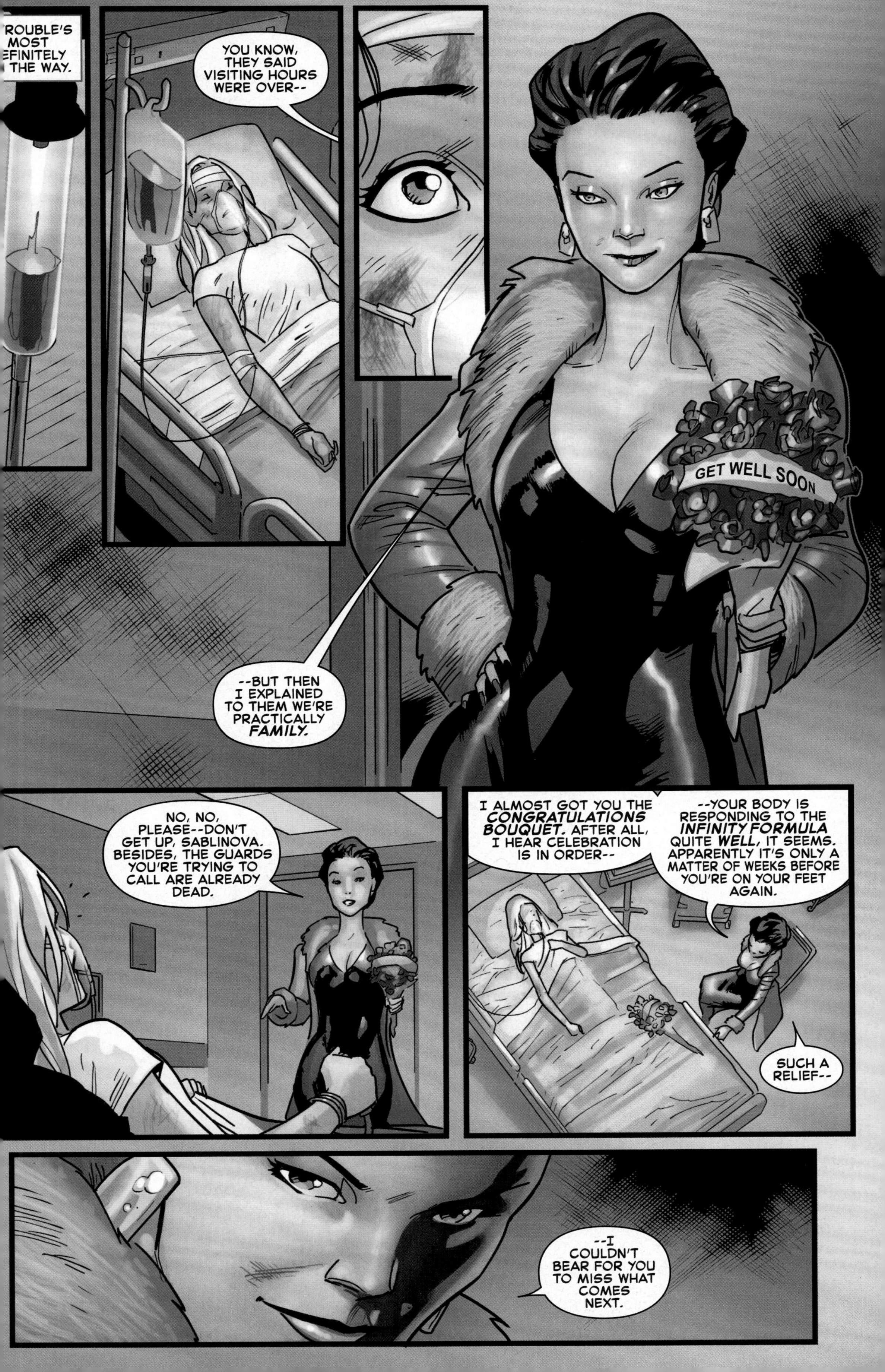
ROUBLE'S MOST EFINITELY THE WAY.
YOU KNOW, THEY SAID VISITING HOURS WERE OVER--
GET WELL SOON
--BUT THEN I EXPLAINED TO THEM WE'RE PRACTICALLY FAMILY.
NO, NO, PLEASE--DON'T GET UP, SABLINOVA. BESIDES, THE GUARDS YOU'RE TRYING TO CALL ARE ALREADY DEAD.
I ALMOST GOT YOU THE CONGRATULATIONS BOUQUET. AFTER ALL, I HEAR CELEBRATION IS IN ORDER--
--YOUR BODY IS RESPONDING TO THE INFINITY FORMULA QUITE WELL, IT SEEMS. APPARENTLY IT'S ONLY A MATTER OF WEEKS BEFORE YOU'RE ON YOUR FEET AGAIN.
SUCH A RELIEF--
--I COULDN'T BEAR FOR YOU TO MISS WHAT COMES NEXT.

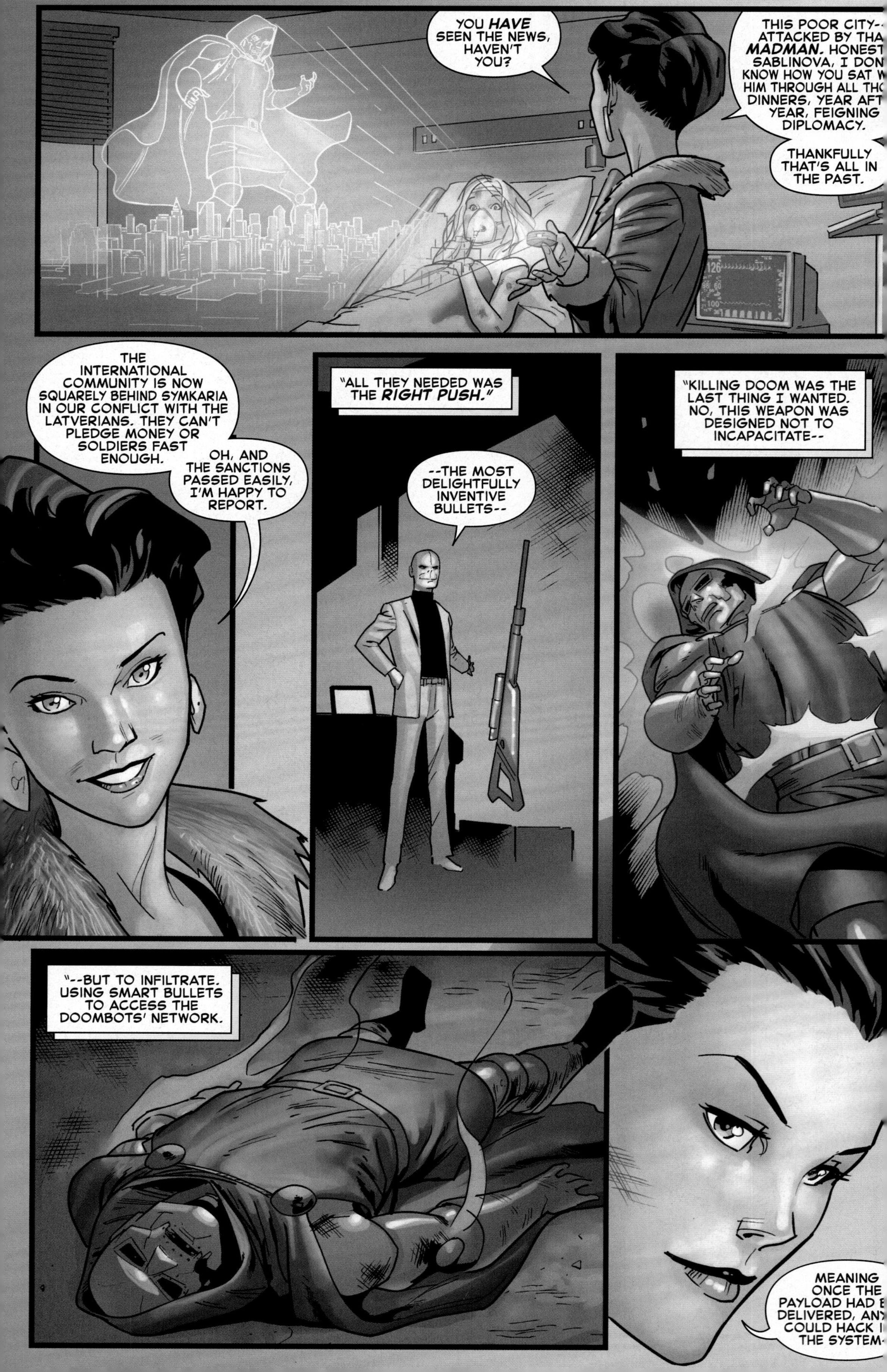

YOU HAVE SEEN THE NEWS, HAVEN'T YOU?
THIS POOR CITY-- ATTACKED BY THA MADMAN. HONEST SABLINOVA, I DON KNOW HOW YOU SAT W HIM THROUGH ALL THO DINNERS, YEAR AFT YEAR, FEIGNING DIPLOMACY.
THANKFULLY THAT'S ALL IN THE PAST.
THE INTERNATIONAL COMMUNITY IS NOW SQUARELY BEHIND SYMKARIA IN OUR CONFLICT WITH THE LATVERIANS. THEY CAN'T PLEDGE MONEY OR SOLDIERS FAST ENOUGH.
OH, AND THE SANCTIONS PASSED EASILY, I'M HAPPY TO REPORT.
"ALL THEY NEEDED WAS THE RIGHT PUSH."
--THE MOST DELIGHTFULLY INVENTIVE BULLETS--
"KILLING DOOM WAS THE LAST THING I WANTED. NO, THIS WEAPON WAS DESIGNED NOT TO INCAPACITATE--
"--BUT TO INFILTRATE. USING SMART BULLETS TO ACCESS THE DOOMBOTS' NETWORK.
MEANING ONCE THE PAYLOAD HAD DELIVERED, AN COULD HACK THE SYSTEM-

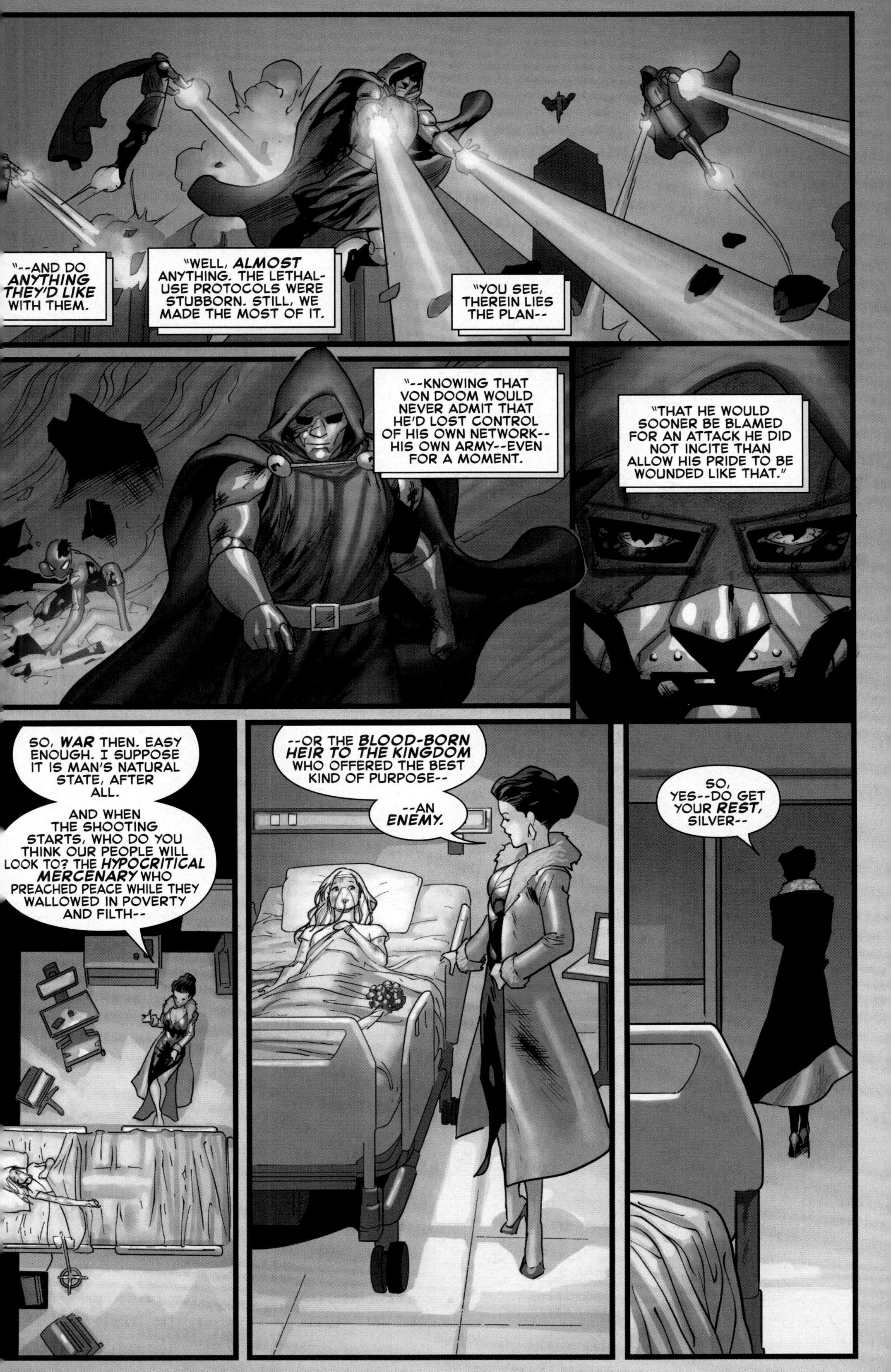
"--AND DO ANYTHING THEY'D LIKE WITH THEM.
"WELL, ALMOST ANYTHING. THE LETHAL-USE PROTOCOLS WERE STUBBORN. STILL, WE MADE THE MOST OF IT.
"YOU SEE, THEREIN LIES THE PLAN--
"--KNOWING THAT VON DOOM WOULD NEVER ADMIT THAT HE'D LOST CONTROL OF HIS OWN NETWORK--HIS OWN ARMY--EVEN FOR A MOMENT.
"THAT HE WOULD SOONER BE BLAMED FOR AN ATTACK HE DID NOT INCITE THAN ALLOW HIS PRIDE TO BE WOUNDED LIKE THAT."
SO, WAR THEN. EASY ENOUGH. I SUPPOSE IT IS MAN'S NATURAL STATE, AFTER ALL.
AND WHEN THE SHOOTING STARTS, WHO DO YOU THINK OUR PEOPLE WILL LOOK TO? THE HYPOCRITICAL MERCENARY WHO PREACHED PEACE WHILE THEY WALLOWED IN POVERTY AND FILTH--
--OR THE BLOOD-BORN HEIR TO THE KINGDOM WHO OFFERED THE BEST KIND OF PURPOSE--
--AN ENEMY.
SO, YES--DO GET YOUR REST, SILVER--

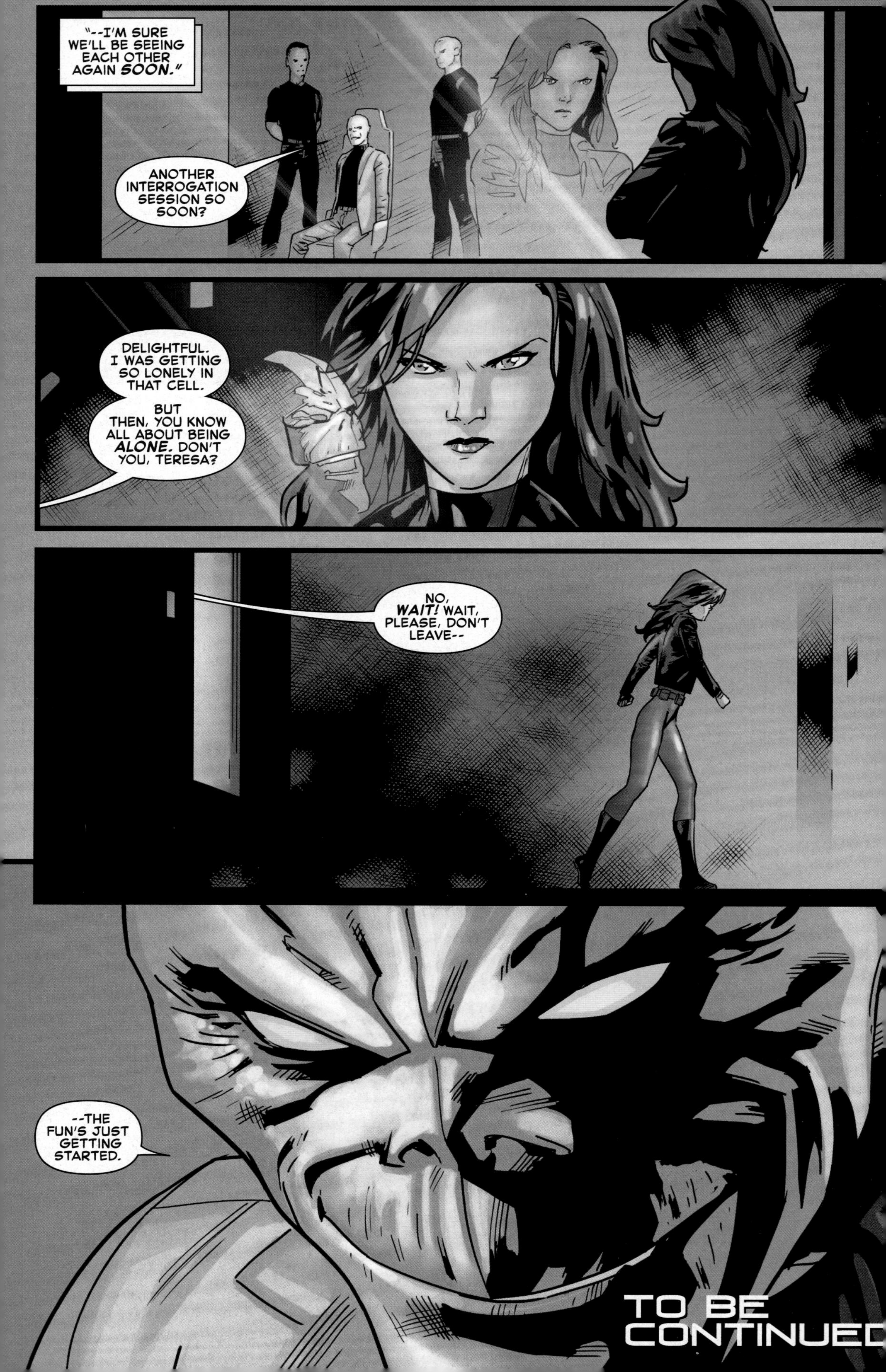
"--I'M SURE WE'LL BE SEEING EACH OTHER AGAIN SOON."
ANOTHER INTERROGATION SESSION SO SOON?
DELIGHTFUL. I WAS GETTING SO LONELY IN THAT CELL.
BUT THEN, YOU KNOW ALL ABOUT BEING ALONE. DON'T YOU, TERESA?
NO, WAIT! WAIT, PLEASE, DON'T LEAVE--
--THE FUN'S JUST GETTING STARTED.
TO BE CONTINUED

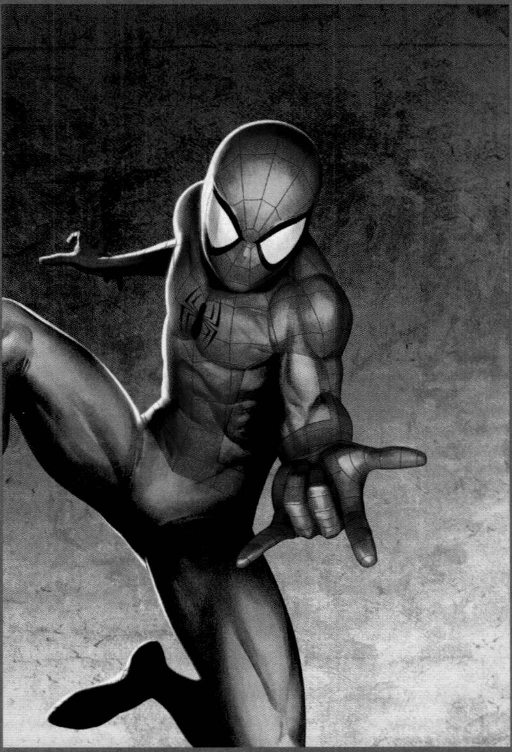

#33 VARIANT
BY SAMI BASRI

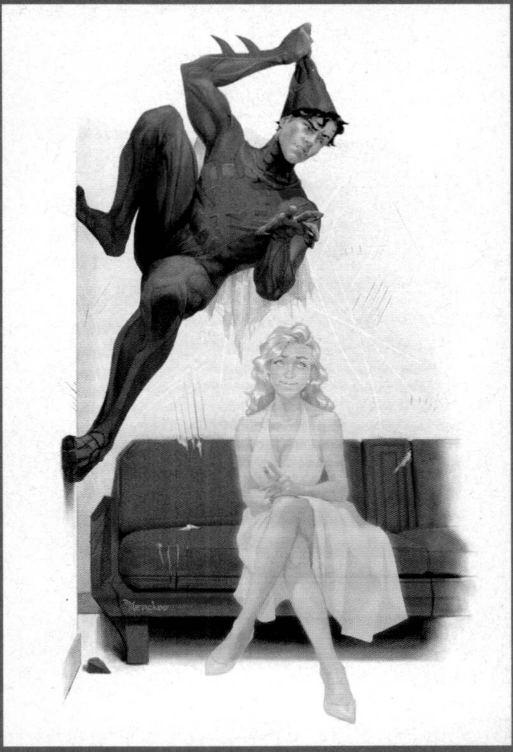

#33 2099 VARIANT
BY MIGUEL MERCADO

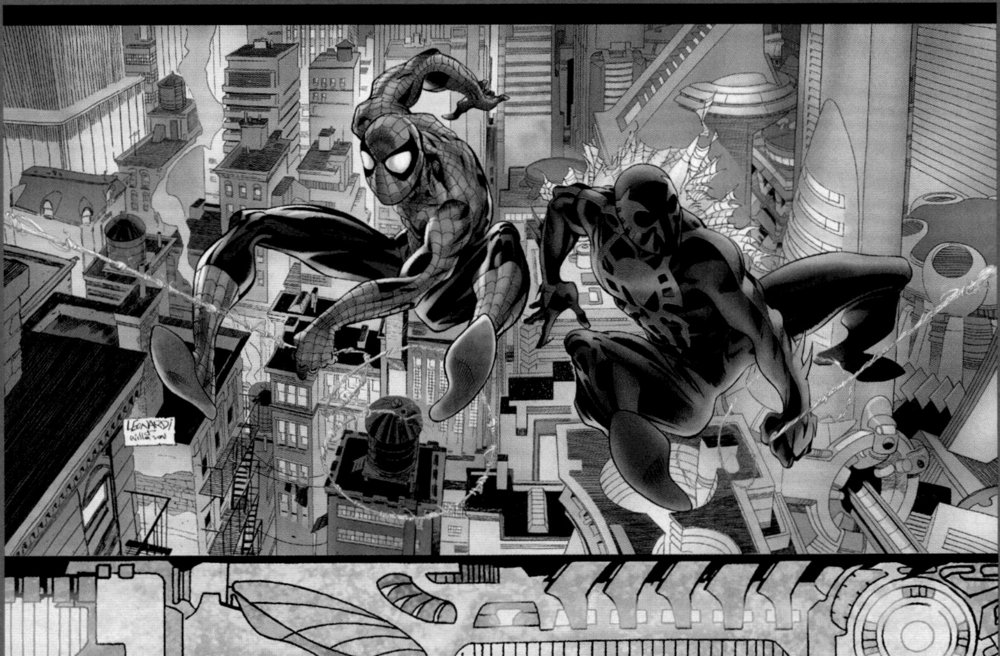

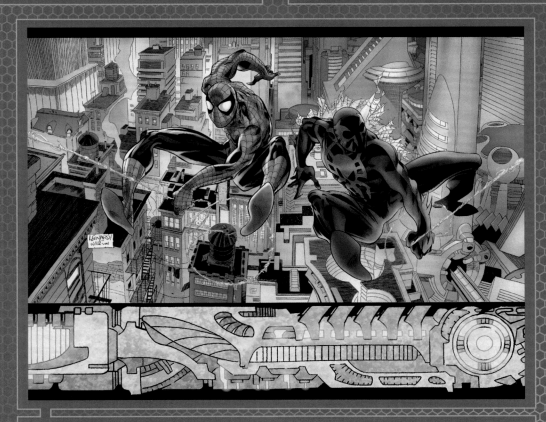

#33 HIDDEN GEM VARIANT
BY RICK LEONARDI & JASON KEITH

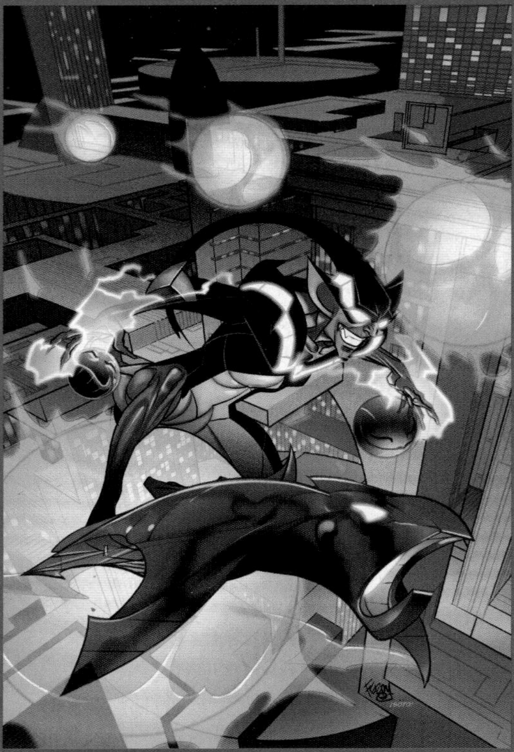

#34 2099 VARIANT
BY PASQUAL FERRY & CHRIS SOTOMAYOR

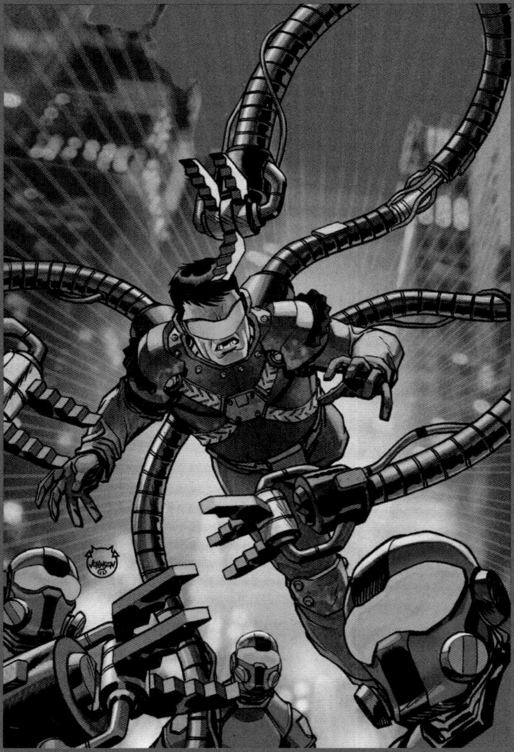

#35 2020 VARIANT
BY DAVE JOHNSON

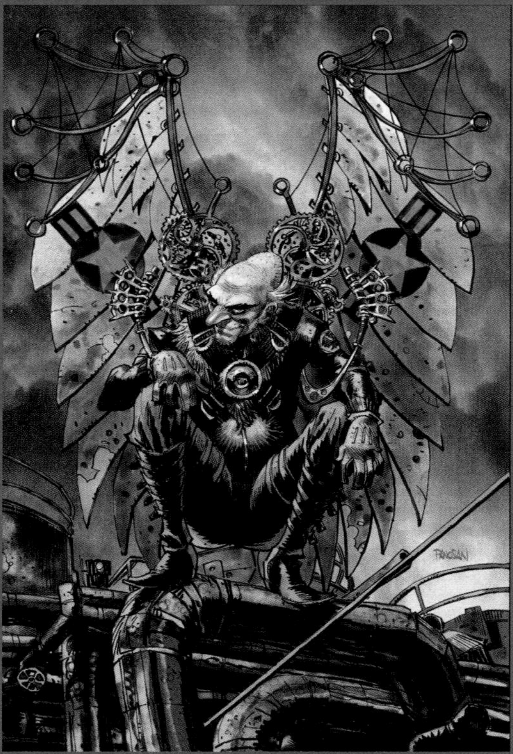
PANOSIAN

#36 2099 VARIANT
BY DAN PANOSIAN

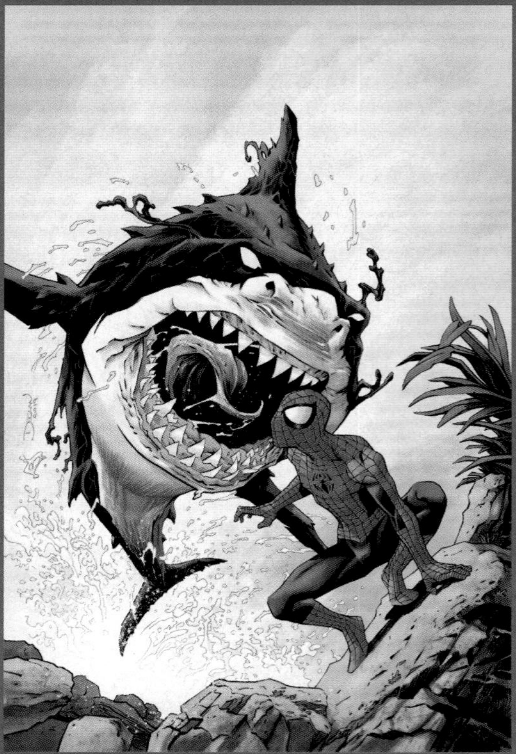

#36 VENOM ISLAND VARIANT
BY DECLAN SHALVEY